W9-AFT-517

High Resolution NMR

Theory and Chemical Applications

High Resolution NMR

Theory and Chemical Applications

EDWIN D. BECKER

National Institutes of Health
Bethesda, Maryland

BRIAR CLIFF COLLEGE
LIBRARY
SIOUX CITY, IOWA

ACADEMIC PRESS   New York and London

QD
476
.B358

COPYRIGHT © 1969, BY ACADEMIC PRESS, INC.
ALL RIGHTS RESERVED
NO PART OF THIS BOOK MAY BE REPRODUCED IN ANY FORM,
BY PHOTOSTAT, MICROFILM, RETRIEVAL SYSTEM, OR ANY
OTHER MEANS, WITHOUT WRITTEN PERMISSION FROM
THE PUBLISHERS.

ACADEMIC PRESS, INC.
111 Fifth Avenue, New York, New York 10003

United Kingdom Edition published by
ACADEMIC PRESS, INC. (LONDON) LTD.
Berkeley Square House, London W1X 6BA

LIBRARY OF CONGRESS CATALOG CARD NUMBER: 68-28898

Second Printing, 1970

PRINTED IN THE UNITED STATES OF AMERICA

Preface

Few techniques involving sophisticated instrumentation have made so rapid an impact on chemistry as has nuclear magnetic resonance. Within five years after the discovery that NMR frequencies depended upon the chemical environments of nuclei, commercial instruments capable of resolving resonance lines separated by less than 0.1 part per million (ppm) were available. Chemists immediately found NMR to be a valuable tool in structure elucidation, in investigations of kinetic phenomena, and in studies of chemical equilibria. Rapid developments in our understanding of NMR phenomena and their relation to properties of chemical interest continue today unabated, and dramatic instrumental developments have improved resolution and sensitivity by factors of ~50 from the first commercial instruments. Today more than 1500 NMR spectrometers are in use, and the scientific literature abounds in reference to NMR data.

In the course of teaching the background and applications of NMR both to graduate students and to established chemists who wanted to learn more of this technique, I have felt the need for a textbook at an "intermediate" level of complexity—one which would provide a systematic treatment of those portions of NMR theory most needed for the intelligent and efficient utilization of the technique in various branches of chemistry and yet one which would avoid the mathematical detail presented in the several excellent treatises on the subject.

In this book I have attempted to present an explanation of NMR theory and to provide sufficient practical examples of the use of NMR to permit the reader to develop a clear idea of the many uses—and the limitations—

v

67680

of this technique. Many practical points of experimental methods are discussed, and pitfalls pointed out. A large collection of problems and spectra of "unknown" compounds of graded difficulty permits the student to test his knowledge of NMR principles. Answers to selected problems are given. I have not attempted to include large compendia of data, but ample literature references and lists of data tabulations and reviews should permit the reader to locate the specialized data needed for specific applications. Many of the literature references are to recent reviews or to other books, rather than to original articles, since the references are intended to provide guides to further reading, not to give credit for original contributions. Under these circumstances an author index would be pointless and has not been included.

EDWIN D. BECKER

Acknowledgments

A preliminary version of this book was used as a text in my class at the NIH Graduate School in 1967, and that version has been read and criticized by several of my colleagues. I wish to express sincere gratitude to Drs. B. L. Shapiro, E. Lustig, R. J. Highet, L. Paolillo, and R. R. Shoup, all of whom made many valuable suggestions for improving the presentation. My thanks go also to Mrs. Sally Pierman, who typed the manuscript, and to Dr. Paolillo, Dr. Highet, and Mr. R. B. Bradley, who provided some of the spectra in Appendix B.

I also wish to acknowledge permission from the following publishers to reproduce copyrighted material: American Association for the Advancement of Science, Figs. 1.4 and 6.8; American Chemical Society, Figs. 1.6, 1.7, 3.7, 3.10, 9.2, and 10.2; Marcel Dekker, Inc., Figs. 3.12 and 3.13; the Faraday Society, Fig. 8.4; American Institute of Physics, Figs. 3.8, 4.9, 4.10, 4.13, 7.3, 7.21, 8.1, 8.2, 8.7, 8.11, 8.12, 8.13, 9.1, 9.3, and 10.4; and *Journal of Chemical Education,* excerpts from an article originally published there [E. D. Becker, *J. Chem. Ed.* **42,** 591 (1965)].

Contents

4.   Chemical Shifts

5.   Electron-Coupled Spin-Spin Interactions

High Resolution NMR

Theory and Chemical Applications

Chapter 1

Introduction

1.1 Historical

Many atomic nuclei behave as though they are spinning, and as a result of this spin they possess angular momentum and magnetic moments. These two nuclear properties were first observed indirectly in the very small splittings of certain atomic spectral lines (hyperfine structure). In 1924 Pauli[1] suggested that this hyperfine structure resulted from the interaction of magnetic moments of nuclei with the already recognized magnetic moments of electrons in the atoms. Analysis of the hyperfine structure permitted the determination of the angular momentum and magnetic moments of many nuclei.

The concept of nuclear spin was strengthened by the discovery (through heat capacity measurements) of *ortho* and *para* hydrogen[2]—molecules that differ only in having the two constituent nuclei spinning in the same or opposite directions, respectively.

In the early 1920's Stern and Gerlach[3] had shown that a beam of atoms sent through an inhomogeneous magnetic field is deflected according to the orientation of the electron magnetic moments relative to the magnetic field. During the 1930's refinements of the Stern-Gerlach technique permitted the measurement of the much smaller values of *nuclear* magnetic moments.[4] A major improvement in this type of experiment was made by Rabi and his co-workers[5] in 1939. They sent a beam of hydrogen molecules through first an inhomogeneous magnetic field and then a homogeneous field, and they applied radio-frequency (rf) electromagnetic energy to the molecules in the homogeneous field. At a sharply defined frequency, energy was absorbed by the molecular beam and caused a small but measurable deflection of the beam.

This actually was the first observation of nuclear magnetic resonance, but such studies were performed only in molecular beams under very high vacuum. It was not until 1946 that nuclear magnetic resonance was found in bulk materials (solids or liquids). In that year Purcell and his co-workers at Harvard reported nuclear resonance absorption in paraffin wax,[6] while Bloch and his colleagues at Stanford found nuclear resonance in liquid water.[7] (They received the 1952 Nobel Prize for their discovery.) When we speak of nuclear magnetic resonance, we are really thinking of the kind of NMR discovered by Bloch and Purcell; that is, nuclear magnetic resonance in bulk materials.

The early work in NMR was concentrated on the elucidation of the basic phenomena and on the accurate determination of nuclear magnetic moments. NMR attracted little attention from chemists until, in 1949 and 1950, it was discovered that the precise resonance frequency of a nucleus depends on the state of its chemical environment.[8] In 1951 separate resonance lines were found for chemically different protons in the same molecule.[9] The discovery of this so-called *chemical shift* set the stage for the use of NMR as a probe into the structure of molecules; this is the aspect of NMR that we shall explore in this book.

1.2 High Resolution NMR

It is found that chemical shifts are very small, and in order to observe such shifts one must study the material in the right state of aggregation. In solids, where intermolecular motion is highly restricted, internuclear inter-actions cause such a great broadening of resonance lines that chemical shift differences are masked. In solution, on the other hand, the rapid molecular tumbling causes these interactions to average to zero, and sharp lines are observed. Thus there is a distinction between *broad line NMR* and *high resolution*, or narrow line, NMR. We shall deal almost exclusively with the latter.

An NMR spectrum is obtained by placing a sample in a homogeneous magnetic field and applying electromagnetic energy at suitable frequencies. In Chapter 2 we shall examine in detail just how NMR spectra arise, and in Chapter 3 we shall delve into the procedures by which NMR is studied. Before we do so, however, it may be helpful to see by a few examples the type of information that can be obtained from an NMR spectrum.

Basically there are three quantities that can be measured in a high resolution NMR spectrum: (1) frequencies, (2) areas, and (3) widths or shapes of the resonance lines. Figure 1.1 shows the spectrum of a simple compound,

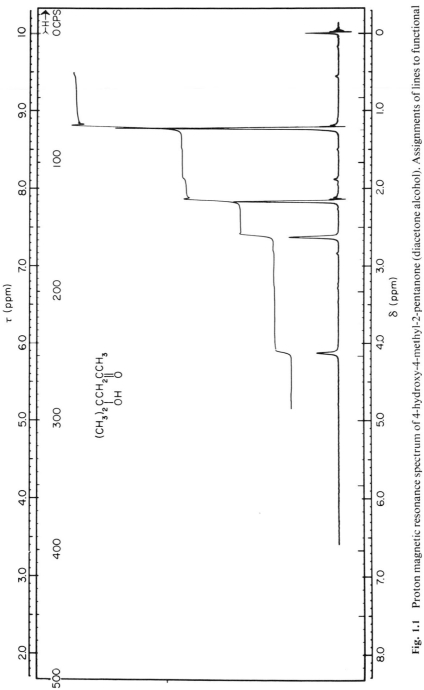

Fig. 1.1 Proton magnetic resonance spectrum of 4-hydroxy-4-methyl-2-pentanone (diacetone alcohol). Assignments of lines to functional groups as follows: $\delta = 1.23$, $(CH_3)_2$; 2.16, $CH_3C=O$; 2.62, CH_2; 4.12, OH. (For definition of δ scale, see Chapter 4.)

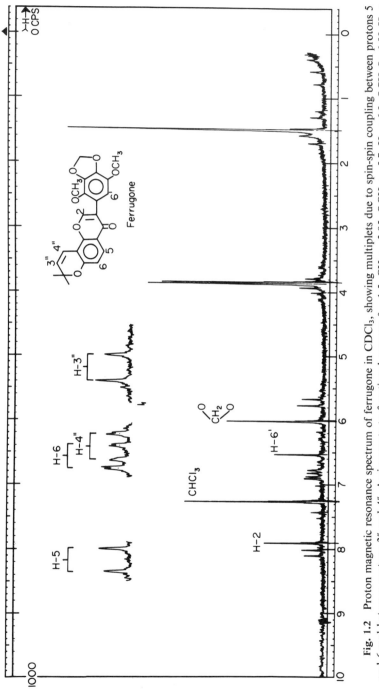

Fig. 1.2 Proton magnetic resonance spectrum of ferrugone in CDCl₃, showing multiplets due to spin-spin coupling between protons 5 and 6 and between protons 3″ and 4″. Assignments to functional groups: $\delta = 1.5$, CH₃; ~3.85, OCH₃; ~5.7, H₃″; 6.0, OCH₂O; 6.55, H₆′; 6.8, H₆; 6.9, H₄″; 7.27, CHCl₃; 7.9, H₂; ~8.1, H₆.

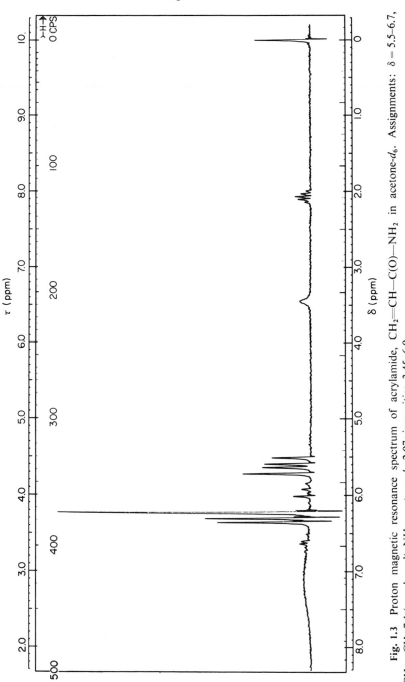

Fig. 1.3 Proton magnetic resonance spectrum of acrylamide, $CH_2{=}CH{-}C(O){-}NH_2$, in acetone-d_6. Assignments: $\delta = 5.5$–6.7, $CH_2{=}CH$; 7.1 (very broad), NH_2; acetone-d_5, 2.07; impurities, 3.45, 6.0.

diacetone alcohol. This spectrum, as well as the others shown in this chapter, arises only from the resonance of the hydrogen nuclei in the molecule. (We shall see in Chapter 2 that we normally obtain a spectrum from only one kind of nucleus and discriminate against the others.) The line at zero on the scale below the spectrum is a reference line (see Chapters 3 and 4). Each of the other lines can be assigned to one of the functional groups in the sample, as indicated in the figure. The step function shown along with the spectrum is an

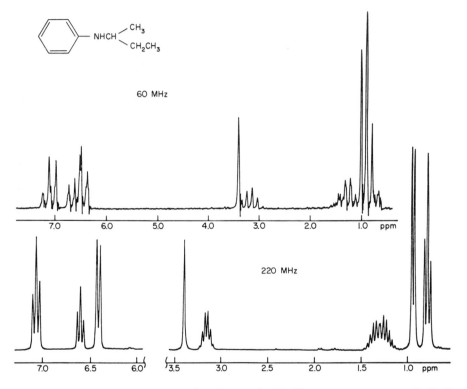

Fig. 1.4 Proton NMR spectrum of *N-sec*-butylaniline. Upper spectrum obtained with a magnetic field of 14,000 gauss and a radio frequency of 60 MHz; lower spectrum, 52,000 gauss and 220 MHz (Ferguson and Phillips[10]).

integral, with the height of each step proportional to the area under the corresponding spectral line. There are several important features illustrated in this spectrum: First, the chemical shift is clearly demonstrated, for the resonance frequencies depend on the chemical environment, as we shall study in detail in Chapter 4. Second, the areas under the lines are different and, as we shall see when we examine the theory in Chapter 2, the area of each line is proportional to the number of nuclei contributing to it. Third, the widths of the lines are different; in particular, the line due to the OH is considerably broader than the others. We shall examine the reasons for different line widths in Chapters 2, 9, and 10.

The spectrum in Figure 1.1 is particularly simple. A more typical spectrum —that of a natural product, ferrugone—is given in Figure 1.2. This spectrum

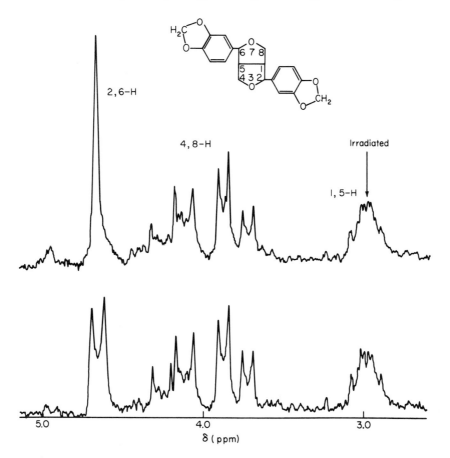

Fig. 1.5 Part of the proton NMR spectrum of sesamin. Bottom, ordinary spectrum; top, with additional radio-frequency irradiation in the vicinity of the complex multiplet at the right of the spectrum.

consists of single lines well separated from each other, as were the lines in Figure 1.1, and of simple multiplets. (The inset shows the multiplets on an expanded abscissa scale.) The splitting of single lines into multiplets arises from interactions between the nuclei called *spin-spin coupling*. This is an important type of information obtainable from an NMR spectrum. In Chapter

5 we shall inquire into the origin of spin coupling and what information of chemical value we can get from it.

Figure 1.3 shows the spectrum of a simple molecule, acrylamide. The three

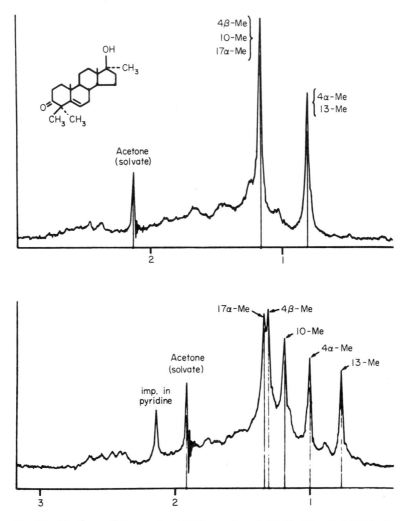

Fig. 1.6 Portions of the proton NMR spectra of 4,4,17α-trimethyl-17β-hydroxy-5-androsten-3-one in $CDCl_3$ (upper) and in pyridine (lower) (Slomp and MacKellar[11]).

vinyl protons give rise to the 12-line spectrum at $\delta = 5.5$–6.7, which shows little regularity in spacing or intensity distribution. A spectrum of this sort must be analyzed by procedures that we shall discuss in detail in Chapter 7.

The appearance of complex spectra often depends on the strength of the magnetic field in which the sample is placed. For example, Figure 1.4 shows marked changes in the spectrum of *N-sec*-butylaniline when observed at

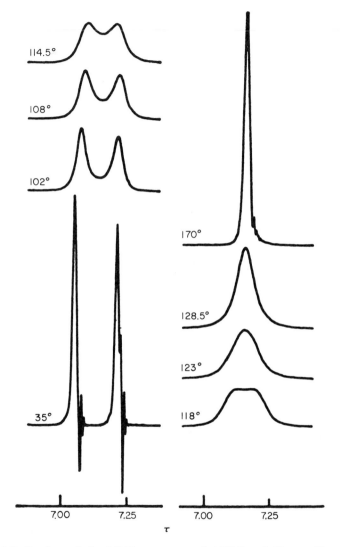

Fig. 1.7 Portion of the NMR spectrum of *N,N*-dimethylformamide at various temperatures (Bovey[12]).

14,000 gauss and at 52,000 gauss. While the former spectrum is rather complex and consists of a number of irregularly spaced lines, the latter consists of simple multiplets that are readily interpreted. In Chapter 3 we shall look into the types of NMR spectrometers available and discuss some experimental techniques, while in Chapters 4 and 5 we shall see why NMR spectra are dependent on magnetic field strength.

A powerful method for unraveling complex spectra is *double resonance*, in which two radio frequencies are applied to the sample simultaneously. Figure 1.5 shows the results of a double resonance experiment with a natural product, sesamin. Application of an intense rf field at the frequency of the complex multiplet at the right of the spectrum causes the doublet at the left of the spectrum to collapse to a single line, while the remainder of the spectrum is unchanged. The theory and application of double resonance will be covered in Chapter 8.

Often the appearance of an NMR spectrum is strongly dependent on intermolecular interactions (or "medium effects"), as well as molecular structure. The upper portion of Figure 1.6 gives the spectrum of a steroid obtained in solution in deuterochloroform. There are five methyl groups in the molecule but only two distinct methyl peaks are observed because of accidental coincidences. On the other hand, the spectrum obtained in pyridine (lower portion of Figure 1.6) shows all five lines. In Chapter 11 we shall explore the effects of solvent interactions and of hydrogen bonding.

NMR spectra are often influenced strongly by rate phenomena. Figure 1.7 shows a portion of the spectrum of N,N-dimethylformamide, in which there is hindered rotation of the $N(CH_3)_2$ group around the CN amide bond. At low temperature there are two distinct peaks for the two separate methyl groups, but with increasing temperature these peaks broaden and eventually coalesce, as the rate of internal rotation of the dimethylamino group increases. In Chapter 10 we shall inquire into the reasons for this type of behavior and the kind of kinetic information that can be obtained from the spectra.

References

1. W. Pauli, Jr., *Naturwiss.* **12**, 741 (1924).

2. D. M. Dennison, *Proc. Roy. Soc.* (*London*) **A115**, 483 (1927).

3. O. Stern, *Z. Physik* 7, 249 (1921); W. Gerlach and O. Stern, *Ann. Phys. Leipzig* **74**, 673 (1924).

4. I. Estermann and O. Stern, *Z. Physik* **85**, 17 (1933).

5. I. I. Rabi, S. Millman, P. Kusch, and J. R. Zacharias, *Phys. Rev.* **55**, 526 (1939); J. M. B. Kellogg, I. I. Rabi, N. F. Ramsey, Jr., and J. R. Zacharias, *ibid.* **56**, 728 (1939).

6. E. M. Purcell, H. C. Torrey, and R. V. Pound, *Phys. Rev.* **69**, 37 (1946).

7. F. Bloch, W. W. Hansen, and M. Packard, *Phys. Rev.* **69**, 127 (1946).

8. W. D. Knight, *Phys. Rev.* **76**, 1259 (1949); W. C. Dickinson, *ibid.* **77**, 736 (1950); G. Lindström, *ibid.* **78**, 817 (1950); W. G. Proctor and F. C. Yu, *ibid.* **77**, 717 (1950).

9. J. T. Arnold, S. S. Dharmatti, and M. E. Packard, *J. Chem. Phys.* **19**, 507 (1951).

10. R. C. Ferguson and W. D. Phillips, *Science* **157**, 257 (1967).

11. G. Slomp and F. MacKellar, *J. Am. Chem. Soc.* **82**, 999 (1960).

12. F. A. Bovey, *Chem. Eng. News* **43**, 98 (August 30, 1965).

Chapter 2

The Theory of NMR

2.1 Nuclear Spin and Magnetic Moment

Nuclei that act as though they are spinning possess angular momentum, which is quantized in units of $\hbar$, where $\hbar$ is Planck's constant divided by 2π. For the maximum observable component of angular momentum, we may write

$$p = I\hbar = \frac{Ih}{2\pi}. \qquad (2.1)$$

The constant of proportionality, which is either an integer or half-integer, is given the symbol I and is referred to as the nuclear spin quantum number or more commonly the *nuclear spin*. We can classify nuclei, then, according to their nuclear spins. There are a number of nuclei that have $I = 0$ and hence possess no angular momentum. This class of nuclei includes all those that have both an even atomic number and an even mass number; for example, ^{12}C, ^{16}O, and ^{32}S. These nuclei, as we shall see, cannot experience magnetic resonance under any circumstances. Appendix A lists the nuclear spins of all isotopes that have $I \neq 0$. A few of the more common nuclei are

$$I = \tfrac{1}{2}: \quad ^{1}H, \, ^{3}H, \, ^{13}C, \, ^{15}N, \, ^{19}F, \, ^{31}P;$$
$$I = 1: \quad ^{2}H(D), \, ^{14}N;$$
$$I > 1: \quad ^{10}B, \, ^{11}B, \, ^{17}O, \, ^{23}Na, \, ^{27}Al, \, ^{35}Cl, \, ^{59}Co.$$

Those nuclei that have $I \geqslant 1$ have nonspherical nuclear charge distribution and hence an electric quadrupole moment Q. We shall consider the effect of the quadrupole moment later. Our present concern is with *all* nuclei that have

12

$I \neq 0$, since each of these possesses a magnetic dipole moment, or a *magnetic moment*, μ. We can think of this moment qualitatively as arising from the motion (spinning) of a charged particle. This is an oversimplified picture, but it nevertheless gives qualitatively the correct results that (a) those nuclei that have a spin have a magnetic moment and (b) the magnetic moment is collinear with the angular momentum vector. We can express these facts by writing

$$\mu = \gamma \mathbf{p}. \tag{2.2}$$

The constant of proportionality γ is called the *magnetogyric ratio* and is different for different nuclei, since it reflects nuclear properties not accounted for by the simple picture of a spinning charged particle. (Sometimes γ is termed the gyromagnetic ratio.) While p is a simple multiple of $\hbar$, μ and hence γ are not and must be determined experimentally for each nucleus (usually by an NMR method). Values of μ are given in Appendix A.

2.2 Classical Mechanical Description of NMR

In considering the interaction of a magnetic moment with an applied magnetic field, we can use either a classical mechanical or a quantum mechanical treatment. Each has some advantages; particularly for the understanding of transient effects and exchange processes, it is very convenient to use a classical approach; whereas in discussing chemical shifts and spin couplings, it is necessary to use energy levels resulting from a quantum treatment.

Consider the interaction of a magnetic field $\mathbf{H}_0$ (typically 10,000–25,000 gauss) with a magnetic moment μ. As shown in Figure 2.1, the moment lies at some angle θ with respect to the field. The magnetic interaction between $\mathbf{H}_0$ and μ generates a torque *tending* to tip the moment toward $\mathbf{H}_0$. Because the nucleus is spinning, the resultant motion does not change θ but rather causes the magnetic moment to *precess* around the magnetic field, as indicated by the dashed path traced out by the end of μ. (The situation is entirely analogous to the precession of a spinning top in the earth's gravitational field.)

Mathematically the torque $\mathbf{L}$ is given by classical magnetic theory as

$$\mathbf{L} = \mu \times \mathbf{H}_0. \tag{2.3}$$

From classical mechanics[1]

$$\frac{d\mathbf{p}}{dt} = \mathbf{L}, \tag{2.4}$$

so

$$\frac{d\mathbf{p}}{dt} = \boldsymbol{\mu} \times \mathbf{H}_0. \tag{2.5}$$

Substituting equation 2.2, we have

$$\frac{d\boldsymbol{\mu}}{dt} = \gamma \frac{d\mathbf{p}}{dt} = \gamma \boldsymbol{\mu} \times \mathbf{H}_0. \tag{2.6}$$

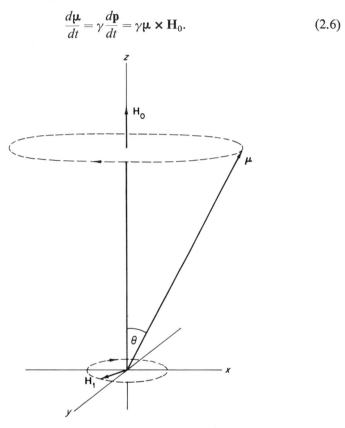

Fig. 2.1   Vectorial representation of Larmor precession.

Since the length of $\boldsymbol{\mu}$ is constant, equation 2.6 expresses the fact that the motion of $\boldsymbol{\mu}$ occurs with only a single degree of freedom, namely, a precession about $\mathbf{H}_0$.[2] Such a precession of $\boldsymbol{\mu}$ with angular velocity and direction given by $\boldsymbol{\omega}_0$ is expressed by

$$\frac{d\boldsymbol{\mu}}{dt} = \boldsymbol{\omega}_0 \times \boldsymbol{\mu}. \tag{2.7}$$

Comparing equations 2.6 and 2.7, we see that

$$\boldsymbol{\omega}_0 = -\gamma \mathbf{H}_0. \tag{2.8}$$

Thus the nuclear moment precesses about $\mathbf{H}_0$ with a frequency

$$\nu_0 = \frac{|\boldsymbol{\omega}_0|}{2\pi} = \frac{\gamma}{2\pi} H_0. \tag{2.9}$$

Equation 2.8 or 2.9 is often called the *Larmor equation*. The precession (or Larmor) frequency is thus directly proportional to the applied magnetic field and also dependent on γ (or $\boldsymbol{\mu}$), which varies from one nucleus to another (see Appendix A).*

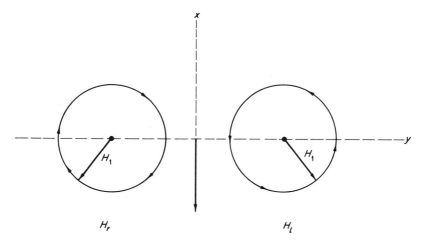

Fig. 2.2 Resolution of a plane (linearly) polarized wave into two counterrotating components.

One significant feature of the Larmor equation is that the angle θ does not appear. Hence the nucleus precesses at a frequency governed by its own characteristic properties and that of the magnetic field. On the other hand, the *energy* of this spin system does depend on θ, since

$$E = -\boldsymbol{\mu} \cdot \mathbf{H}_0 = -\mu H_0 \cos \theta. \tag{2.10}$$

If a small magnetic field $\mathbf{H}_1$ is placed at right angles to $\mathbf{H}_0$, and is made to rotate about $\mathbf{H}_0$ at a frequency ν_0 (see Figure 2.1), then $\boldsymbol{\mu}$ experiences the resultant of $\mathbf{H}_0$ and $\mathbf{H}_1$ and θ changes by $d\theta$. Energy is thus absorbed from the field $\mathbf{H}_1$ into the nuclear spin system. If $\mathbf{H}_1$ rotates at any frequency $\nu \neq \nu_0$, then it is alternately in and out of phase with $\boldsymbol{\mu}$, and no net energy

---

* By analogy to the electron magnetic moment, which is expressed in Bohr magnetons, a *nuclear Bohr magneton* μ_0 is defined as

$$\mu_0 \equiv e\hbar/2Mc = 5.0500 \times 10^{-24} \text{ erg/gauss,}$$

where e and M are the charge and mass of the proton. In Appendix A values of μ are given in units of μ_0'.

absorption occurs. Hence the absorption of energy is a resonance phenomenon, sharply tuned to the natural nuclear precession frequency.

In practice, the rotating field $\mathbf{H}_1$ is obtained from a linearly polarized electromagnetic field that results from the passage of electric current at frequency ν through a coil. If this field is polarized along the x axis, it may be thought of as resulting from two equal fields counterrotating in the xy plane, as indicated in Figure 2.2. Mathematically

$$H_r = (H_1)_x \cos 2\pi\nu t + (H_1)_y \sin 2\pi\nu t,$$
$$H_l = (H_1)_x \cos 2\pi\nu t - (H_1)_y \sin 2\pi\nu t. \tag{2.11}$$

Obviously the sum of H_r and H_l has only an x component. With respect to the precessing nuclei, the counterrotating field is at a frequency $2\nu_0$ away and may be ignored.

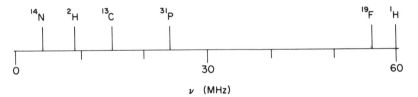

Fig. 2.3   Resonance frequencies for several nuclei in a magnetic field of approximately 14,100 gauss.

We might say a few words about the orders of magnitude involved in NMR. Applied fields H_0 of 10–25 kilogauss (kG) are commonly employed; Larmor frequencies with such fields are in the radio-frequency (rf) range of several megahertz (MHz).* The values of ν_0 for a field H_0 of 14,100 gauss are given for a few important nuclei in Figure 2.3, and other values of ν_0 (for a 10,000-gauss field) are listed in Appendix A.

In conventional spectroscopy the spectrum is scanned by varying the frequency of incident radiation. In NMR either the radio frequency or the magnetic field may be varied, since by the Larmor relation (equation 2.9) ν_0 is proportional to H_0. In either case the range needed to encompass all the resonances from a given type of nucleus is small—usually less than a few kilohertz or a few gauss. Therefore, *in a given experiment we study the resonance of only one type of nucleus.*

The magnitude selected for H_1 depends on factors that we shall take up later in this chapter. Usually H_1 is only a few milligauss or less, so that $H_1 \ll H_0$.

---

* The hertz (Hz) is now by international agreement preferred for the unit of frequency rather than the older cycle per second (cps); 1 Hz ≡ 1 cps.

2.3 Quantum Mechanical Description of NMR

As with other branches of spectroscopy, an explanation of many aspects of NMR requires the use of quantum mechanics. Fortunately, the particular equations needed are simple and can be solved exactly.

In quantum theory, the energy of interaction between a magnetic moment and an applied field, given by equation 2.10, appears in the Hamiltonian operator $\mathscr{H}$,

$$\mathscr{H} = -\mu \cdot H_0. \tag{2.12}$$

By substituting from equations 2.1 and 2.2, we have

$$\mathscr{H} = -\gamma \hbar H_0 \cdot I. \tag{2.13}$$

Here I is interpreted as an operator. From the general properties of spin angular momentum in quantum mechanics,[3] it has been shown that the solution of this Hamiltonian gives energy levels in which

$$E_m = -\gamma \hbar m H_0. \tag{2.14}$$

The quantum number m may assume the values

$$-I, -I+1, \ldots, I-1, I.$$

There are thus $2I + 1$ energy levels, each of which may be thought of as arising from an orientation of μ with respect to H_0 such that its projection on H_0 is quantized (see Figure 2.4). For the particularly important case of $I = \frac{1}{2}$ there are just two energy levels; in this case we often speak of a nuclear spin as having "flipped" from an orientation with the field to one opposed to the field. The energy separation between the states is linearly dependent on the magnetic field.

In these terms NMR arises from transitions between energy levels, just as in other branches of spectroscopy. Transitions are induced by the absorption of energy from an applied electromagnetic field. The presence of this field is treated by adding to the Hamiltonian a term expressing interaction between the spin system and the applied radio-frequency field H_1:

$$\mathscr{H}' = 2\mu_x H_1 \cos 2\pi \nu t. \tag{2.15}$$

From the well-established results of time-dependent perturbation theory[4] we find that the probability of transition per unit time between levels m and m' is

$$P_{mm'} = \gamma^2 H_1^2 |(m|I_x|m')|^2 \delta(\nu_{mm'} - \nu). \tag{2.16}$$

$2H_1$ is the magnitude of the radio-frequency field applied in the x direction, with H_0 in the z direction; $(m|I_x|m')$ is the quantum mechanical matrix element of the x component of the nuclear spin operator and is zero unless $m = m' \pm 1$; and $\delta(\nu_{mm'} - \nu)$ is the Dirac delta function, which is zero unless $\nu_{mm'} = \nu$. $\nu_{mm'}$ is the frequency corresponding to the energy difference between states m and m', as given by the Bohr relation,

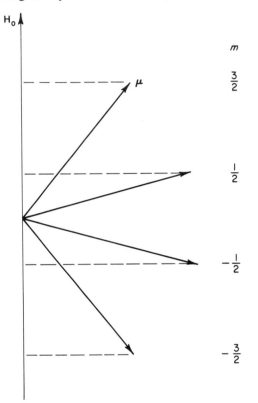

Fig. 2.4   The $2I + 1$ orientations of μ with respect to $\mathbf{H}_0$ and the quantization of the projection of μ on $\mathbf{H}_0$. The case illustrated is $I = \frac{3}{2}$.

$$\nu_{mm'} = \frac{\varDelta E_{mm'}}{h}$$

$$= \frac{\gamma H_0 |m' - m|}{2\pi}. \tag{2.17}$$

Several important points are contained in equation 2.16. First, the transition probability increases with γ and with the applied field H_1.* (This

* While the power absorbed varies as H_1^2 according to equation 2.16, the observed NMR signal, which is proportional to an induced *voltage* in a coil (see Chapter 3), varies linearly with H_1.[5]

latter relation will be modified in Section 2.5.) Second, the matrix element furnishes the selection rule $\Delta m = \pm 1$, so that transitions are permitted only between adjacent energy levels and thus give only a single line at a frequency

$$\nu = \frac{\gamma}{2\pi} H_0. \tag{2.18}$$

Third, the resonance condition is expressed in the delta function. Actually the delta function would predict an infinitely sharp line, which is unrealistic; therefore, it is replaced by a line shape function $g(\nu)$, which has the property that

$$\int_0^\infty g(\nu)\, d\nu = 1. \tag{2.19}$$

(In practice $g(\nu)$ often turns out to be Lorentzian or approximately Lorentzian in shape.) Equation 2.16 becomes then

$$P_{mm'} = \gamma^2\, H_1^2 |(m|I_x|m')|^2\, g(\nu). \tag{2.20}$$

For nuclei with $I = \tfrac{1}{2}$ there is only one transition, so equation 2.20 becomes[4]

$$P = \tfrac{1}{4}\gamma^2\, H_1^2\, g(\nu). \tag{2.21}$$

2.4 Effect of the Boltzmann Distribution

The tendency of nuclei to align with the magnetic field and thus to drop into the lowest energy level is opposed by thermal motions, which tend to equalize the populations in the $2I + 1$ levels. The resultant equilibrium distribution is the usual compromise predicted by the Boltzmann equation. For simplicity we shall consider only nuclei with $I = \tfrac{1}{2}$, so that we need include only two energy levels, the lower corresponding to $m = -\tfrac{1}{2}$ and the upper to $m = +\tfrac{1}{2}$.* We shall designate the levels by the subscripts $-$ and $+$, respectively. For the $I = \tfrac{1}{2}$ system the Boltzmann equation is

$$\frac{n_+}{n_-} = \exp\left(-\frac{\Delta E}{kT}\right). \tag{2.22}$$

---

* The level with $m = -\tfrac{1}{2}$ is of lower energy if the field H_0 is taken along the negative z axis, and m refers to the projection of I on the z axis. This convention is consistent with that employed in Chapter 7.

By substitution of the values of E from equation 2.14, and by introducing equations 2.1 and 2.2, we find that this becomes

$$\frac{n_+}{n_-} = \exp\left(-\frac{\gamma \hbar H_0}{kT}\right)$$

$$= \exp\left(-\frac{2\mu H_0}{kT}\right). \tag{2.23}$$

For small values of the argument in the exponential the approximation $e^{-x} = 1 - x$ may be employed to show that the fractional excess population in the lower level is

$$\frac{n_- - n_+}{n_-} = \frac{2\mu H_0}{kT}. \tag{2.24}$$

For ^{1}H, which has a large magnetic moment, in a field of 14,000 gauss this fractional excess is only about 1×10^{-5} at room temperature.*

One consequence of this slight excess population in the lower level is the appearance of a very small macroscopic magnetic moment directed along $\mathbf{H_0}$. The mean value $\bar{\mu}$ is given by the weighted average of the oppositely directed moments from the two states:

$$\bar{\mu} = \frac{n_-}{n_+ + n_-}\mu + \frac{n_+}{n_+ + n_-}(-\mu). \tag{2.25}$$

From the Boltzmann distribution, equation 2.23, together with the fact that $2\mu H_0/kT \ll 1$, we see that

$$\frac{n_-}{n_+ + n_-} \approx \frac{1}{2}\left(1 + \frac{\mu H_0}{kT}\right),$$

$$\frac{n_+}{n_+ + n_-} \approx \frac{1}{2}\left(1 - \frac{\mu H_0}{kT}\right). \tag{2.26}$$

Then

$$\bar{\mu} = \frac{1}{2}\left(1 + \frac{\mu H_0}{kT}\right)\mu - \frac{1}{2}\left(1 - \frac{\mu H_0}{kT}\right)\mu = \frac{\mu^2 H_0}{kT}. \tag{2.27}$$

For N nuclei per unit volume, the total magnetization is N times as large, and the *volume magnetic susceptibility* is

$$K = \frac{N\bar{\mu}}{H_0} = \frac{N\mu^2}{kT}. \tag{2.28}$$

For protons in water at room temperature this is about 3×10^{-10}. This nuclear paramagnetic susceptibility is ordinarily completely masked by the diamagnetic

---

* This very small difference in population occurs because the energy levels are only slightly separated from each other. In this case ΔE is only ~6 *millicalories*.

susceptibility due to the electrons, which is about 10^{-6}, but has been measured at very low temperature.

The near equality of population in the two levels is an important factor in determining the intensity of the NMR signal. According to the Einstein formulation, the radiative transition probability between two levels is given by [3]

$$P_+ \propto B_+ \rho(v) n_-,$$
$$P_- \propto B_- \rho(v) n_+ + A_- n_+. \tag{2.29}$$

P_+ and P_- are the probabilities for absorption and emission, respectively; B_+ and B_- are the coefficients of absorption and of *induced* emission, respectively; A_- is the coefficient of *spontaneous* emission; and $\rho(v)$ is the density of radiation at the frequency that induces the transition. Einstein showed that $B_+ = B_-$, while $A_- \propto v^3 B_-$. As a result of this strong frequency dependence, spontaneous emission (fluorescence), which usually dominates in the visible region of the spectrum, is an extremely improbable process in the rf region and may be disregarded. Thus the *net* probability of absorption of rf energy, which is proportional to the strength of the NMR signal, is

$$P \propto B\rho(v)(n_- - n_+). \tag{2.30}$$

The small value of $(n_- - n_+)$ accounts in large part for the insensitivity of NMR relative to other spectroscopic methods (see Chapter 3).

2.5 Spin-Lattice Relaxation

It is important now to consider the manner in which the Boltzmann distribution is established. Again we shall for simplicity treat only the case $I = \frac{1}{2}$. If initially the sample containing the nuclear spin system is outside a polarizing magnetic field, the difference in energy between the two levels is zero, and the populations n_+ and n_- must be equal. When the sample is placed in the field, the Boltzmann distribution is not established instantaneously. Since spontaneous emission is negligible, the redistribution of population must come about from an interaction of the nuclei with their surroundings (the "lattice"). As we shall see, this is a nonradiative first-order rate process characterized by a "lifetime," T_1, called the *spin-lattice relaxation time*. The origin of this process may be seen in the following: Let $n = (n_- - n_+)$ be the difference in population; let $n_0 = (n_- + n_+)$; let $W_+ =$ the probability for a nucleus to undergo a transition from the lower to the upper level as a result of an interaction with the environment, and let W_- be the analogous probability for the downward transition. Unlike the radiative transition probabilities, W_+ and W_- are not equal; in fact, at equilibrium, where the number of upward and downward transitions are equal,

$$W_+ n_- = W_- n_+. \tag{2.31}$$

From equations 2.23 and 2.31

$$\frac{W_+}{W_-} = \left(\frac{n_+}{n_-}\right)_{\text{eq}} = \exp\left(-\frac{2\mu H_0}{kT}\right). \tag{2.32}$$

Using the same approximations as in Section 2.4 for $2\mu H_0/kT \ll 1$, and defining W as the mean of W_+ and W_-, we may write

$$\frac{W_+}{W} = \frac{(n_+)_{\text{eq}}}{n_0/2} = 1 - \frac{\mu H_0}{kT},$$

$$\frac{W_-}{W} = \frac{(n_-)_{\text{eq}}}{n_0/2} = 1 + \frac{\mu H_0}{kT}. \tag{2.33}$$

The total rate of change of n is

$$\frac{dn}{dt} = \frac{dn_-}{dt} - \frac{dn_+}{dt} = 2\frac{dn_-}{dt}. \tag{2.34}$$

But by definition of W_+ and W_-

$$\frac{dn_-}{dt} = n_+ W_- - n_- W_+. \tag{2.35}$$

So, from equations 2.33 to 2.35,

$$\frac{dn}{dt} = -2W\left(n - n_0 \frac{\mu H_0}{kT}\right). \tag{2.36}$$

By introducing equation 2.26, we obtain

$$\frac{dn}{dt} = -2W(n - n_{\text{eq}}). \tag{2.37}$$

This rate equation describes a first-order decay process, characterized by a rate constant $2W$. If we define a time T_1

$$T_1 = \frac{1}{2W}, \tag{2.38}$$

and integrate, we obtain

$$n - n_{\text{eq}} = (n - n_{\text{eq}})_{t=0} \exp\left(-\frac{t}{T_1}\right). \tag{2.39}$$

T_1 thus serves as a measure of the rate with which the spin system comes into equilibrium with its environment and hence is called the spin-lattice relaxation time.

The magnitude of T_1 is highly dependent on the type of nucleus and on factors such as the physical state of the sample and the temperature. For liquids T_1 is usually between 10^{-2} and 100 sec, but in some cases may be as short as 10^{-4} sec. In solids T_1 may be much longer—sometimes days. The mechanisms of spin-lattice relaxation and some chemical applications will be taken up in Chapter 9.

If T_1 is long enough (>10 sec), the effect of spin-lattice relaxation may be seen readily in a series of scans made immediately after the sample is placed in the magnetic field. An example is given in Figure 2.5. Shorter T_1's must be measured by more elaborate techniques, to be discussed in Chapter 9.

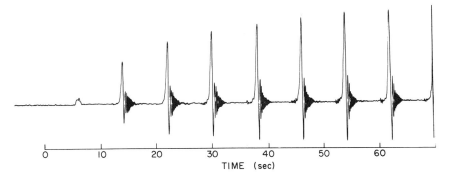

Fig. 2.5 Spin-lattice relaxation in benzene (60 MHz). The sample was placed in the magnetic field H_0 at $t = 0$ and the spectrum scanned repetitively using a small value of H_1.

2.6 Line Widths

We pointed out in Section 2.3 that an NMR line is not infinitely sharp, and we assumed some function $g(\nu)$ as the line shape. The existence of spin-lattice relaxation implies that the line must have a width at least as great as can be estimated from the Uncertainty Principle:

$$\Delta E \cdot \Delta t \sim h. \tag{2.40}$$

Since the average lifetime of the upper state cannot exceed T_1, this energy level must be broadened to the extent of h/T_1, and thus the half-width of the NMR line resulting from this transition must be *at least* of the order of $1/T_1$.

For liquids line widths of from 10^{-2} to 10^2 Hz would be expected from the range of T_1 given in Section 2.5.

There are, however, other processes that can increase line widths substantially over the value expected from spin-lattice relaxation. The most important of these involves the interaction between nearby nuclear magnetic moments. The field experienced by one nuclear moment and caused by another of magnitude μ at a distance r is proportional to μ/r^3. A given nucleus experiences a field of this magnitude from each of its neighbors, and each such contribution may either augment the field applied to the sample or detract from it, depending on the orientation of each magnetic moment with respect to the applied field. It is apparent that not all nuclei in a macroscopic sample will experience the same internuclear field; thus the resonance frequencies of the nuclei will differ, and the observed line will be broadened. The theory will be taken up in more detail in Chapter 9, where it will be shown that this interaction averages almost completely to zero when the molecules in the sample are in rapid random motion with respect to the applied field. Thus this interaction, which is the major source of line width in solids, is negligible in most liquids or solutions containing small molecules. For polymers the situation is intermediate. Typical line widths are: liquids, <0.1–10 Hz; polymers, 10–10^4 Hz; solids, 10^4–10^5 Hz.

When the line width is greater than that predicted from T_1, it is convenient to define another time T_2 (shorter than T_1), which is called *the spin-spin relaxation time*. T_2 is defined so as to be consistent with the Uncertainty Principle order of magnitude relation

$$\nu_{1/2} T_2 \sim 1, \tag{2.41}$$

where $\nu_{1/2}$ is the width of the line at half maximum intensity. For consistency with T_2 introduced in an alternative manner (see Section 2.8), we can formulate the precise definition of T_2 in terms of the line shape function $g(\nu)$ as follows:

$$T_2 \equiv \tfrac{1}{2}[g(\nu)]_{max}. \tag{2.42}$$

We can easily show that this apparently arbitrary definition of T_2 gives the desired relationship expressed in equation 2.41. If the line has a Lorentzian shape, as is predicted theoretically and usually verified experimentally, then $g(\nu)$ obeys the equation

$$g(\nu) = \frac{a}{b^2 + (\nu - \nu_0)^2}, \tag{2.43}$$

where ν_0 is the frequency of the peak, and a and b are constants. By introducing equations 2.42 and 2.43 into equation 2.19, we find that

$$T_2 = \frac{1}{\pi \nu_{1/2}}. \tag{2.44}$$

For a line shape other than Lorentzian the definition of T_2 given in equation 2.42 leads to a relation between T_2 and $\nu_{1/2}$ differing in the constant factor but otherwise consistent with the Uncertainty Principle relation (cf. Problem 7).

The "natural" widths of very sharp NMR lines cannot be measured directly because even the best existing apparatus has a magnetic field inhomogeneity equivalent to $\sim$0.05–0.1 Hz.

2.7 Saturation

In the presence of an rf field the fundamental rate equation for spin-lattice relaxation (2.37) must be modified by including a term like that in equation 2.30, which expresses the fact that the rf field causes net upward transitions proportional to the difference in population n. The resultant differential equation is

$$\frac{dn}{dt} = -\frac{n - n_{eq}}{T_1} - 2nP. \tag{2.45}$$

Substituting for P from equation 2.21 and solving the differential equation, we find that the steady-state value n_{ss} is

$$n_{ss} = \frac{n_{eq}}{1 + \frac{1}{2}\gamma^2 H_1^2 T_1 g(\nu)}. \tag{2.46}$$

The decrease in n below the Boltzmann equilibrium value naturally decreases the magnitude of the NMR signal below what would be expected. This process is called *saturation* and in extreme cases can lead to a virtual disappearance of an NMR signal. The denominator of equation 2.46 is largest when $g(\nu)$ is at its maximum value. Substituting for $g(\nu)_{max}$ from equation 2.42, we obtain

$$n_{ss} = \frac{n_{eq}}{1 + \gamma^2 H_1^2 T_1 T_2} = n_{eq} Z. \tag{2.47}$$

The quantity Z, which is defined by equation 2.47, is called the *saturation factor*. We shall refer to this factor in Section 3.7, when we consider the practical effects of saturation on signal strength.

2.8 The Bloch Equations; Nuclear Induction

Bloch successfully explained many aspects of NMR phenomena by means of a set of classical mechanical equations based, not on the magnetic properties of an individual nucleus, but on the macroscopic, measurable magnetization resulting from an ensemble of nuclei.

The rationale for the treatment can perhaps best be understood by reference to Figure 2.6. In the absence of an rf field the nuclei (assumed identical) all precess at the Larmor frequency and make some angle with respect to the imposed field. For the case $I = \frac{1}{2}$ there are two possible orientations of the nuclear moments with respect to the field, the one with lower energy being slightly more populated, as indicated by the number of nuclear

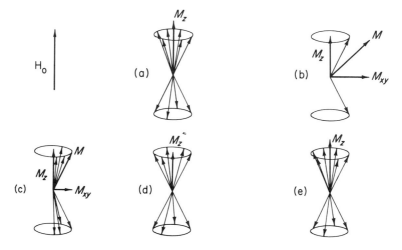

Fig. 2.6 Relation between the macroscopic nuclear magnetization **M** and individual nuclear moments **μ**. The nuclear moments are shown as light arrows and the macroscopic magnetization as dark arrows. (a) Equilibrium situation, with resultant **M** oriented along the z axis. (b) Nuclear moments forced into phase by rf field, with generation of component of **M** in the xy plane. (c) Nuclear moments begin to lose phase coherence, with resultant decrease of M_{xy}. (d) Nuclear moments lose all phase coherence, so that $M_{xy} = 0$. Little change occurs in M_z. (e) Populations of nuclei in states $m = \frac{1}{2}$ and $m = -\frac{1}{2}$ are reestablished at the Boltzmann value, with M_z assuming its equilibrium value.

vectors in Figure 2.6a. With a large collection of nuclei precessing at random phase, the *resultant* macroscopic magnetization points along the z direction. This is the equilibrium magnetization M_0 that is responsible for the small nuclear magnetic susceptibility calculated in equation 2.28.

An imposed rf field H_1 at the Larmor frequency has two effects: (1) some nuclei flip by absorbing energy from H_1 so that the populations in the two states become more nearly equal, thus decreasing M_z; and (2) the nuclei are forced by the rf field to precess in phase, thus creating a component of magnetization M_{xy} in the xy plane. The situation just described, which occurs at resonance, is depicted in Figure 2.6b.

After resonance is passed, the nuclei gradually get out of phase with each other. The lifetime for this loss of phase coherence turns out to be just T_2, the spin-spin relaxation time. Thus M_{xy} decays to zero in time T_2. (Since T_2 measures relaxation in a plane normal to the direction of $\mathbf{H}_0$, T_2 is also called

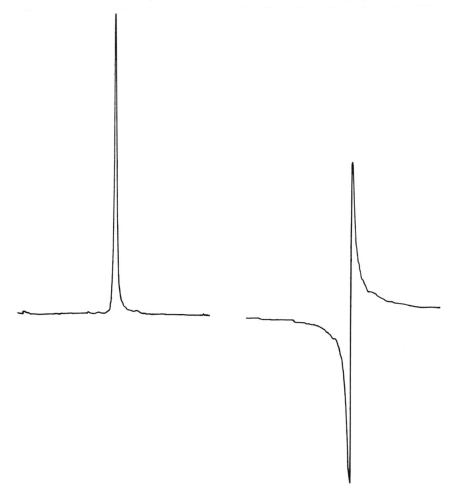

Fig. 2.7 Typical absorption and dispersion modes.

the *transverse relaxation time*.) By spin-lattice relaxation the Boltzmann distribution of spins is restored, so that M_z decays back to its equilibrium value M_0 with a time constant T_1. (Hence T_1 is also called the *longitudinal* relaxation time.) This decay is indicated in Figure 2.6c. If $T_1 \approx T_2$, the original equilibrium situation is restored, as shown in Figure 2.6e. On the other hand, if $T_1 \gg T_2$, an intermediate situation occurs (Figure 2.6d) in which M_{xy} has decayed to zero, while M_z still retains its smaller nonequilibrium value.

Bloch treated the behavior of the magnetization components M_z and M_{xy} under the assumption of two relaxation times T_1 and T_2 and with a field H_1 rotating in the xy plane (see equation 2.11). The differential equations and their solution are given elsewhere.[4] The results of the Bloch treatment show that the rf field H_1 produces a magnetization in the xy plane, which leads to two measurable signals: (1) the *absorption* signal, a component out of phase with H_1, which has a Lorentzian line shape; and (2) the *dispersion* signal, which is in phase with H_1. The shapes of these signals are shown in Figure 2.7. By appropriate electronic means (see Section 3.3) we can select one of these two signals for study. Usually the absorption mode is used, but the dispersion mode has some advantages (Section 3.15).

Bloch showed that the rotating magnetization M_{xy} can induce a small rf signal in a coil placed along the y axis, while the field H_1 is supplied by a coil on the x axis. The induced signal can be amplified and detected to give the NMR spectrum. This procedure, *nuclear induction*, is used in many NMR spectrometers (see Section 3.1). From considerations of the magnitude of the induced signal it is possible to derive an expression for the NMR signal strength.[4] For $T_1 = T_2$, the peak intensity at constant field is proportional to

$$\frac{I+1}{I^2} \mu^3 H_0^2. \tag{2.48}$$

2.9 Ringing

The solutions of the Bloch equations discussed above are the steady-state or "slow passage" solutions, that is, those obeying the "adiabatic" condition[6] that the rate of change of H_0 is sufficiently slow:

$$\frac{dH_0}{dt} \ll |\gamma| H_0^2. \tag{2.49}$$

In addition, there are a number of transient phenomena that can also be explained by the Bloch equations. At present we shall treat only one, *ringing* or "wiggles." A resonance line scanned very slowly has the Lorentzian shape predicted by the Bloch equations, but most sharp lines scanned at the usual speeds (see Section 3.5) exhibit a ringing pattern following the center of the line, as indicated in Figure 2.8. Ringing is easily understood from Figure 2.6. Suppose that the rf frequency is held constant at ν_0, and the spectrum is scanned by increasing the magnetic field so that the Larmor frequency of the nuclei increases through the value ν_0. Immediately after the resonance condition is passed, the magnetization is depicted by Figure 2.6b, with a component rotating at the Larmor frequency in the xy plane. H_1 is still rotating in the xy plane at ν_0, and as the Larmor frequency increases due to the steadily increasing field H_0, there is interference between H_1 and M_{xy}, leading to the beat pattern typical of two close-lying frequencies. As M_{xy} decays with a time constant

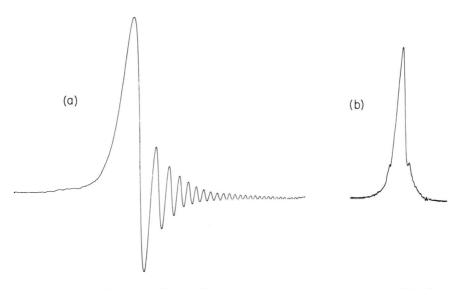

Fig. 2.8   (a) Ringing (or "wiggles") seen after passage through resonance. Direction of scan is from left to right. (b) Same spectral scan at a slower rate, approaching that of "slow passage." Discontinuities near the base of the resonance line are due to spectrometer instability at the very slow scanning speed.

T_2, the envelope of the ringing pattern should in principle furnish a measure of T_2. In practice, the decay is often due principally to inhomogeneities in the magnetic field. Because of field inhomogeneity, nuclei in different portions of the sample experience slightly different values of H_0, hence have different Larmor frequencies. Thus they not only undergo resonance at a slightly different H_0, leading to a somewhat broadened line, but after resonance they get out of phase more quickly (i.e., in a time less than T_2). The decay rate then is characteristic of field homogeneity, rather than the molecular T_2. The appearance of ringing is often a useful practical criterion of homogeneity, with more intense and longer-lived ringing indicating a more homogeneous field.

References

1. See, for example, H. Goldstein, "Classical Mechanics." Addison-Wesley, Reading, Massachusetts, 1950.

2. For details see, for example, P. L. Corio, "Structure of High Resolution NMR Spectra," pp. 16–19. Academic Press, New York, 1966.

3. See reference 2, pp. 60–62.

4. See, for example, J. A. Pople, W. G. Schneider, and H. J. Bernstein, "High Resolution Nuclear Magnetic Resonance," pp. 31–43. McGraw-Hill, New York, 1959.

5. R. A. Hoffman and S. Forsen, *Progr. NMR Spectroscopy* 1, 26 (1966).

6. See reference 2, p. 22.

Problems

1. Using the values for μ and I given in Appendix A, verify that the resonance frequencies in Appendix A for ^{1}H, ^{2}H, ^{14}N, and ^{31}P are correct.

2. Show that the sensitivity data for constant field given in Appendix A for the four nuclei of Problem 1 are in accord with equation 2.48.

3. Find values for $(n_- - n_+)/n_-$ for ^{19}F, ^{31}P, and ^{15}N at (a) 14,100 gauss and 300°K; (b) 14,100 gauss and 5°K; and (c) 50,000 gauss and 300°K.

4. Derive an equation for signal strength as a function of time that can be used to calculate T_1.

5. Use the equation derived in Problem 4 and the data in Figure 2.5 to calculate T_1 for benzene.

6. Fill in the details of the derivation of equation 2.37 from equation 2.34.

7. Derive an expression in terms of T_2 for the width at half-height of a Gaussian-shaped line.

8. Find the value of the volume nuclear paramagnetic susceptibility K for PF_5 at −90°C and at 2°K. Assume a density of 1.0 at both temperatures.

9. Use equation 2.47 to find the maximum value of H_1 that can be used for protons with $T_1 = T_2 = 4$ sec if Z is to be maintained as large as 0.95. (Note that equation 2.47 is derived for slow passage and that in practice larger values of H_1 are used with correspondingly faster sweep rates.)

Chapter 3

Instrumentation and Techniques

3.1 Basic NMR Apparatus

The basic instrumentation needed for NMR spectroscopy is shown schematically in Figure 3.1. The essential components are as follows.

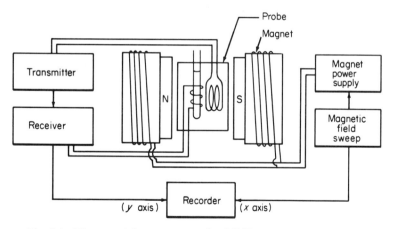

Fig. 3.1 The essential components of an NMR spectrometer system.

(1) A *magnet*, usually capable of producing a field of at least 14,000 gauss. In general, a higher field is desirable for increased sensitivity (Section 2.4) and for reasons to be discussed in Chapter 4. The magnet may be one of three types: a permanent magnet; an electromagnet; or a superconducting solenoid. Permanent magnets are generally simpler and cheaper, but are limited to

about 14,000 gauss and do not possess the flexibility of the more commonly used electromagnets. An electromagnet, of course, requires a suitable power supply of high stability. Superconducting solenoids, which are just coming into use, will be discussed in Section 3.6.

(2) A source of rf power, the *transmitter*. This may be designed for use over a range of frequencies, but for most high resolution NMR work the transmitter is crystal controlled at a single frequency.

(3) A *probe*, which fits into the magnet gap and holds the sample, as well as electrical coils to carry rf power to and from the sample. The probe may be of a single coil or double coil type. In the latter, one coil is attached to the transmitter, while the other, which is placed at right angles to the first, picks up the induced signal from the resonant change in nuclear magnetization. (The double coil type is illustrated in Figure 3.1.)

(4) A *receiver*, which amplifies, detects, and filters the NMR signal.

(5) *Sweep circuitry* to vary either the rf frequency or the magnetic field in a controlled manner. (The latter is shown in Figure 3.1.)

(6) A *recorder* or other means of displaying the NMR spectrum. The recorder or oscilloscope sweep is preferably synchronized with the spectral sweep.

3.2 Requirements for High Resolution NMR

In practice the components listed in the preceding section actually involve apparatus that is mechanically and electronically quite sophisticated. Particularly for the study of the narrow lines that make up the NMR spectrum of a liquid or solution (high resolution NMR), there are very stringent requirements on the magnet and the electronic systems.

Homogeneity. Adequate magnetic field homogeneity across the sample is the *sine qua non* for NMR. As we saw in Section 2.6, NMR lines from small molecules in the liquid phase are usually <0.6 Hz in width, and as we shall see in Chapter 5, lines separated from each other by <1 Hz can frequently provide information of chemical value. For proton resonance, rf frequencies of 60 or 100 MHz are usually used; hence a resolution of at least 5×10^{-9} is required. This phenomenal homogeneity requirement is realized by several means.

First, the sample volume is restricted. In most instruments the "effective volume" of the sample (i.e., that within the rf receiver coil) is restricted to about 0.04 cm^3. The sample is usually placed in a cylindrical tube, and considerably more sample may actually be required in practice; this point will be taken up in Section 3.5.

Second, the magnet must have large-diameter pole pieces relative to the width of the air gap. All parts must be machined and aligned carefully and the pole faces must be polished almost to optical flatness.

Third, electromagnets are often *cycled*, that is, increased for a few minutes to a field higher than that desired for the NMR studies. Because of hysteresis

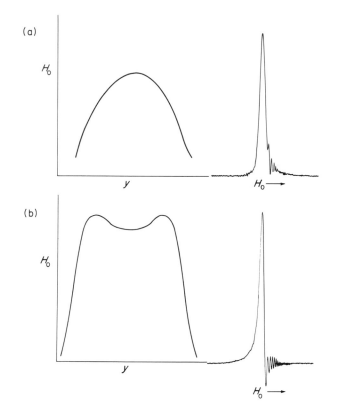

Fig. 3.2 Typical field gradients and line shapes resulting from improper cycling of an electromagnet: (a) undercycled; (b) overcycled.

effects this procedure substantially reduces the field gradients across a sample. A magnet that has not been adequately cycled has a field gradient of a "domed" shape, as indicated in Figure 3.2a. The center of the sample, containing the bulk of the nuclei, comes into resonance then at the lowest applied field as the spectrum is scanned, while the remainder of the sample resonates at a higher applied field. The result is a line shape of the form shown in Figure 3.2a. A field that has been overcycled has a "dished" gradient and gives a line shape of the form in Figure 3.2b. Magnets operating at high field strength (near

24,000 gauss) are generally not cycled, but satisfactory field homogeneity can be obtained as described below.

Fourth, the temperature of the cooling water for an electromagnet and the air temperature for any magnet (especially a permanent magnet) must be carefully controlled. Usually the magnet yoke is insulated to decrease thermal fluctuations.

Fifth, electrical coils of carefully chosen geometry are placed on the pole faces of the magnets, and small dc currents are passed through them. The small magnetic fields thus generated are adjusted to compensate any inhomogeneity in the main magnetic field. With these so-called *shim coils*, linear field gradients in the x, y, and z directions can be reduced by about an order of magnitude, and a second-order, or "curvature," control permits in effect a fine control over the cycling. For magnets that cannot be cycled, additional coils provide correction of higher-order field gradients. Some spectrometers are equipped with a device that automatically adjusts the current in one of the shim coils to maintain optimum homogeneity.

Finally, a considerable improvement in *effective* homogeneity is achieved by spinning the sample tube about its axis. If the field gradient across the sample in a direction transverse to the spinning axis is ΔH, then it has been shown[1] that a spinning rate

$$R > \frac{\gamma \Delta H}{2\pi} \frac{\text{rev}}{\text{sec}} \tag{3.1}$$

averages out much of the inhomogeneity by causing each portion of the sample to move periodically through the entire gradient. The sample thus behaves as though it experiences only the average field rather than the entire range of field. This procedure is so effective that it is used almost universally in high resolution NMR work. Sample spinning is usually accomplished by means of a small air turbine mounted on the probe. Rotation of the order of 30 rev/sec is typical, but may need to be as high as 100–200 rev/sec in the less homogeneous fields of superconducting magnets.

There is one practical drawback to the spinning technique: the periodic spinning modulates the magnetic field and leads to the appearance of *sidebands* (i.e., "images" of the spectral peaks) symmetrically placed and separated by the spinning frequency and integral multiples of it. Spinning sidebands can usually be reduced to less than 1% of the ordinary peak intensity by proper adjustment of the electrical shim coils and by use of high-precision sample tubes and spinning apparatus. Spinning sidebands can easily be recognized by their change in position when the spinning speed is altered. A higher speed not only causes them to move farther from the parent peak but also reduces their intensity. Examples of spinning effects and spinning sidebands are shown in Figure 3.3.

Stability. A highly homogeneous field is of little practical value in measuring sharp line NMR spectra if there are significant fluctuations of field or rf frequency during the period of observation. To forestall such effects, the early high resolution NMR measurements were simply made rapidly; such fast scans, however, obscure much of the detail in the spectra and, as we shall see in Section 3.5, lead to a poorer signal/noise ratio.

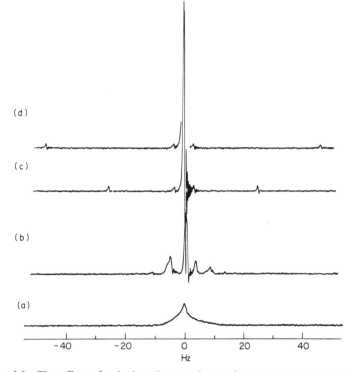

Fig. 3.3 The effect of spinning the sample on the proton resonance spectrum of tetramethylsilane (TMS): (a) Without spinning, showing a line about 3.5 Hz wide; (b) spinning at the slow rate of about 4 rev/sec; (c) spinning rate 25 rev/sec; (d) spinning rate 46.5 rev/sec. (The small peaks seen in (c) and (d) near the base of the principal line are not spinning sidebands, but arise from molecules of TMS containing ^{29}Si. See Section 7.24 for details.)

The first real efforts to achieve adequate stability for high resolution NMR aimed at stabilizing the radio frequency by means of a crystal-controlled oscillator operating at the Larmor frequency (e.g., 60 MHz) for the particular nucleus involved. The magnetic field was stabilized independently by a flux stabilizer, which sensed changes in the field and applied correction currents through the magnet power supply.

It is apparent that because of the Larmor relationship the field and frequency need not be individually held extremely constant; only their ratio is important. Most of the spectrometers now in use employ a field/frequency control procedure that incorporates some sort of feedback loop. The means for accomplishing such control will be taken up in Section 3.4.

3.3 Modulation and Phase Detection

Many features of NMR instrumentation depend on the periodic modulation of either the rf frequency or the magnetic field. Because of the Larmor relationship, the two types of modulation give essentially the same results. Field modulation is usually employed because it is simpler to obtain, but often we express the results as though the rf were modulated.

It has been shown[2] that the modulation of the field at an audio frequency that is large compared with the widths of NMR lines (a frequency typically in the range 1–10 kHz) results in the appearance of sidebands at multiples of the audio frequency. By altering the *modulation index*, which involves the amount of audio power applied, the intensity distribution in the sidebands may be varied. For most purposes only the first sideband is needed.

Almost all high resolution NMR spectrometers now employ *phase detection* of the NMR signal, in both the rf and the audio range. This is accomplished by using a signal from the transmitter as a reference and electronically detecting the amplified output signal from the NMR probe that is either in phase or 90° out of phase with the transmitter signal. The rf phase detection thus selects the absorption or dispersion mode of the NMR signal (see Section 2.8), while the audio phase detection discriminates against spurious signals at other frequencies (e.g., erratic changes in amplifier gain or transmitter level). The latter procedure thereby eliminates much low-frequency noise and leads to a more stable spectral base line. This is particularly important in measuring the areas under NMR lines (see Section 3.7). Field modulation and phase detection also furnish an effective means of stabilizing the field/frequency relation in an NMR spectrometer.

3.4 Field/Frequency Control

The principles of audio modulation of the magnetic field may be used for stabilization of the field/rf frequency ratio in two ways. In both, the audio modulation frequency is chosen to be larger than the range over which chemically shifted resonance lines are to be expected. For proton resonance at 60 or 100 MHz a frequency of 2 kHz is adequate; for other nuclei the frequency must usually be several times as large. A spectrum thus appears as indicated schematically in Figure 3.4. The range of variation of the field

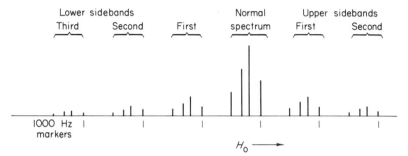

Fig. 3.4 Schematic representation of a spectrum spanning 500 Hz with audio modulation of 1000 Hz.

may then be restricted to encompass only the spectrum generated by, say, the first upper sideband.

One method of field/frequency control uses a "nuclear sideband oscillator," in which the centerband frequency is determined by a crystal at a constant

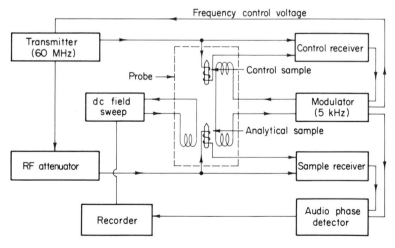

Fig. 3.5 Block diagram of an external lock system. The audio modulator, control sample, and control receiver are the components of a feedback loop that alters the audio frequency or radio frequency, or both, in order to maintain the control sample at resonance when the magnetic field strength fluctuates. The analytical sample is subjected to the same frequencies and magnetic field as the control sample, but in addition is exposed to a linearly varying sweep field from a separate coil.

frequency, but the modulation frequency is varied by a feedback loop that maintains resonance at the upper sideband frequency for a particular sample.[2a] This type of operation requires two samples placed as close together as possible in the magnetic field. The "control sample" (e.g., water) is part of the feedback loop that determines one sideband frequency, while the sample to be studied is subjected also to a controllable "sweep field," which is varied through resonance. A block diagram of the Varian A-60 spectrometer, which employs this scheme, is given in Figure 3.5. Since the control sample is in a separate tube from the analytical sample, this type of system is often referred to as an *external lock* system. A good external lock system maintains stability better than 2×10^{-8}/hour.

An *internal lock* system, based on sideband responses, is also in widespread use. In this case, two sideband frequencies are used, one held very constant, the other variable. The feedback loop normally is applied to the magnetic field to maintain resonance, but in addition some of the feedback current may be applied to "pull" the crystal-controlled centerband frequency very slightly ($<$ a few hertz) from its nominal value. Either the fixed or variable frequency sideband may be used in the control loop. If the fixed frequency is used for control, the field and frequency are locked together, and the spectrum is then scanned by varying the second modulating frequency (preferably linearly with time) and displaying the NMR signal obtained from a second phase sensitive detector referenced to this frequency. This constitutes a true *frequency sweep*, rather than the conventional field sweep, and is advantageous for double resonance experiments (see Chapter 8). *Field sweep* may also be obtained with this system if the variable frequency is used in the feedback loop, while the fixed frequency is used for the observed signal. In this case, the linearly varying audio frequency causes a linear change in the field (in addition to any other small changes in field needed to compensate for frequency fluctuations). A block diagram illustrating the system and sweep modes is given in Figure 3.6. The resonance line used to maintain the locking or feedback channel may be a separate sample, as in the case described above, but there is no need that this be so. Normally the locking signal is derived from a sharp NMR line in the sample being studied; frequently this is a compound deliberately added as a reference, such as $Si(CH_3)_4$ for proton resonance. Spectrometers such as the Varian HA-100 and HA-60-IL use this internal lock system. Since the field/frequency control is derived from the sample tube containing the substance being studied, it is possible to discriminate better against small field fluctuations than it is in the external lock systems, and the stability is about 1×10^{-9}/hour.

Both of the locking systems just described have been used most extensively for proton and ^{19}F resonances. Their use for other nuclei is limited by the low sensitivity and unfavorable relaxation times often encountered, but significant progress has been made in using internal lock systems for ^{2}H, ^{13}C, and ^{31}P. In addition, an internal lock system is sometimes employed with the control loop depending on one nucleus (e.g., ^{1}H), while the observation frequency is that of another nucleus (e.g., ^{13}C). This, of course, requires the use of two radio frequencies and a probe that is tuned for both frequencies. There are a number

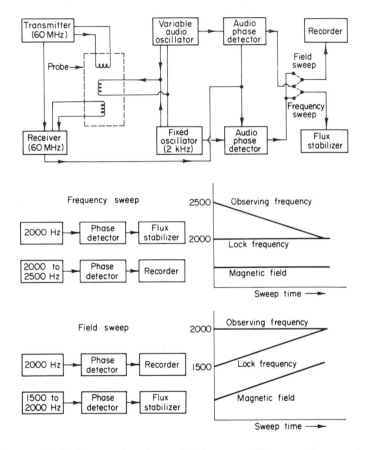

Fig. 3.6 Block diagram of an internal lock system. The transmitter, receiver, and modulation coils in the probe actually are placed orthogonally around the sample but are separated here for clarity. A control signal is derived from one of the audio responses and is fed to the magnetic flux stabilizer, which adjusts the magnetic field to compensate for field fluctuations and drift. The frequency sweep and field sweep modes of operation are illustrated for a total sweep equivalent to 500 Hz over nuclei that are less "shielded" than those of the "lock" material, with a fixed audio frequency of 2000 Hz. These illustrations are based on the use of the first *upper* sideband. If the first *lower* sideband is selected, frequency sweep requires that the observing frequency cover the range 1500–2000 Hz, while field sweep requires a range of 2500–2000 Hz for the lock frequency. (Shielding is discussed in Chapter 4; the example given here is typical for protons with tetramethylsilane as the lock material.)

of practical problems, but such systems using two separate rf oscillators have been successfully employed in ^{13}C, ^{31}P, and ^{11}B resonance studies. Some instruments, such as the JEOLCO C-60-H, can be operated with either internal or external lock.

The most elegant manner of obtaining two accurately controlled radio frequencies is the use of a *frequency synthesizer*, which is a variable frequency rf oscillator whose frequency can be precisely controlled (usually to 0.1 or 0.01 Hz). It is possible to extract from the frequency synthesizer two rf frequencies, one fixed at the proton resonance frequency for the control loop, and the other variable over a very wide range. Several instruments employing frequency synthesizers have been built. The use of frequency synthesizers in NMR spectroscopy seems destined to increase rapidly.

3.5 Signal/Noise and Size of Sample

Several factors determine the signal/noise ratio in NMR and hence limit the minimum size of sample that may be studied. We have already seen in Section 2.8 that an NMR signal for a given nucleus should in principle increase quadratically with field strength, so that large values of H_0 are preferred. The inherent sensitivity varies substantially from one nucleus to another, as indicated in Appendix A. The electronic circuits employed and the care used in manufacture of the probe are, of course, important factors. The "filling factor," that is, the fraction of the volume of the receiver coil that is actually filled by sample, not glass of the sample tube or air space, is especially important. The use of thin pieces of glass on which the coil is wound, as well as the use of thin-walled sample tubes, is mandatory to obtain a high filling factor.

From the practical standpoint, the commercially available spectrometers operating at 60 MHz display a signal somewhat above the noise level from a single sharp line due to protons present at about 0.005–0.02 M. When possible, concentrations of $\gtrsim 0.2$ M are usually preferred. Normally, for proton resonance a sample of about 0.4 ml is contained in a precision, thin-walled glass tube of about 5 mm outer diameter. In some instruments larger-diameter sample tubes may be used to gain some sensitivity at the expense of a larger total amount of solution required. The resulting loss in resolution from the larger tube prevents very significant gains in sensitivity from being made in this way. Microcells, in which the sample is contained in a spherically shaped cavity of 25–50 μl can be used to reduce the total *amount* of sample required, but their greater wall thickness usually requires higher concentrations than the minimum values quoted above (cf. Section 3.14).

The greater the long-term stability of the spectrometer, the longer the time that can be spent in scanning a spectrum. A longer scan time permits additional electronic filtering to reduce some of the noise and thereby improve the signal/noise ratio. Particularly with internal lock spectrometers a scan duration of hours is possible. With very slow scans, however, the rf power must be kept low to avoid saturation (see Sections 2.7 and 3.7).

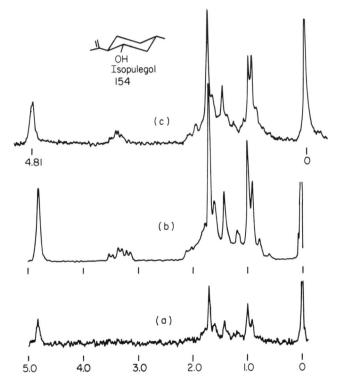

Fig. 3.7 Enhancement of the proton resonance of isopulegol (0.8 mg) by time averaging. (a) Single scan on Varian A-60 spectrometer with sweep rate of 1 Hz/sec; (b) average of 210 scans with sweep rate of 2 Hz/sec; (c) single scan on the more sensitive Varian HA-100 spectrometer with sweep rate of 1 Hz/sec (Lundin et al.[4]).

An alternative method of improving signal/noise by the expenditure of additional scanning time is the use of *time averaging*. Instead of displaying a spectrum on a chart, the spectral information is placed in digital form in the memory of a small special-purpose computer. The information from repetitive scans is then added to that in the computer memory, so that after N scans, the signal is N times as great as would be obtained with one scan. Since noise is random, it can be shown[3] that the noise after N scans has only increased by

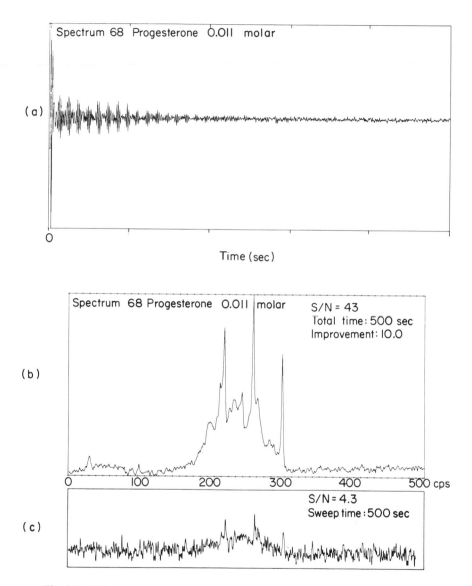

Fig. 3.8 Enhancement of the proton resonance of progesterone by Fourier transform spectroscopy. (a) Observed response to a short pulse, summed 500 times with a time-averaging computer. The response to each pulse is recorded for 1 sec. (b) Fourier transform of (a). (c) Ordinary spectrum of progesterone obtained with a 500-sec sweep time (Ernst and Anderson[5]).

$\sqrt{N}$, so that there is a signal/noise improvement of $\sqrt{N}$. An example is shown in Figure 3.7. Instrumentation for time averaging is commercially available.*

A recent development that holds great promise for signal enhancement is the technique of *Fourier transform spectroscopy*. A strong rf pulse of about 100-μsec duration is applied to the sample and the resultant spectral response pattern is recorded in the memory of a small computer for about 1 sec. Since the spectrum of the sample generally consists of many lines, not just one, this pattern is not a simple free induction decay but is modulated by interference effects. It can be shown that the response pattern is just the Fourier transform of the spectrum,[5] and the spectrum can be extracted by taking the inverse Fourier transform, a task easily done by a large digital computer. The advantage of this technique is that the pulse can be repeated about once per second, and repetitive traces added in the small storage computer before the Fourier transform is taken. Thus in a period of, say, 500 sec, which is a typical time for a routine proton resonance spectrum, 500 pulses can be used, and the resultant signal/noise is theoretically improved by $\sqrt{500} = 22$. In practice, a factor of about 10 has actually been realized. Careful analysis of this technique indicates that its value is greatest for those cases where $T_1 \sim T_2 \approx 1$ sec, and the total spectral scan is great compared with a typical line width. This situation occurs ideally for proton resonance. Figure 3.8 shows a typical pulse response and the resultant spectrum of a complex molecule.

The entire topic of signal/noise enhancement has been treated in detail.[6]

3.6 Superconducting Magnets

The advantages of high magnetic fields have been pointed out with respect to sensitivity. In addition, as we shall see in Chapters 4–6, many spectra are more readily interpreted if they are obtained at high fields. The practical field limits for sufficiently homogeneous magnets are about 14,000 gauss for permanent magnets and 24,000 gauss for conventional electromagnets. With solenoids made of superconducting materials, fields of the order of 100,000 gauss become feasible. The task of developing solenoids that provide such high fields of sufficient homogeneity for NMR work is monumental. Thus far, the highest field achieved for a high resolution NMR magnet is about 52,000 gauss (220 MHz for proton resonance). Particularly for nuclei other than

---

* With a microcell of 50-μl volume (see Section 3.14), time averaging over a weekend with a 100-MHz spectrometer (using a normal scan of 8–10 ppm) should permit the observation of a single, moderately narrow line from a single proton/molecule with a sample of about 0.04 μmole.

hydrogen, where as we shall see, chemical shifts are large and line widths frequently rather great, the superconducting solenoids offer great promise, for in this case homogeneity requirements can be considerably eased.

3.7 Intensity Measurements

In Section 2.4 we saw that the strength of an NMR signal, which is measured by the area under the NMR line, is proportional to the number of

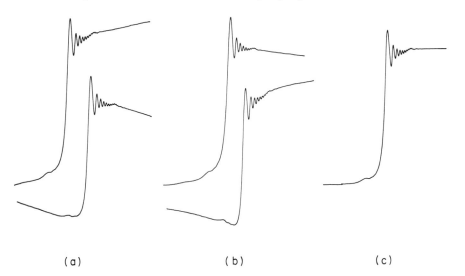

(a)   (b)   (c)

Fig. 3.9 Effect of phasing and integrator adjustments on a spectrum and on an integral: (a) amplifier balance incorrectly set; (b) phase incorrectly set; (c) correct adjustments.

nuclei contributing to the line. Accurate measurements of these areas greatly facilitate the interpretation of spectra and also provide a means of conducting quantitative analyses. Most NMR spectrometers are equipped with electronic integrators, which record relative areas of spectral lines as a step function such as the one in Figure 1.1. In principle such integrations can be accurate to within 1–2% provided signal/noise ratio is sufficiently high. To achieve this precision in practice it is necessary to observe several precautions. First, the phase detector must be carefully adjusted to insure that the signal is a pure absorption mode with no dispersion characteristics. Second, there must be no drift in the amplifying or integrating system. The proper adjustments are illustrated in Figure 3.9. Third, the value of H_1 must be low enough to insure that appreciable saturation does not occur. Since the saturation parameter (equation 2.44) depends on the values of T_1 and T_2, which can differ appreciably between chemically different nuclei of the same species (see Chapter 9), even the measurement of relative areas can be appreciably in error if saturation occurs. In practice, saturation is often somewhat less serious than the Bloch equations would indicate since they are derived for slow passage, and most NMR spectra are obtained with more rapid sweeps.[6] In fact, if the scanning speed is sufficiently rapid and the rf power H_1 is kept low, the values of integrals can be made essentially independent of relaxation times. The sensitivity lost by using a more rapid scan can be regained by time averaging.

3.8 References

As we shall see in detail in Chapter 4, the range of resonance frequencies encompassed by the chemical shifts for a given nucleus is very small relative to the resonance frequencies of the nuclei. The latter are in the range of 1–100 MHz at the magnetic fields usually used, while the former seldom span more than several kilohertz. Within this range we wish to make measurements accurate to a small fraction of the line width, that is, in many cases to about 0.1 Hz or less. While it is possible with sufficiently elaborate instruments to measure frequencies in the megahertz range to <0.1 Hz, there is no means known by which the magnetic field could be independently measured to the necessary accuracy of 1 part in about 10^8 or 10^9. Thus an *absolute* measure of the resonance condition is impossible for high resolution NMR, and all measurements reported are merely made relative to some agreed-upon standard or reference for each nucleus. Unfortunately, an "ideal" reference is not always available, and for experimental reasons it is not always convenient to use a given reference. Hence, NMR data have often been expressed in different ways, and it is important to know how a reference compound can be used and how to convert from one to another.

Two types of reference are used in NMR: *internal* and *external*. An internal reference is a compound, usually giving a sharp NMR line, that is dissolved directly in the sample solution under study. The reference is then dispersed uniformly at a molecular level through the sample. The magnetic field acts equally on the sample and reference molecules, so that a determination of the *difference* in resonance frequency between the two, together with an *approximate* knowledge of the magnetic field or the imposed rf frequency, is adequate for a meaningful measurement. Internal references are used most commonly and are generally advantageous. Provided the reference compound does not react chemically with the sample, the only serious drawback to an internal reference is the possibility that intermolecular interactions will influence the resonance frequency of the reference. Usually, by careful choice of relatively inert compounds this effect can be made small enough to be disregarded. The internal reference of choice for proton resonance is tetramethylsilane. Other references, as well as scales for expressing data, will be given in Chapter 4.

An external reference is a compound placed in a separate container from the sample. Usually an external reference is placed either in a small sealed capillary tube inside the sample tube or in the thin annulus formed by two precision coaxial tubes. In either case, the usual rapid sample rotation (Section 3.2) makes the reference signal appear as a sharp line superimposed on the spectrum of the sample. An external reference is advantageous in eliminating the possibility of intermolecular interactions or chemical reaction with the sample. Also, there are no problems with solubility of the reference in the sample solution. There is, however, a serious difficulty raised by the difference in bulk magnetic susceptibility between sample and reference. In all substances with completely paired electrons, the motion of the electrons in a magnetic field is such as to make the substance diamagnetic, that is, repellant to a magnetic field. The magnetization per unit volume induced in the sample is given by

$$\mathbf{M} = K\mathbf{H}_0 \tag{3.2}$$

where K, the *volume magnetic susceptibility*, is negative for all diamagnetic materials. For the sample, K_S is approximately the weighted average of the values for solute and solvent; for sufficiently dilute solutions this is nearly the value for the solvent. But the external reference in general will have a value $K_R \neq K_S$. As a result, the magnetic field experienced by a molecule in the sample will be slightly different from that experienced by a molecule in the reference. Standard electromagnetic theory[7] shows that these fields $(H_0)_S$ and $(H_0)_R$, are

$$(H_0)_S = H_0[1 + (\tfrac{4}{3}\pi - \alpha) K_S],$$
$$(H_0)_R = H_0[1 + (\tfrac{4}{3}\pi - \alpha) K_R]. \tag{3.3}$$

The quantity α is called the *shape factor* and depends upon the shape of the interface between sample and reference phases. If this interface is a sphere, $\alpha = \tfrac{4}{3}\pi$, so that the susceptibility correction reduces to zero. Spherical cells are sometimes used, but they are generally inconvenient, and imperfections in the glass wall can introduce spurious effects.[8] For the usual cylindrical sample tubes that are long relative to their diameter, $\alpha = 2\pi$, and

$$(H_0)_S = H_0(1 - \tfrac{2}{3}\pi K_S),$$
$$(H_0)_R = H_0(1 - \tfrac{2}{3}\pi K_R) \tag{3.4}$$

(K_S and K_R are normally negative). The use of equation 3.4 in correcting observed data will be discussed in Chapter 4.

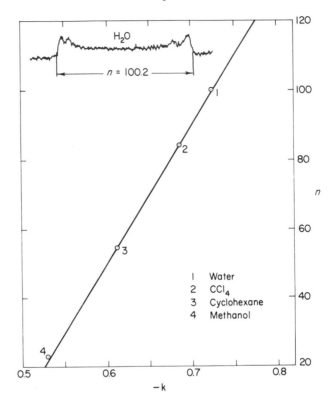

Fig. 3.10 The use of NMR in measurements of volume magnetic susceptibility. Insert: Typical signal observed from the liquid in the annulus of a nonspinning coaxial tube. Plot: Typical calibration curve showing the linear relation between volume magnetic susceptibility K and the separation of the maxima in the resonance curve n (Li et al.[12a]).

3.9 Magnetic Susceptibility Measurements

The magnetic susceptibility data needed for application of equation 3.4 can frequently be found in the literature, as determined by classical procedures.[9] The accuracy of such data is sometimes questionable. Fairly reliable measurements of magnetic susceptibilities can often be made from NMR measurements by employing the precision coaxial cell mentioned above. Careful analysis of the magnetic field distribution in such a cell[10] shows that when the cell is spun rapidly, as in normal NMR spectral measurements, the material in the outer annulus behaves as though it were in a single tube, but when the cell is not spun, the substance in the annulus gives rise to a broad two-peaked resonance, as shown in Figure 3.10. The separation n (in hertz) of the two maxima is given by

$$n = 4\pi\nu_0 \left[(K_1 - K_2)\left(\frac{a}{r}\right)^2 + (K_2 - K_3)\left(\frac{b}{r}\right)^2 \right], \tag{3.5}$$

where ν_0 is the fixed radio frequency; a and b are the internal and external radii, respectively, of the inner glass tube; r is the mean radius of the annulus; and the K's are the volume magnetic susceptibilities of (1) the solution in the inner tube, (2) glass, and (3) the liquid in the annulus.[11] Equation 3.5 may be applied most easily by constructing a calibration curve from a series of substances of known susceptibility placed in turn in the inner tube. With constant cell geometry and with one given liquid in the annulus, equation 3.5 shows that n is directly proportional to K_1. From a calibration chart, such as that in Figure 3.10, susceptibilities of other solutions may be determined. Several articles have treated in detail this and related methods for measuring magnetic susceptibilities by NMR.[12]

3.10 Frequency Calibration

With adequate field/frequency control, spectra are usually recorded on precalibrated charts, and it is normally unnecessary to record a calibration marker other than the one internal or external reference peak with each spectrum. However, the built-in calibration must be checked and adjusted regularly, and for more accurate measurements, calibration markers should be recorded directly with the spectrum of the sample. The most convenient procedure involves the modulation of the field at a measured audio frequency so as to produce sidebands, as in Figure 3.4. The spacing on the chart paper may thus be accurately determined. Often two sidebands of different frequency are used to bracket a peak of interest. With an internal lock spectrometer, the greatest accuracy is obtained by stopping the scan at the peak of interest and determining with a frequency counter the difference between the locking and observing frequencies.

For the accurate determination of the separation of two lines that are very close together (<5 Hz) the method of "wiggle-beats" is sometimes used. The exponentially decaying ringing pattern shows a modulation envelope due to interference between the ringing patterns for the two or more evenly spaced peaks. The separation in seconds between successive modulation maxima can be shown to be the reciprocal of the separation (in hertz) between the peaks themselves.[13]

3.11 Control of Sample Temperature

Most NMR spectrometers are equipped to vary the temperature of the sample by passing preheated or precooled nitrogen past the spinning sample tube. The commercially available instruments are usually limited, by the materials used in the probe, to temperatures between $-100°$ and $200°C$, but some high resolution probes have been constructed to operate at temperatures as low as $-190°$ and as high as $300°C$. At extreme temperatures some deterioration of magnetic field homogeneity is often found. It is important that adequate time be allowed for temperature equilibration of the system, and that the homogeneity adjustments be optimized at each temperature. Instrument calibration is also subject to variation with temperature. The uniformity of temperature through the sample and the stability of temperature control have not been thoroughly checked with different instruments, but constancy of the order of $\pm2°C$ is usually claimed.

Changes in temperature of the sample will alter the Boltzmann distribution of spins in the various energy levels. For the case of $I = \frac{1}{2}$, equations 2.24 and 2.30 show that a reduction in temperature from $27°C$ ($300°K$) to $-60°C$ causes an increase in signal intensity of 40%; a corresponding decrease in intensity is obtained on increasing sample temperature.

3.12 Useful Solvents

In addition to the desired solvation property itself, the major considerations in selecting a solvent for NMR spectroscopy are the minimization of interaction or reaction between solvent and sample and the avoidance of strong NMR signals from the solvent. For proton NMR a list of commonly employed solvents is given in Table 3.1. Solvents that contain no hydrogen atoms are, of course, desirable, but all the hydrogen-containing solvents listed in Table 3.1 are available commercially in deuterated form of $98–99.7\%$ isotopic purity. (Even so a small signal from the residual protons must be expected in the region indicated.) Chloroform-d is relatively inexpensive, and is the most commonly employed solvent for proton NMR. Samples with readily exchangeable hydrogen atoms (such as OH or NH groups) will, of course, lose these hydrogens to a solvent containing exchangeable deuterium atoms.

Table 3.1

Some Useful Solvents for Proton NMR

Solvent	δ (Residual proton signal)[a]
$CDCl_3$	7.27
CD_3OD	3.35, 4.8[b]
Acetone-d_6	2.05
D_2O	4.7[b]
p-Dioxane-d_8	3.55
Dimethylsulfoxide-d_6	2.50
Pyridine-d_5	6.98, 7.35, 8.50
Benzene-d_6	7.20
Acetic acid-d_4	2.05, 8.5[b]
CCl_4	—
CS_2	—
SO_2	—
Hexafluoroacetone	—

[a] δ is given in parts per million relative to tetramethylsilane (internal reference). See Chapter 4 for definition of δ.

[b] Highly variable, depending on solute and temperature. (See discussion of hydrogen bonding, Chapter 11.)

Many substances that are vapors at room temperature and atmospheric pressure may be used as NMR solvents in sealed tubes or at reduced temperature. SO_2, for example, has a vapor pressure of about 3 atm at room temperature and can be easily contained in sealed thin-walled, 5-mm-diameter NMR sample tubes. For use of SO_2 above room temperature, sample tubes with 1-mm wall thickness are used.

For NMR studies of nuclei other than hydrogen, suitable solvents that do not contain the nucleus being studied are usually readily available. Frequently, the use of two or more solvents can provide valuable information on molecular structure. A discussion of solvent effects will be given in Chapter 11.

3.13 Sampling Techniques

The selection of solvents and choice of concentration usually requires a compromise among several competing factors. For example, a relatively inert solvent (saturated hydrocarbon or CCl_4) is often desirable to minimize molecular interactions, but solubilities of many samples often require strongly interacting polar solvents. Likewise, a low concentration both minimizes solute–solute interactions and usually reduces viscosity, thus leading to sharper lines (see Chapter 9). However, improved signal/noise naturally results from higher concentrations. In practice most proton NMR spectra are obtained where possible with samples at a concentration of 0.2 M or greater. The lower sensitivity or lower natural abundance, or both, of most other nuclei usually requires considerably higher concentrations.

Spectra of gases can be obtained, but pressures of several atmospheres are usually necessary in the absence of time averaging to obtain an adequate amount of sample. Solids must, of course, be dissolved to permit rapid molecular tumbling to average out the interactions that lead to signal broadening (see Section 2.6).

For proton resonance, solvents containing exchangeable protons are limited in use. If a proton in the sample exchanges rapidly with a solvent proton, separate signals for the two types of protons are not observed; instead, only a single peak appears at the weighted average of the two frequencies (see Chapter 10). Because of the preponderance of solvent molecules this is essentially the solvent frequency. Even small amounts of hydrogen or hydroxyl ion or of water often catalyze exchange. At intermediate rates of exchange, lines are often broadened, sometimes beyond recognition. An illustration of exchange broadening was given in the OH peak in Figure 1.1, and further examples are shown in Chapter 10.

The presence of paramagnetic materials (those containing unpaired electrons) in NMR samples often causes line broadening due to the decrease in spin-lattice or spin-spin relaxation time. (The effects will be discussed in Chapter 9.) Ions such as Fe^{+++}, Cu^{++}, and Mn^{++} can cause very substantial broadening of some NMR lines if the ions are complexed to the sample being studied. Even molecular oxygen from the atmosphere causes some broadening; hence for optimum resolution of narrow lines, the sample should be deoxygenated, either by evacuation or by bubbling nitrogen through the sample.

Small solid particles floating in the sample cause local magnetic field inhomogeneities and often lead to line broadening. The effect is especially pronounced if the particle is ferromagnetic. For example, a small piece of steel thinner than a fine hair can cause the deterioration of resolution and appearance of an erratic base line depicted in Figure 3.11. The presence of a ferromagnetic particle is best confirmed by examining the sample under a bright light while moving a small permanent magnet (ca. 100-gauss field) beside the sample tube. The magnet can also be used to retain the particle in the tube while the solution is withdrawn into a long disposable pipet for transfer to another tube.* Low-retention microfilters are available for filtering NMR samples.[14]

As an aid to spectral interpretation it is often desirable to exchange all active hydrogen atoms in a sample by deuterium. This can be accomplished

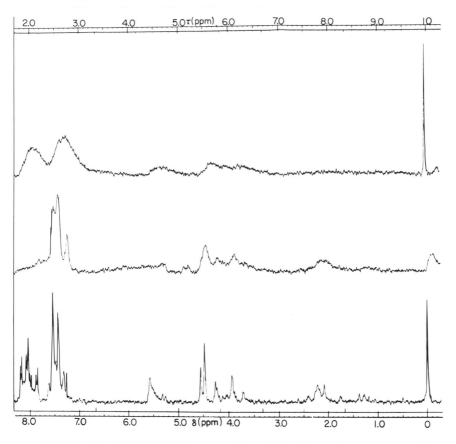

Fig. 3.11 The effect of a tiny ferromagnetic particle on the proton resonance spectrum of a benzoylated sugar. The top and middle curves are repeat runs with the particle present; the bottom curve is the spectrum with the particle removed.

most readily by adding a drop of D_2O to the sample tube and shaking for a few minutes.[15] If the water is immiscible with the sample solution, the layers usually separate readily when the sample is spun, but care must be taken that

* The ubiquitousness of ferromagnetic particles in NMR samples is often not appreciated. In our laboratory we have found a substantial percentage (10–15%) of "routine" but fairly pure organic samples to contain tiny ferromagnetic particles, in some cases probably coming from steel spatulas.

small water droplets do not adhere to the wall of the sample tube in the region of the receiver coil, for a deterioration of resolution may result. A small peak due to water dissolved in the solvent may appear, in any event, since water is not completely insoluble in most organic solvents.

3.14 Micro Techniques

Several types of microcells are in use for confining a small amount of sample to the region of the receiver coil in the probe. Some are illustrated in Figure 3.12. The nylon plugs in Figure 3.12a can be pushed together to form

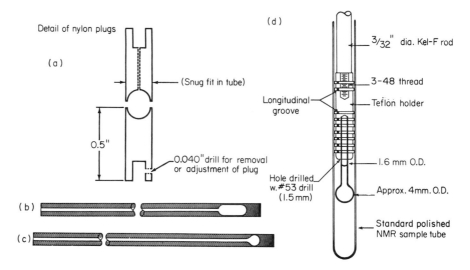

Fig. 3.12   Some NMR microcells. (a) Nylon plugs for use in open-end sample tubes (Varian Associates). (b), (c) All glass cells (Wilmad Glass Co. and NMR Specialties). (d) Thin glass spherical cell (Kontes Glass Co.). Figures from Lundin et al.[16]

a spherical cavity of volume 25 μl or used with a separation of about 5 mm to form a sample reservoir of 100 μl. In the latter case there is no loss in spectrometer sensitivity, whereas in the former the thick walls result in a smaller filling factor for the receiver coil, and a threefold reduction in signal is found. This is, of course, more than compensated by the higher concentration, provided the sample is sufficiently soluble. The other cells are made entirely of glass and are generally more convenient to use. The volumes of these cells are 30–100 μl.

One of the microcells has been adapted to the collection of samples from a gas chromatograph,[17] as indicated in Figure 3.13. When a species to be collected emerges from the gas chromatograph, it is trapped in the sample tube by diverting the gas stream through the long needle into the spherical cavity

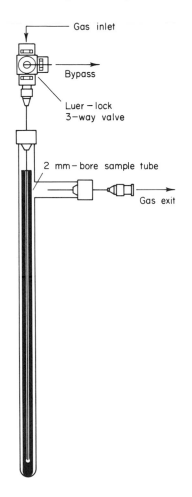

Gas inlet

Bypass

Luer − lock
3−way valve

2 mm − bore sample tube

Gas exit

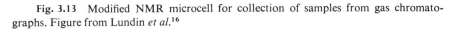

Fig. 3.13 Modified NMR microcell for collection of samples from gas chromatographs. Figure from Lundin *et al.*[16]

in the sample tube. Solvent is then added and the spectrum obtained. A minimum of about 100–400 μg of sample is usually required for a satisfactory spectrum without the use of time averaging. Further details of micro techniques in NMR are given in an excellent review.[16]

3.15 Adiabatic Rapid Passage

In the study of nuclei that give weak signals either because of low inherent sensitivity or low abundance, it is common to use large values of rf field to enhance the signal and to sweep the spectrum rapidly to avoid saturation. For nuclei such as ^{13}C, for which T_1 is sometimes of the order of minutes, the dispersion mode is used since this saturates less readily than the absorption signal. Even so, some saturation usually occurs so that the second half of the dispersion curve (cf. Section 2.8) does not appear. Repetitive scans in opposite directions are averaged to obtain reliable frequencies. The rapid sweep obscures many details, and whenever possible this technique is giving way to normal absorption measurements with more sensitive instruments.

3.16 Pulse Techniques

Some types of NMR data are more readily obtained by imposition of a short intense pulse of rf power, rather than a continuous wave of more moderate power. One example of pulsed NMR, Fourier transform spectroscopy, was mentioned in Section 3.5. Most use is made of pulse techniques, however, in connection with measurement of relaxation times. Some further aspects of pulses in this connection will be discussed in Chapter 9.

3.17 Double Resonance Techniques

A variety of interesting and important data can be obtained by simultaneously applying rf power at two or more frequencies. A discussion of the experimental technique will be deferred to Chapter 8.

References

1. F. Bloch, *Phys. Rev.* **94**, 496 (1954); see also G. A. Williams and H. S. Gutowsky, *ibid.* **104**, 278 (1956); and J. I. Kaplan, *J. Chem. Phys.* **27**, 1426 (1957).

2. For comprehensive treatments of modulation in NMR, see (a) W. A. Anderson, *Rev. Sci. Instr.* **33**, 1160 (1962); (b) O. Haworth and R. E. Richards, *Progr. NMR Spectroscopy* **1**, 1 (1966).

3. R. R. Ernst, *Rev. Sci. Instr.* **36**, 1689 (1965).

4. R. E. Lundin, R. H. Elsken, R. A. Flath, N. Henderson, T. R. Mon, and R. Teranishi, *Anal. Chem.* **38**, 291 (1966).

5. R. R. Ernst and W. A. Anderson, *Rev. Sci. Instr.* **37**, 93 (1966).

6. R. R. Ernst, *Advan. Magn. Resonance* **2**, 1 (1966).

7. See, for example, J. A. Pople, W. G. Schneider, and H. J. Bernstein, "High Resolution NMR," p. 80. McGraw-Hill, New York, 1959.

8. D. J. Frost and G. E. Hall, *Mol. Phys.* **10**, 191 (1966).

9. See, for example, "Handbook of Chemistry and Physics," Chemical Rubber Co., Cleveland, 1964.

10. J. R. Zimmerman and M. R. Foster, *J. Phys. Chem.* **61**, 282 (1957).

11. C. A. Reilly, H. M. McConnell, and R. G. Meisenheimer, *Phys. Rev.* **98**, 264A (1955).

12. (a) N. C. Li, R. L. Scruggs, and E. D. Becker, *J. Am. Chem. Soc.* **84**, 4650 (1962); (b) D. C. Douglass and A. Fratiello, *J. Chem. Phys.* **39**, 3161 (1963); (c) D. F. Evans, *J. Chem. Soc.* p. 2003 (1959); (d) H. A. Lauers and G. P. Van der Kelen, *Bull. Soc. Chim. Belges* **75**, 238 (1966); (e) R. F. Spanier, T. Vladimiroff, and E. R. Malinowski, *J. Chem. Phys.* **45**, 4355 (1966).

13. C. A. Reilly, *J. Chem. Phys.* **25**, 604 (1956).

14. "Flath-Lundin Filter Assembly," obtainable from Hamilton Syringe Company, Whittier, California.

15. H. M. Fales and A. V. Robertson, *Tetrahedron Letters* p. 111 (1962).

16. R. E. Lundin, R. H. Elsken, R. A. Flath, and R. Teranishi, *Appl. Spectroscopy Rev.* **1**, 131 (1967).

17. E. G. Brame, Jr., *Anal. Chem.* **37**, 1183 (1965).

Problems

1. Most NMR spectrometers provide for spinning the sample about an axis designated as the y axis, while the field H_0 is placed along the z axis. Which

electrical shim coil would you expect to require the most careful adjustment, that correcting for inhomogeneity along the x, y, or z axis? Why?

2. Modulation of radio frequencies can be accomplished by altering the *frequency* or the *amplitude* of the rf wave. Show by trigonometric relations that a modulation of the *amplitude* of a wave described by the relation $A\cos(2\pi\nu_0 t)$ by an audio wave described by $B\cos(2\pi\nu_m t)$ results in the appearance of two sidebands at frequencies $\nu_0 + \nu_m$ and $\nu_0 - \nu_m$.

3. External lock proton NMR spectrometers have a control that must usually be adjusted for each sample to place the internal reference TMS at the zero position on the chart paper, while internal lock spectrometers do not need such adjustment. Why is there a difference between these two instruments in this respect?

4. What sensitivity enhancement can theoretically be obtained by time averaging over a weekend (5 P.M. Friday to 9 A.M. Monday) relative to a single 500-sec scan?

Chapter 4

Chemical Shifts

4.1 The Origin of Chemical Shifts

The chemical shift, which is really the cornerstone of chemical applications of NMR, has its origin in the magnetic screening produced by electrons. Thus a nucleus experiences not the magnetic field that is applied to the sample (H_0), but rather the field after it has been altered by the screening or shielding of the electrons surrounding the nucleus. Since electrons are magnetic particles also, their motion is influenced by the imposition of an external field; in general, the motion induced by an applied field is in a direction so as to oppose that field (Lenz's law[1]). Thus at the nucleus the magnetic field is

$$H(\text{nucleus}) = H_0 - \sigma H_0$$
$$= H_0(1 - \sigma). \tag{4.1}$$

The screening factor, or *shielding factor*, σ is found to be small (roughly 10^{-5} for protons and $<10^{-3}$ for most other nuclei); σ is actually a second-rank tensor, so that the magnitude of the shielding depends on the orientation of the molecule relative to the applied field. For molecules in rapid motion, however, the directional (anisotropic) part of σ averages out, so that σ may be treated as a simple number. (Effects of the anisotropy will be mentioned in Sections 7.25 and 9.3.) Actually σ cannot generally be determined experimentally, for that would require measurements of a "bare" nucleus stripped of all electrons. For most applications it is sufficient to make all measurements relative to some agreed-upon reference compound.

59

4.2 Reference Compounds

As we saw in Section 3.9, both internal and external references are used, and for various reasons different chemical substances may be selected for use as a reference. There is at present general agreement that for ^1H resonance, data should be reported with respect to an internal reference of tetramethylsilane (TMS) for nonaqueous solvents in which TMS is soluble. For aqueous solutions no single reference is predominant.

Some of the more frequently used reference compounds for several different nuclei are given in Table 4.1. For each nucleus, the reference that at

Table 4.1

FREQUENTLY USED REFERENCE COMPOUNDS

Nucleus	Reference compounds
^1H	$Si(CH_3)_4$, cyclohexane, benzene; aqueous solutions: $(CH_3)_3Si(CH_2)_3)SO_3^-Na^+$, acetone, $(CH_3)_3COH$, dioxane, $CH_3C{\equiv}N$
^{13}C	$^{13}CS_2$, $CH_3^{13}COOH$, $K_2^{13}CO_3$(aqueous)
^{19}F	CCl_3F, CF_3COOH, F_2, CF_4, C_6F_6, C_4F_8
^{31}P	P_4O_6, H_3PO_4 (85% in water)
^{14}N, ^{15}N	NH_3, NH_4^+, NO_3^-, CH_3NO_2, HNO_3
^{17}O	H_2O
^{11}B	$B(OCH_3)_3$, $BF_3:O(C_2H_5)_2$, BCl_3

present seems most likely to be universally adopted is given in boldface type, and all chemical shift data in this book are given with respect to these references. At present, however, the majority of data in the literature for ^{19}F are expressed with respect to CF_3COOH; for ^{13}C, $CH_3^{13}COOH$; and for ^{31}P, H_3PO_4 (85%). By means of double resonance techniques it is possible in principle to refer chemical shifts of nuclei other than ^1H to TMS (see Section 8.6).

4.3 Chemical Shift Scales

NMR data are usually *measured* in frequency units (hertz) from the chosen reference, as pointed out in Sections 3.3 and 3.10. In cases where complex spectra occur or where spin-spin coupling constants are to be given, the results should be *reported* in frequency units as well. For chemical shifts, however, the use of frequency units has the disadvantage that the reported chemical shift is dependent on the value of the magnetic field (and through the Larmor relation, equation 2.9, on the rf frequency), since the chemical shift is induced by the field (see equation 4.1). Hence it is customary and highly desirable to *report* chemical shifts in the dimensionless unit of parts per million (ppm), which is independent of the rf frequency or magnetic field strength. We can see the relation between such a dimensionless scale and the shielding factor. With the inclusion of the shielding factor, the Larmor equation (2.9) relating the resonance frequency and the *applied* magnetic field (H_0) is

$$\nu_0 = \frac{\gamma}{2\pi} H_0 (1 - \sigma). \tag{4.2}$$

We can now distinguish two cases: (a) Suppose the field is held fixed at H_0 and the frequency is varied to scan the spectrum. The resonance frequencies of sample and reference are

$$\nu_S = \frac{\gamma}{2\pi} H_0 (1 - \sigma_S),$$
$$\nu_R = \frac{\gamma}{2\pi} H_0 (1 - \sigma_R). \tag{4.3}$$

The chemical shift on the dimensionless scale is usually given the symbol δ. If we define

$$\delta \equiv \frac{\nu_S - \nu_R}{\nu_R} \times 10^6, \tag{4.4}$$

then by substitution of equation 4.3, we have

$$\delta = \frac{\sigma_R - \sigma_S}{1 - \sigma_R} \times 10^6 \approx (\sigma_R - \sigma_S) \times 10^6, \tag{4.5}$$

since $\sigma \ll 1$. (b) Suppose, alternatively, that the radio frequency is held constant at ν_0 and the magnetic field varied. The resonances of sample and reference will then be found at the values of the applied field given by

$$\nu_0 = \frac{\gamma}{2\pi} H_S (1 - \sigma_S),$$
$$\nu_0 = \frac{\gamma}{2\pi} H_R (1 - \sigma_R). \tag{4.6}$$

To obtain consistency with the foregoing definition of δ (equation 4.4) we must define

$$\delta = \frac{H_R - H_S}{H_R} \times 10^6. \tag{4.7}$$

Then by substitution of equation (4.6) into (4.7), we obtain

$$\delta = \frac{\sigma_R - \sigma_S}{1 - \sigma_S} \times 10^6 \approx (\sigma_R - \sigma_S) \times 10^6. \tag{4.8}$$

Two important points should be noted from the results of the last paragraph. First, a more *highly shielded* nucleus (larger σ) will show its resonance at a *higher applied field* when the field is scanned, but at a *lower frequency* when frequency is varied. Second, a sample that is *less shielded* than the reference will be assigned a *larger* value of the *chemical shift δ*.

It is apparent that the definitions of δ in equations 4.4 and 4.7 could both have had sample and reference reversed, so that the value of δ would increase with increasing shielding. Both conventions are used. For ^1H resonance, the protons in the reference compound TMS prove to be more shielded than almost all other protons; hence the definition embodied in equations 4.4 and 4.7 is generally used, since it permits virtually all chemical shifts to be expressed as positive numbers. For some other nuclei, however, the most convenient reference compound has relatively unshielded nuclei, so that the alternative convention is more convenient. It is essential that the user of NMR data ascertain in each case the convention employed.

With the convention normally used for ^1H resonance, a larger chemical shift δ (measured with respect to TMS) implies a nucleus that is less shielded and hence resonates at lower field. Since it is often convenient to think of increasing chemical shifts in the direction of increasing, rather than decreasing, shielding, an alternative scale, the τ scale, has gained wide popularity. This scale is a dimensionless scale that assigns to TMS (internal reference) the value 10.000 ppm. Chemical shifts are then expressed in parts per million with decreasing numbers corresponding to decreasing shielding. Most ^1H chemical shifts, as we shall see in Section 4.5, lie within 10 ppm to the low field side of TMS; thus most τ values lie between 0 and 10. The τ scale and the δ scale as defined in equations 4.4 and 4.7 are obviously related; and values can be converted from one to the other by the equation

$$\tau = 10.000 - \delta. \tag{4.9}$$

Both δ and τ scales are given, whenever possible, on ^1H resonance spectra in this book. In tables the δ scale has been used since it is the scale officially recommended by, among others, the American Society for Testing and Materials (ASTM).[2]

In summary, then, chemical shifts can be expressed in three ways: (1) in frequency units (hertz)—this procedure is generally not encouraged and is permissible *only* when the approximate value of the observation field (e.g., 14,000 gauss) or radio frequency (e.g., 60 MHz) is explicitly stated; (2) in parts per million with a *clearly stated reference* as zero (if there is any ambiguity, the direction of increasing δ should also be given); and (3) for ^{1}H resonance only, in parts per million on the τ scale.

4.4 Magnetic Susceptibility Correction

In Section 3.8 we saw that the magnetic field experienced by a molecule depends on the bulk magnetic susceptibility of the medium in which the molecule resides. If molecules of sample and reference compounds are in a single solution (internal reference), the same magnetic susceptibility effect applies to both; hence the difference in magnetic field between the two is independent of the susceptibility of the solution. However, if an interface exists between sample and reference (external reference), we found in equation 3.4 that there is a difference in field between sample and reference given by

$$(H_0)_S - (H_0)_R = H_0[\tfrac{2}{3}\pi(K_R - K_S)]. \tag{4.10}$$

(It should be recalled that equations 3.4 and 4.10 apply to the usual cylindrical sample tube and that K_S and K_R are negative for ordinary diamagnetic materials.) By substituting the expressions for $(H_0)_S$ and $(H_0)_R$ from equations 3.4 in place of H_0 in equations 4.3, and by using the definition of δ in equation 4.4, we find that

$$\delta = \frac{H_0(1 - \tfrac{2}{3}\pi K_S)(1 - \sigma_S) - H_0(1 - \tfrac{2}{3}\pi K_R)(1 - \sigma_R)}{H_0(1 - \tfrac{2}{3}\pi K_R)(1 - \sigma_R)} \times 10^6. \tag{4.11}$$

Since K's are of the order of 10^{-6} and σ's are of the order of 10^{-4} to 10^{-6}, terms in the numerator of equation 4.11 involving products of K and σ can be dropped, and in the denominator both K_R and σ_R are negligible relative to unity. Thus we obtain

$$\delta = [(\sigma_R - \sigma_S) + \tfrac{2}{3}\pi(K_R - K_S)] \times 10^6. \tag{4.12}$$

Hence, the true chemical shift is

$$\delta(\text{true}) \equiv (\sigma_R - \sigma_S) \times 10^6 = \delta(\text{measured}) - \tfrac{2}{3}\pi \times 10^6(K_R - K_S). \tag{4.13}$$

Obviously, if the alternative definition of $\delta = (\sigma_S - \sigma_R) \times 10^6$ is used, K_R and K_S in equation 4.13 must be interchanged.

For pairs of diamagnetic materials $|K_R - K_S|$ is typically 0–0.4×10^{-6}, thus introducing a susceptibility correction of <1 ppm. For nuclei with large chemical shifts (e.g., ^{13}C, ^{19}F, ^{31}P), the accuracy of the data in the past often has not warranted making susceptibility corrections, but recent instrumental improvements promise to produce accurate frequency data for these nuclei.

For proton resonance the small range of chemical shifts makes it mandatory to correct for susceptibility if an external reference is used. If the sample solution is sufficiently dilute, conversions to internal TMS reference from various external references may be made readily by means of measured frequency differences for TMS in different solvents. Some useful figures for such conversions are given in Figure 4.1. For example, from Figure 4.1 we see that a proton with $\delta = 2.13$ ppm downfield from external acetone would have $\delta = 2.37$ ppm with respect to external cyclohexane, and if the proton in question were in a dilute solution in CCl_4, it would have $\delta = 3.57$ ppm relative to *internal* TMS. Further examples of interconversion of scales are given in the problems at the end of the chapter.

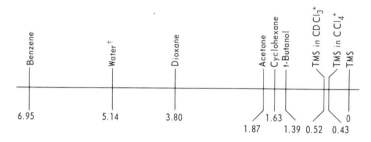

Fig. 4.1   Relative resonance frequencies for various ^1H reference compounds. Except where solutions are indicated, all data refer to the undiluted liquid.* For dilute solutions (<1% by volume); † temperature-dependent.

4.5 Empirical Correlations of Chemical Shifts

As we shall see in the next section, the bases for chemical shifts can be accounted for theoretically in principle, but a priori calculations in general cannot at present provide exact values for these quantities. For predictions of chemical shifts for nuclei in particular chemical environments, it is therefore necessary to rely very largely on empirical correlations between observed shifts and chemical structure. Figures 4.2–4.7 provide a general orientation of the orders of magnitude involved and the effects of various functional groups for the chemical shifts of six of the most widely studied nuclei. These figures are meant to be illustrative of the usual values observed. There may be individual compounds in some cases that fall outside the ranges given; likewise,

Fig. 4.2   Approximate chemical shifts for protons in various functional groups. Data refer to proton given in boldface type and are taken from various sources.[3-5] * Chemical shift highly dependent on hydrogen bonding (see Chapter 11); also influenced by exchange effects (see Chapter 10). Reference: TMS (internal).

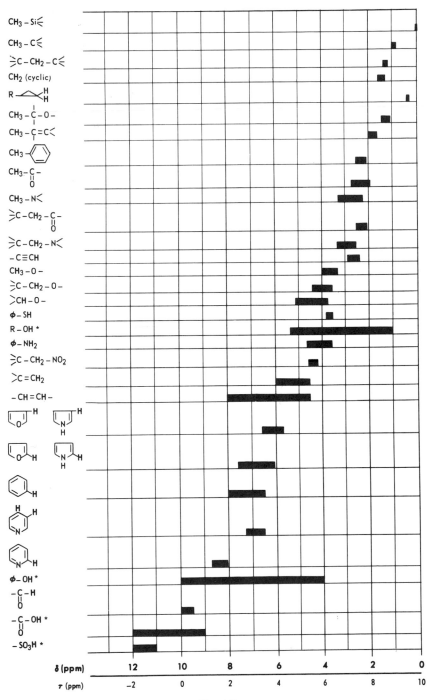

Fig. 4.2

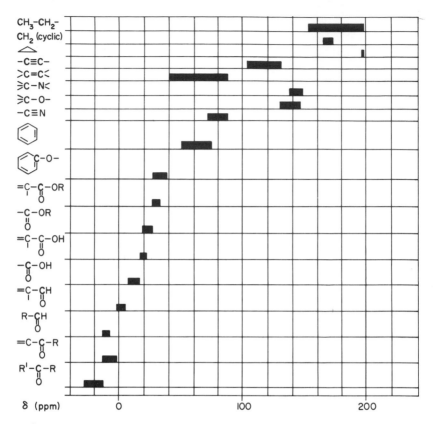

Fig. 4.3   Approximate chemical shifts for ^{13}C in various functional groups. Data refer to ^{13}C given in boldface type and are taken from the review by Stothers.[6] Reference: CS_2.

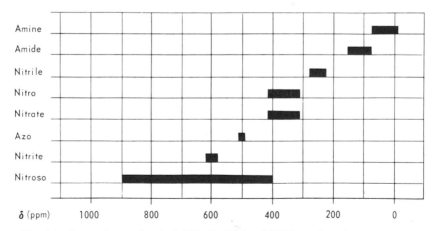

Fig. 4.4   Approximate chemical shifts for ^{14}N and ^{15}N in various functional groups. Data are taken from several sources.[7,8] Reference: ammonia.

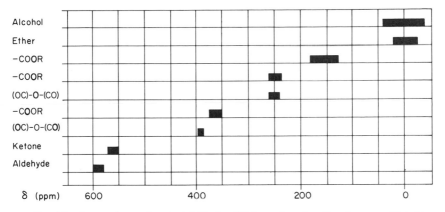

Fig. 4.5 Approximate chemical shifts for ^{17}O in various functional groups. Data from Christ[9] and Emsley, Feeney, and Sutcliffe.[10] Reference: H_2O.

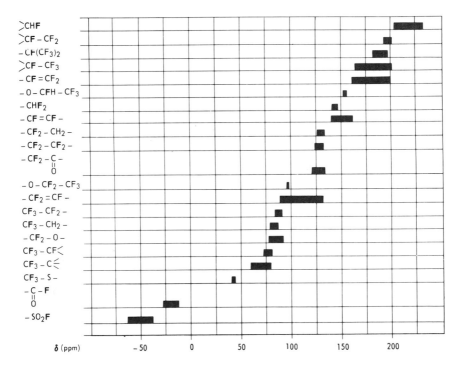

Fig. 4.6 Approximate chemical shifts for ^{19}F in various functional groups. Data are taken from the review by Brame.[11] Reference: CCl_3F.

it is often possible to restrict the range more narrowly if specific classes of compounds are considered.

The most striking feature of Figures 4.2–4.7 is the very small range of chemical shifts for hydrogen nuclei (ca. 12 ppm) relative to the much larger range (but still small on an absolute basis) for the heavier nuclei. As we shall

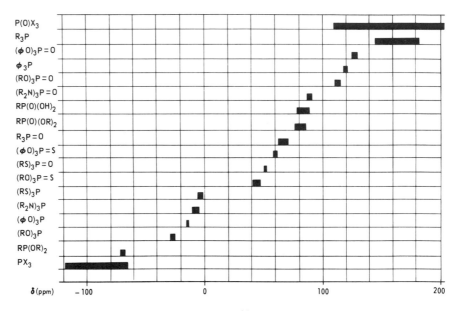

Fig. 4.7   Approximate chemical shifts for ^{31}P in various functional groups. Data from several sources.[12–14] Reference: P_4O_6.[15]

see in Section 4.6, this difference is associated with the presence of $2p$ electrons in the heavier nuclei and their absence in hydrogen. We shall discuss other features of these figures in the following sections.

4.6 Theory of Chemical Shifts

For a single free *atom* in a spherically symmetric S electronic state, Lamb[16] showed that the effect of an imposed magnetic field is to induce an electron current that leads to a shielding factor,

$$\sigma_D = \frac{4\pi e^2}{3mc^2} \int_0^\infty r\rho(r)\, dr. \tag{4.14}$$

Here $\rho(r)$ is the density of electrons as a function of radial distance from the nucleus, and e, m, and c are the usual fundamental constants.

For molecules the Lamb theory is inadequate because it assumes that the electrons are free to move in any direction, whereas in a molecule electronic motion is severely restricted. Ramsey[17] used second-order perturbation theory to develop a formula that in principle accounts for the shielding factor in molecules. Ramsey's expression for σ, which is not reproduced here, is the sum of two terms.[18] The first, σ_D, is essentially the Lamb expression and is often called the diamagnetic term since $\sigma_D > 0$. It leads to a shielding of the nucleus. The second term, σ_P, is negative and is sometimes referred to as the temperature-independent paramagnetic term. (This distinguishes it from the temperature-dependent paramagnetism that results from unpaired electrons.) This term corrects for the fact that the electrons in a molecule are not disposed with spherical symmetry about the nucleus in question. Thus the presence of p electrons near the nucleus is an important factor in determining σ_P. The mathematical expression for σ_P includes in the denominator energies of excitation, that is, differences in energy between ground and excited electronic states. For most molecules Ramsey's expression cannot be evaluated to any degree of accuracy because insufficient data are available for the energies of all the excited states and the electron distribution. For the hydrogen molecule it has been possible to make a reliable semiempirical evaluation for both σ_D and σ_P. The result is

$$\sigma = \sigma_D + \sigma_P = 32.1 \times 10^{-6} + (-5.5 \times 10^{-6})$$

$$= 26.6 \times 10^{-6}.$$

The Ramsey formulation is probably most useful in furnishing a framework for discussing chemical shifts, and the factors that are important. In general, we might list five terms that could contribute to σ: (a) the diamagnetic contribution from the atom in question, σ_D; (b) the paramagnetic contribution from the atom in question, σ_P; (c) the effect of neighboring atoms; (d) interatomic currents; and (e) the effect of external electric fields.

Contribution (e) arises in practice primarily from neighboring molecules and will be discussed in connection with solvent effects in Chapter 11. For protons, the paramagnetic contribution (b) is likely to be small because a hydrogen atom has large electronic excitation energies and no low-lying p orbitals. Consequently, it is generally considered that term (b) is negligible for protons. For other nuclei, however, the paramagnetic term is often the dominant term. We shall place emphasis first on chemical shifts of protons in the following treatment of effects (a), (c), and (d), with a discussion of heavier nuclei in Section 4.11.

4.7 Effect of Electron Density

Term (a) in the preceding section can be evaluated approximately for protons by the Lamb formula to give

$$\sigma(\text{local diamagnetic}) \approx 20 \times 10^{-6} \lambda, \qquad (4.15)$$

where λ is the effective number of electrons in the $1s$ orbital of the hydrogen. For a completely screened hydrogen atom, λ would approach 1; for a hydrogen ion, it would be 0. Thus the local diamagnetic effect is in the range of a few parts per million, which is just the range of chemical shifts observed for protons.

Equation 4.15 suggests that there ought to be some sort of correlation between the shielding factor and the electron density around the hydrogen. For example, a more acidic proton, such as the OH proton in phenol, should be less shielded than the corresponding less acidic proton in an alcohol. This is indeed found to be the case, the chemical shift for the OH proton of phenol occurring about 4 ppm to lower field than that of ethanol. (Hydrogen bonding can alter these chemical shifts substantially, as we shall see in Chapter 11.)

The presence of a formal charge near a magnetic nucleus leads to a substantial shielding or deshielding. For example, Figure 4.8 shows the spectra of 1-methylcytosine and its hydrochloride. In the hydrochloride the positive charge is shared primarily between positions 3 and 7, but the effect can be seen on all proton resonances, which are shifted downfield. Similar, but larger, effects are found with charged aromatic systems. Comparison of the chemical shifts in the symmetric molecules $C_5H_5^-$, C_6H_6, and $C_7H_7^+$ shows that a charge localized on one of the carbon atoms of benzene would result in a shielding or deshielding of the attached proton by about 9 ppm/electron.[19] This value may be used to calculate from NMR data the approximate change in charge density resulting from the introduction of an electron-donating or electron-withdrawing substituent. In general, electron densities obtained this way have been in rather good agreement with those calculated from molecular orbital treatments.

A strongly electronegative atom or group attached to or near a magnetic nucleus has the expected effect of deshielding the nucleus. Thus rough correlations are found between chemical shift and electronegativity of substituents. Figure 4.9 shows typical results for CH_3CH_2X. Note the parallelism between the correlations for ^1H and ^{13}C chemical shifts, but the vastly different range of δ encompassed.

Substitution on an aromatic ring causes changes in shielding of protons resulting from addition or withdrawal of charge. The generalizations used by chemists in predicting electron density at *ortho*, *meta*, and *para* positions apply

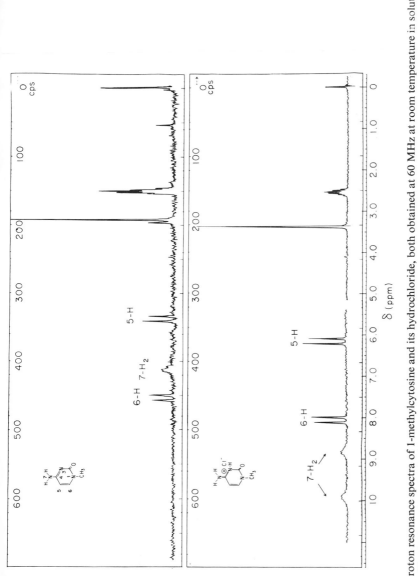

Fig. 4.8 Proton resonance spectra of 1-methylcytosine and its hydrochloride, both obtained at 60 MHz at room temperature in solution in dimethylsulfoxide-d_6. Note downfield shifts of all peaks on formation of the cation. The separate lines for the two NH_2 protons in the cation arise from hindered rotation of the amino group. (See Chapter 10 for further details.)

in large measure to NMR spectra, as indicated for some typical substituents in Figure 4.10. To a large extent, substituent effects are approximately additive for aromatic systems. Extensive studies[22] have provided tables of substituent

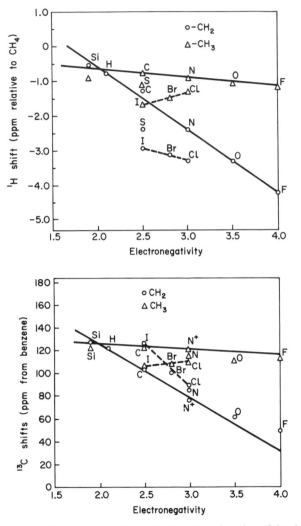

Fig. 4.9 ^{1}H and ^{13}C chemical shifts of CH_3CH_2X as a function of the electronegativity of X (Spiesecke and Schneider[20]).

contributions.[23] Such empirical methods of predicting chemical shifts are quite useful, but their limitations should be recognized. In aromatic systems, for example, additivity provides surprisingly good results for many *meta* and *para* disubstituted benzenes, but gives only fair agreement with experiment for substituted benzenes containing appreciable dipole moments.

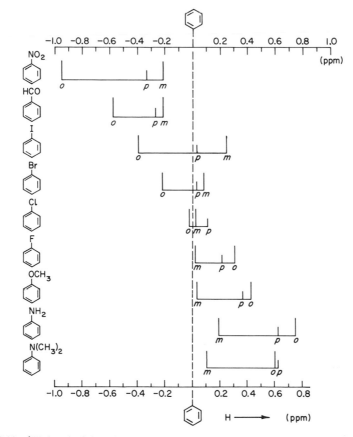

Fig. 4.10 ^{1}H chemical shifts in monosubstituted benzenes (Spiesecke and Schneider[21]).

4.8 Magnetic Anisotropy and Chemical Shifts

While variation in electron density around a proton is probably the most important factor influencing its chemical shift, many exceptions are found to a correlation between δ and electron density. To account for these cases, we must consider the induced magnetic fields that have their origins in atoms or functional groups near the atom in question.

Suppose we consider a simple system, H—Y, where Y is an atom or a more complex part of a molecule. If a magnetic field H_0 is imposed on this molecule, the electrons around Y are forced to move in some fashion, and as a result there is a magnetic dipole moment μ_Y generated at Y. The magnitude of μ_Y is

$$\mu_Y = \chi_Y H_0. \tag{4.16}$$

where χ_Y is the magnetic susceptibility of Y. Since $\chi_Y < 0$ for diamagnetic materials, μ_Y points in a direction opposite H_0. We can obtain better insight into the effect of μ_Y on the local field at the proton if we look separately at the

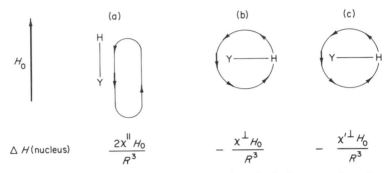

Fig. 4.11   Secondary magnetic field generated at the hydrogen nucleus due to the diamagnetism of the neighboring group Y. Arrows indicate closed lines of flux due to a point magnetic dipole located at the center of electric charge of Y but shown slightly displaced for clarity. (a) H—Y bond parallel to H_0; (b), (c) H—Y bond perpendicular to H_0. Parts (b) and (c) are identical if Y has axial symmetry.

H—Y bond oriented along three mutually perpendicular directions, one of which coincides with that of H_0. The situation is depicted in Figure 4.11. Since field strength arising from a point magnetic dipole varies inversely as the cube of the distance from the dipole, the increment of magnetic field experienced by the proton H due to the induced moment at Y is the average of the three contributions shown in Figure 4.11.

$$\Delta H(\text{nucleus}) = \frac{H_0}{3R^3}(2\chi^{\parallel} - \chi^{\perp} - \chi'^{\perp}), \tag{4.17}$$

where R is the distance between the proton H and the center of electric charge in Y. The notations $\parallel$ and $\perp$ refer to the direction of the H—Y bond relative to H_0. The factor of 2 in the parallel component arises from the spatial degeneracy present in this orientation; that is, the lines of flux illustrated in the plane of the page are duplicated in a plane perpendicular to the page. The orientations depicted in Figure 4.11b, c are, in general, different, since one represents a view of the "edge" of group Y and the other the "face" of Y.

Equation 4.17 shows that the magnitude of the field increment at the proton depends on a *magnetic anisotropy* in Y; that is, a lack of equality of the three susceptibility components. (This is sometimes referred to as the *neighbor anisotropy effect*.) The field increment from equation 4.17 thus results in a change in shielding.

$$\Delta\sigma = -\frac{1}{3R^3}(2\chi^\| - \chi^\perp - \chi'^\perp). \tag{4.18}$$

One particularly simple example of this effect occurs in HC≡CH, where the anisotropy arises from the freedom of the electrons in the triple bond to circulate at will around the axis of the molecule. If Y in Figure 4.11 represents the C≡CH fragment, then $\chi^\|$ is large in magnitude because the flow of electrons around the bond generates a moment along the H—Y axis. On the other hand, the electrons are less likely to circulate perpendicular to the H—Y axis because they then would cut through chemical bonds. Consequently $\chi^\perp$ and $\chi'^\perp$ are small (and equal because of the axial symmetry). Keeping in mind that both $\chi^\|$ and $\chi^\perp$ are negative, we expect from equation 4.18 a large *positive* $\Delta\sigma$. Thus the resonance is predicted to be at a higher field than it would be in the absence of this large neighbor anisotropy effect. A comparison of the proton chemical shifts of the series C_2H_6, CH_2=CH_2, and HC≡CH shows that the HC≡CH line is only 0.6 ppm lower in field than the line of C_2H_6, while C_2H_4 lies 4.4 ppm lower in field than C_2H_6. On electronegativity grounds alone C_2H_2 should be lower in field than C_2H_4.

Nothing in our discussion has required H to be chemically bonded to Y. In general, where the proton in question does not lie on one of the principal axes of magnetic susceptibility, the neighbor anisotropy effect may be calculated from the relation[24]

$$\Delta\sigma = \frac{1}{3R^3}[(2 - 3\cos^2\theta)(\chi^\| - \chi^\perp) - (\chi^\| - \chi'^\perp)], \tag{4.19}$$

where the proton is at a distance R from the center of the anisotropic group or bond in a direction inclined at an angle θ to the direction of $\chi^\|$. If $\chi^\perp = \chi'^\perp$, equation 4.19 becomes simpler:

$$\Delta\sigma = \frac{1}{3R^3}(1 - 3\cos^2\theta)(\chi^\| - \chi^\perp). \tag{4.20}$$

Susceptibility differences of various bonds may be estimated empirically by comparisons of data from different molecules or may be calculated with quantum mechanical models. Since the theoretical calculations require severe approximations, most attention has been devoted to the empirical approach. Here, however, two major difficulties occur: first, the isolation of neighbor anisotropy effects from other effects; and second, the approximations of a point magnetic dipole centered at some often arbitrary position in group Y. As a result, rather different values of magnetic anisotropies are sometimes reported for such important groups as C—H, C—C, C=C, and C=O. For the C=O group, for example, there is general agreement that a proton directly above the plane of the $\diagdown$C=O group is shielded and a proton at certain positions in the plane (such as an aldehyde proton) is deshielded; but the magnitudes of the anisotropies are disputed.[25] A generalized version of equation 4.19, which is based on a magnetic dipole of finite length, rather than a point dipole, has been derived and applied to a number of molecules of known

Table 4.2

CHEMICAL SHIFTS[a] OF PROTONS α TO OXYGEN ATOMS[27]

X	CH_3X	$C—CH_2X$	$\begin{smallmatrix}C\diagdown\\C\diagup\end{smallmatrix}CHX$
OR	3.29	3.40	
OH	3.38	3.56	3.85
OC_6H_5	3.73	3.90	
OCR $\overset{\|}{O}$	3.65	4.10	5.01
$OC—C_6H_5$ $\overset{\|}{O}$	3.90	4.23	5.12
$OCCF_3$ $\overset{\|}{O}$	3.96	4.34	

[a] In ppm relative to TMS (internal).

geometry.[26] This treatment should provide more reliable values of χ's since it is valid at shorter distances than equation 4.19 (which should not be used for $R < 3$ Å).

A commonly recognized factor in determining chemical shifts is called the "C—C bond effect," which refers to the decrease in proton shielding with addition of C—C bonds, for example, CH_3X, $C—CH_2X$, $\begin{smallmatrix}C\diagdown\\C\diagup\end{smallmatrix}CHX$. The origin of this effect is not entirely clear; it may be due to the neighbor anisotropy effect or it may be an intrusion of the paramagnetic effect, to which we referred earlier. Examples of the C—C bond effect may be seen in Figure 4.2 and Table 4.2.

4.9 Ring Currents

A special, and quite important, type of anisotropy effect occurs when it is possible to have *inter*atomic circulation of electrons within a molecule. A circulation of π electrons around the periphery of an aromatic ring, for example, gives rise to a "ring current" and resultant induced shielding effects.*

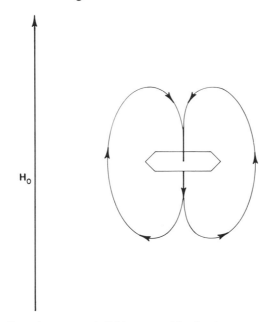

H_0

Fig. 4.12 Secondary magnetic field generated by the ring current in benzene.

If an aromatic ring is oriented perpendicular to the applied field H_0, as in Figure 4.12, the π electrons are relatively free to circulate around the ring and will move in a direction such that the magnetic moment resulting from their motion opposes the applied field. This moment may be pictured as a point magnetic dipole at the center of the ring, with the dipole field falling off as the cube of the distance. If we construct closed lines of magnetic flux, as in Figure 4.12, we find that the sign of the ring current effect is highly dependent upon geometry. An aromatic proton in the plane of the ring experiences a ring current field that enhances the applied field; hence its resonance occurs

---

* In principle, one could consider the sum of magnetic anisotropies for the atoms of the ring,[28] but in practice the inclusion of ring currents as a separate contribution to the chemical shift is useful.

at a lower applied field than might otherwise be anticipated. In fact, the chemical shift of benzene is about 1.7 ppm lower in field than that of ethylene, which is very similar from the standpoint of hybridization and electronegativity. A proton held over the aromatic ring, on the other hand, would be expected to experience an upfield shift.

The magnitude of the shielding due to a ring current may be estimated from a point dipole calculation[29] or more accurately from a model that treats

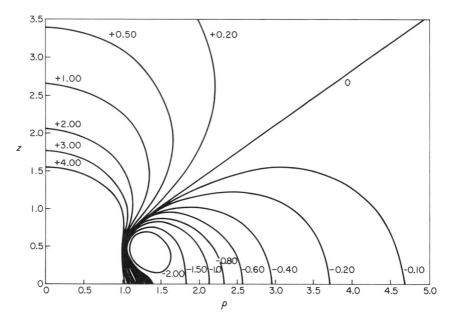

Fig. 4.13 Effect on the chemical shifts of a nucleus at various positions due to the ring current in benzene. The plot represents one quadrant of a plane passing normally through the center of the ring, which lies horizontally. A positive sign denotes an upfield contribution to the chemical shift; ρ and z are in units of the benzene C—C distance, 1.39 Å (Johnson and Bovey[30]).

the π electrons as rings above and below the atomic plane.[30] (In the calculations, averages are taken over all orientations of the aromatic ring in the magnetic field, not just the one shown in Figure 4.12.) The ring model may be used to calculate semiquantitatively the ring current effect at various positions relative to a benzene ring. The results of such a calculation have been tabulated[31] and are illustrated in the contour diagram of Figure 4.13.

The ring model may also be used to interpret data on such molecules as porphyrins, whose large ring currents lead to substantial downfield shifts for protons outside the ring and a very large upfield shift for the NH protons inside the electron ring. Typical porphyrin data are given in Figure 4.14.

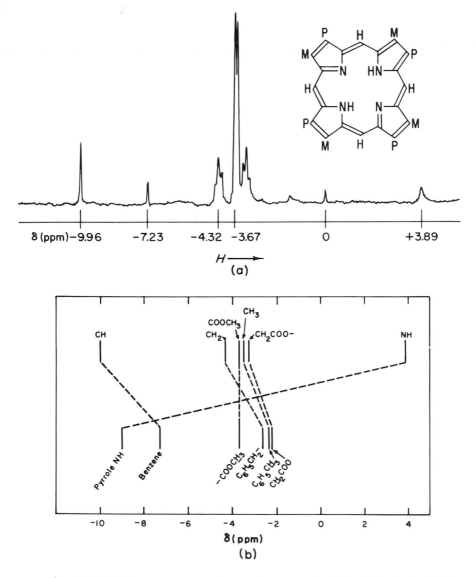

Fig. 4.14 (a) Proton resonance spectrum of coproporphyrin-1 methyl ester in CDCl₃ at 60 MHz. M, CH₃; P, —CH₂CH₂COOCH₃. (b) Differences in chemical shifts of protons in porphyrin esters (above) and in related nonporphyrin compounds (below), showing the effect of ring currents.

4.10 Paramagnetic Species

Metallo-organic compounds in which the metal is diamagnetic display chemical shifts for proton resonance that cover a range only slightly larger than that found for other organic molecules. If the metal is paramagnetic, however, chemical shifts for protons often cover a range of 200 ppm. These large chemical shifts arise from what is termed a *contact interaction* or pseudo-contact interaction, which involves the transfer of some unpaired electron density from the metal to the ligand. This unpaired spin density can cause positive or negative chemical shifts, depending on the electron distribution. The presence of unpaired electrons usually causes a rapid nuclear relaxation and leads to line broadening (see Sections 2.6 and 9.5). Proton resonance in paramagnetic complexes can be observed only in cases where the relaxation time is favorable. The theory and applications of such studies have been reviewed recently.[32]

4.11 Nuclei Other Than Hydrogen

Our discussion of the factors affecting chemical shifts has focused almost entirely on proton resonance, but the various effects that we listed are equally applicable to other nuclei. The paramagnetic effect σ_P will, however, be much larger for other nuclei than it is for the proton, as pointed out in Section 4.6. In fact, the paramagnetic effect is the dominant feature for most other nuclei and accounts qualitatively for the larger range of chemical shifts, as illustrated in Figures 4.2–4.7. For example, the difference in chemical shift between F_2 and F^- of approximately 500 ppm is attributed to σ_P. For a spherically symmetric ion, σ_P can be ignored, but in a molecule such as F_2 with considerable p bond character it is very significant. Similar conclusions can be drawn for ^{13}C, ^{31}P, and many other nuclei.

4.12 Tabulations of Chemical Shifts and Spectra

In this chapter we have considered some of the major effects that determine chemical shifts. It is worthwhile reiterating the point made in Section 4.5 that theory alone is insufficient for predicting accurate chemical shifts and that recourse must be had to empirical data. It is beyond the scope of this book to include extensive tabulations of data beyond those few examples in the preceding sections. However, as an aid in finding chemical shift data, we present the following summary of a number of the more recent and extensive compilations of chemical shift data or complete spectra:

1. "Varian High Resolution NMR Spectra Catalog," Vols. 1 and 2 (Varian Associates, Palo Alto, Calif.). An excellent collection of 700 proton resonance spectra of many types of compounds, together with indexes by name, functional groups, and chemical shifts.

2. American Petroleum Institute—Manufacturing Chemists Association compilation of NMR spectra (Chemical Thermodynamic Properties Center, Texas A and M College, College Station, Texas). A continuing compilation of proton resonance spectra of hydrocarbons (API) and other compounds (MCA).

3. F. A. Bovey, "NMR Data Tables for Organic Compounds," Wiley (Interscience), New York, 1967. A compilation of chemical shifts and spin-spin coupling constants for more than 4200 organic compounds.

4. G. V. D. Tiers, Table of τ Values (reproduced in reference 4). Precisely determined chemical shifts for approximately 700 compounds.

5. G. Slomp and J. G. Lindberg, "Chemical Shifts of Protons in Nitrogen-Containing Organic Compounds," *Anal. Chem.* **39**, 60 (1967). A correlation of chemical shift with functional groups, based on data for 2300 protons.

6. "Sadtler Standard NMR Spectra" (Sadtler Research Laboratories, Philadelphia, Penna.). A continuing compilation of more than 4000 proton resonance spectra.

7. J. W. Emsley, J. Feeney, and L. H. Sutcliffe (reference 4). Volume 2 contains a wealth of data on empirical correlations of chemical shifts and molecular structure.

8. N. S. Bhacca and D. H. Williams, "Application of NMR Spectroscopy in Organic Chemistry," Holden-Day, San Francisco, 1965. A detailed guide to proton resonance spectra of steroids.

9. M. G. Howell, A. S. Kende, and J. S. Webb, "Formula Index to NMR Literature Data," Plenum Press, New York, 1966, Vols. 1 and 2. An empirical formula index to NMR spectra published in about 30 journals through 1962.

10. R. F. Zürcher, *Helv. Chim. Acta* **46**, 2054 (1963). An extensive tabulation of chemical shifts of the angular methyl protons in steroids.

11. H. Suhr, "Anwendungen der Kernmagnetischen Resonanz in der Organischen Chemie," Springer, New York, 1965. Many useful tabulations of chemical shifts.

12. W. Brügel, "NMR Spectra and Chemical Structure," Academic Press, New York, 1967. A compilation of proton chemical shifts and spin-spin coupling constants for 88 general classes of organic compounds; also some data on ^{19}F, ^{31}P, and ^{11}B.

4.13 Empirical Estimation of Chemical Shifts

When the spectra of suitable model compounds are not available, an approximate calculation of the expected chemical shift of a proton in a given environment may be helpful. To the extent that substituent effects are additive, a table of constants may be prepared for each substituent on the carbon bearing the proton in question. Most attempts at such tabulations[33, 34] have met with only limited success, since many complexities of chemical shifts and the presence of through-space interactions are not accounted for by such a simple treatment.

References

1. See, for example, F. W. Sears, "Principles of Physics II," p. 288. Addison-Wesley, Reading, Mass., 1947.

2. Recommendation on Standards, Conventions, and Referencing, Committee E-13, American Society for Testing and Materials, Philadelphia, Pennsylvania.

3. E. Mohacsi, *J. Chem. Ed.* **41**, 38 (1964).

4. J. W. Emsley, J. Feeney, and L. H. Sutcliffe, "High Resolution NMR Spectroscopy," pp. 1115–1136. Macmillan (Pergamon), New York, 1965.

5. C. F. Hammer, Notes for Georgetown Univ. NMR Workshop (1965).

6. J. B. Stothers, *Quart. Rev. (London)* **19**, 144 (1965).

7. E. W. Randall and D. G. Gillies, *Progr. NMR Spectroscopy* (to be published).

8. J. B. Lambert, B. W. Roberts, G. Binsch, and J. D. Roberts, *in* B. Pesce (editor), "NMR in Chemistry." Academic Press, New York, 1965.

9. H. A. Christ, *Helv. Phys. Acta* **33**, 572 (1960).

10. Reference 4, p. 1046.

11. E. G. Brame, Jr., *Anal. Chem.* **34**, 591 (1962).

12. H. Finegold, *Ann. N.Y. Acad. Sci.* **70**, 875 (1958).

13. R. A. Y. Jones and A. R. Katritzky, *Angew. Chem., Internat. Edit.* **1**, 32 (1962).

14. Reference 4, pp. 1054–1067.

15. A. C. Chapman, J. Homer, D. J. Mowthorpe, and R. T. Jones, *Chem. Comm.* p. 121 (1965).

16. W. E. Lamb, Jr., *Phys. Rev.* **60**, 817 (1941).

17. N. F. Ramsey, *Phys. Rev.* **78**, 699 (1950).

18. For details, see reference 4, pp. 68–76.

19. See reference 4, pp. 779–782.

20. H. Spiesecke and W. G. Schneider, *J. Chem. Phys.* **35**, 722 (1961).

21. H. Spiesecke and W. G. Schneider, *J. Chem. Phys.* **35**, 731 (1961). More extensive tabulations have also been given by S. Castellano, R. Kostelnik, and C. Sun, *Tetrahedron Letters*, 4635, 5205 (1967).

22. For a concise summary and references, see reference 4, pp. 754–765.

23. P. Diehl, *Helv. Chim. Acta* **44**, 829 (1961); J. S. Martin and B. P. Dailey, *J. Chem. Phys*, **39**, 1722 (1963); J. J. R. Reed, *Anal. Chem.* **39**, 1586 (1967); see also reference 4, pp. 1140–1142.

24. See, for example, reference 4, pp. 130 ff.

25. G. J. Karabatsos, G. C. Sonnichsen, N. Hsi, and D. J. Fenoglio, *J. Am. Chem. Soc.* **89**, 5067 (1967).

26. J. W. ApSimon, W. G. Craig, P. V. Demarco, D. W. Mathieson, L. Saunders, and W. B. Whalley, *Tetrahedron* **23**, 2339 (1967).

27. L. M. Jackman, "Applications of NMR Spectroscopy in Organic Chemistry," p. 5 5 Macmillan (Pergamon), New York, 1959.

28. J. I. Musher, *Advan. Magn. Resonance* **2**, 177 (1966).

29. J. A. Pople, *J. Chem. Phys.* **24**, 1111 (1956).

30. C. E. Johnson, Jr., and F. A. Bovey, *J. Chem. Phys.* **29**, 1012 (1958).

31. This tabulation is reproduced in reference 4, pp. 595–604.

32. D. R. Eaton and W. D. Phillips, *Advan. Magn. Resonance* **1**, 103 (1965).

33. J. N. Shoolery, "Technical Information Bulletin," Varian Associates, Palo Alto, California, 1959. The table is reproduced in reference 24, p. 59.

34. H. Primas, R. Arndt, and R. Ernst, "Advances in Molecular Spectroscopy," pp. 1246–1252. Macmillan (Pergamon), New York, 1962. The table is reproduced in reference 4, pp. 838–841.

Problems

1. With the aid of the chemical shift correlation chart, Figure 4.2, deduce the structure of the molecules giving Spectra 1–4, Appendix B.

2. The methylene protons of ethanol in CCl_4 have a chemical shift δ measured as 215 Hz from TMS (internal reference) at 60-MHz rf field. Express δ in parts per million and give τ (ppm) for these protons. How many hertz from TMS would you expect the chemical shift of these protons to be at 100 MHz? At $H_0 = 10,000$ gauss?

3. The difference in chemical shift between the α and β protons of naphthalene in dioxane solution has been reported as 14.34 Hz at 40 MHz. Express the difference in parts per million. Do you expect the α or β protons to resonate at lower field? Why?

4. The chemical shift of dioxane in CCl_4 is $\tau = 6.43$ ppm. What would be the chemical shift of dioxane in CCl_4 when measured with respect to external dioxane as a reference?

5. The methyl resonance lines of three chemically related substances (A, B, C), each dissolved in CCl_4, are reported as follows: A, $\tau = 9.06$ ppm; B, $\delta = 61$ Hz at 60 MHz, with respect to internal TMS; C, $\delta = -0.20$ ppm, with respect to external cyclohexane. Which of the three actually resonates at highest field?

6. Benzene in CCl_4 (very dilute solution) has its proton resonance at $\tau = 2.734$ ppm. Express this chemical shift relative to external benzene. What portion of the difference is attributable to magnetic susceptibility effects? (Use susceptibility data from the "Handbook of Chemistry and Physics".)

7. The proton chemical shift of $CHCl_3$, measured with respect to external benzene, is 49.5 Hz at 60 MHz ($CHCl_3$ at lower field). The ^{13}C chemical shift of $CHCl_3$ is 52 ppm upfield from external benzene. What percentages of these reported chemical shifts are due to magnetic susceptibility effects?

8. From Figure 4.14, what is the effect of the ring current on a proton at a distance 3.1 Å above the plane of a benzene ring and with a projected distance in the plane of 1.8 Å from the center of the ring?

9. Show that for a 60-MHz proton resonance experiment, a frequency sweep of 1500–2000 Hz is required to span the range $\delta = 8.33$–0 ppm relative to TMS if TMS is used as an internal lock with fixed audio frequency of 2 kHz, with operation on the first lower sideband. (See Figure 3.6.)

Chapter 5

Electron-Coupled Spin-Spin Interactions

5.1 Origin of Spin-Spin Coupling

From the discussion in Chapters 2 and 4, one might anticipate that an NMR spectrum would be made up of a number of single lines of different areas and widths, each arising from one or more chemically discrete nuclei. Actually, most NMR spectra consist not only of individual lines, but also of groups of lines termed *multiplets*. The multiplet structure arises from interactions between nuclei which cause splitting of energy levels and hence several transitions in place of the single transition expected otherwise. This type of interaction is commonly called *spin-spin coupling*.

There is another kind of spin-spin coupling that we described in Section 2.6: the magnetic dipole-dipole interaction between two different nuclear moments. We found that the magnitude of this dipole-dipole interaction is proportional to $1/R^3$, where R is the distance between the nuclei, but that it depends also on the angle between $\mathbf{R}$ and $\mathbf{H}_0$. When the nuclei are in molecules that are in rapid, random motion, as are most small molecules in solution, this interaction averages almost completely to zero. The coupling interaction in which we are now interested is normally manifested in solution; hence it must arise from a mechanism that is independent of the rotation of the molecule.

Ramsey and Purcell[1] suggested a mechanism for the coupling interaction that involves the electrons that form chemical bonds. Consider, for example, two nuclei, A and B, each with $I = \frac{1}{2}$. Suppose nucleus A has its spin oriented parallel to $\mathbf{H}_0$. An electron near nucleus A will tend to orient its spin anti-parallel to that of A because of the tendency of magnetic moments to pair in antiparallel fashion. If this electron is in an orbital with another electron, then by the Pauli exclusion principle the spin of the second electron must be antiparallel to the first or parallel to that of nucleus A. Now if the second electron is near nucleus B, it will tend to orient the spin of B. Thus, information about the spin orientation of A is transmitted to B via the bonding electrons. In this situation, which is illustrated in Figure 5.1a, the most favorable (i.e., lowest energy) situation occurs when nuclei A and B are antiparallel to each other. This does not mean that the opposite situation, where the spins of A and B are parallel, does not occur. These magnetic interactions are small, so that the parallel orientation of spins A and B (see Figure 5.1b) is a state of

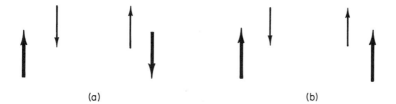

(a)   (b)

Fig. 5.1 The origin of electron-coupled spin-spin interaction. (a) Antiparallel orientation of nuclear spins; (b) parallel orientation of nuclear spins. Nuclear spins are denoted by boldface arrows, electron spins by lightface arrows.

only slightly higher energy and occurs with almost equal probability (i.e., in about half the molecules). Thus when nucleus A undergoes resonance and 'flips" its spin orientation with respect to H_0, the energy of its transition depends on the initial orientation of B relative to A, and two spectral lines result, the difference in their frequency being proportional to the energy of interaction (coupling) between A and B.

The foregoing explanation of the origin of spin-spin coupling does not depend on the molecule being in an external field. Unlike the chemical shift, which is induced by and hence proportional to the applied field, spin-spin coupling is characteristic of the molecule. The magnitude of the interaction between nuclei A and B is given by the spin-spin coupling constant J_{AB}, which is always expressed in hertz (a unit of convenient magnitude, which is directly proportional to energy).

Spin coupling can occur where two nuclei are bonded together, such as ^{13}C—H or ^{31}P—H, or where several bonds intervene, such as H_A—^{12}C—^{12}C—H_B. In general, then, the spin coupling information is carried by electrons through chemical bonds, not through space. (Possible exceptions, especially with nuclei other than hydrogen, have been suggested.)

From this electron spin polarization mechanism the magnitude of the coupling is *generally* expected to decrease as the number of intervening bonds increases. Magnitudes of couplings will be discussed in later sections.

For nuclei with $I > \frac{1}{2}$, more lines result from spin interactions, since there are $2I + 1$ possible orientations of a nuclear spin I relative to the applied field. Thus for the molecule HD (deuterium has $I = 1$), the proton resonance consists of three lines, while the deuterium resonance consists of two lines. It will be recalled from Section 2.1, however, that nuclei with $I > \frac{1}{2}$ possess a nuclear electric quadrupole moment. In an asymmetric electrical environment such nuclei usually relax rapidly and, as shown in Chapters 9 and 10, rapid relaxation can "decouple" two spin-coupled nuclei and lead to loss of multiplet structure. The halogens Cl, Br, and I almost always relax rapidly, as do most of the heavier nuclei with $I > \frac{1}{2}$. ^{14}N and ^{2}H sometimes relax fast enough to be partially or completely decoupled.

5.2 Coupling between Groups of Equivalent Nuclei

Let us consider the case in which there is coupling involving a set of equivalent nuclei—for example, CH_3CHO, where coupling occurs between the CH_3 protons and the aldehyde proton. As a result, any one of the CH_3 protons "senses" the *two* possible orientations of the aldehyde proton spin, and the CH_3 line is split into a doublet, as shown in Figure 5.2. The aldehyde proton, however, experiences *four* possible orientations of the CH_3 proton spins—all three protons oriented parallel to the field ("up" in Figure 5.2), two protons up and one down, two down and one up, or all three down. These two intermediate situations can occur in three ways, as depicted in Figure 5.2, so that relative probability of the four states is $1:3:3:1$. The aldehyde proton resonance, then, consists of four lines corresponding to these four different states and two of them will be three times as intense because these states are three times as probable.

One might well inquire at this point about the failure to observe additional splitting of lines due to spin coupling between pairs of CH_3 protons. While such *coupling* between equivalent protons does indeed exist, it does not lead to any observable *splitting* of lines. We shall say more about this point in the next section and in Chapter 7.

Our discussion thus far of the origin of spin-spin coupling has been only a qualitative exposition of the general mechanism for this important interaction. The analysis of spin-spin multiplets of the sort given in Figure 5.2 is applicable only under certain conditions. This type of treatment, which is termed *first-order analysis*, is so widely used (and frequently misused) that we shall devote the next section to a detailed explanation.

5.3 First-Order Analysis

Spectra arising from coupled nuclei—both individual nuclei and groups of equivalent nuclei—may be treated by first-order analysis *only* when two conditions are satisfied:

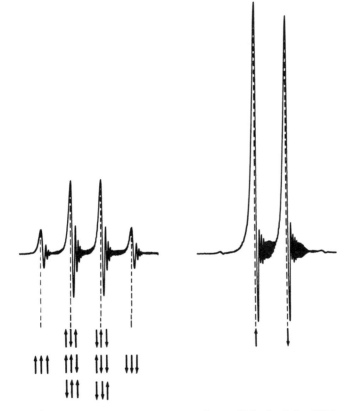

Fig. 5.2 The proton resonance spectrum of acetaldehyde: left, CHO resonance; right, CH_3 resonance. Under the CH_3 resonance is a schematic representation of the two spin orientations of the CHO proton, while the four orientations of the CH_3 protons are indicated beneath the CHO resonance.

1. *The chemical shift difference between nuclei (or groups of nuclei) must be much larger than the spin coupling between them.* For this comparison the chemical shift difference, $\nu_A - \nu_B$, and the spin coupling constant J_{AB} must clearly be expressed in the same units. The unit of frequency hertz (Hz; or cycles per second, cps), is universally employed. Since chemical shifts expressed

in frequency units increase linearly with applied field (and radio frequency), spectra obtained at higher field strength are more likely to adhere to this relation than those obtained at lower field strength.

2. *Coupling must involve groups of nuclei that are magnetically equivalent, not just chemically equivalent.* Nuclei are said to be *chemically* equivalent when they have the same chemical shift, usually as a result of molecular symmetry (e.g., the 2 and 6 protons, or the 3 and 5 protons in phenol) but occasionally as a result of an accidental coincidence of shielding effects. Nuclei in a set are *magnetically* equivalent when they all possess the same chemical shift *and* all nuclei in the set are coupled equally with *any* other single nucleus in the molecule. Thus, in the tetrahedral molecule difluoromethane (I)

(I)

H_a and H_b *are* magnetically equivalent since they are by symmetry equally coupled to F_a and they are equally coupled to F_b. On the other hand, in 1,1-difluoroethylene (II) H_a and H_b *are not* magnetically equivalent, since

(II)

H_a and F_a are coupled by $J(cis)$, while H_b and F_a are coupled by $J(trans)$, and in general $J(cis) \neq J(trans)$.*

When there is *rapid* internal motion in a molecule, such as internal rotation or inversion, the equivalence of nuclei should be determined on an overall average basis, rather than in one of the individual conformations. For example, in CH_3CH_2Br, the three CH_3 protons are magnetically equivalent because they couple equally on the average with each of the methylene protons, even though in any one of the three stable conformations they would be magnetically nonequivalent. Further discussion of rate phenomena and conformational isomers will be presented in Chapter 10.

When first-order analysis is applicable, the number of components in a multiplet, their spacing, and their relative intensities can be determined easily from the following rules.

1. A nucleus or group of nuclei coupled to a set of n nuclei with spin I

---

* The term "equivalent nuclei" has been widely used, in some cases to denote chemical equivalence[2] and in others magnetic equivalence.[3]

will have its resonance split into $2nI + 1$ lines. For the common case of $I - \frac{1}{2}$ there are then $n + 1$ lines.

2. The relative intensities of the $2nI + 1$ lines can be determined from the number of ways each spin state may be formed. For the case of $I = \frac{1}{2}$ the intensities of the $n + 1$ lines correspond to the coefficients of the binomial theorem, as indicated in Table 5.1.

Table 5.1

RELATIVE INTENSITIES OF FIRST-ORDER MULTIPLETS FROM COUPLING
WITH n NUCLEI OF SPIN $\frac{1}{2}$

n	Relative intensity								
0					1				
1					1	1			
2				1	2	1			
3				1	3	3	1		
4			1	4	6	4	1		
5		1	5	10	10	5	1		
6		1	6	15	20	15	6	1	
7	1	7	21	35	35	21	7	1	
8	1	8	28	56	70	56	28	8	1

3. The $2nI + 1$ lines are equally spaced, with the frequency separation between adjacent lines being equal to J, the coupling constant.

4. Coupling between nuclei within a magnetically equivalent set does not affect the spectrum.

Two examples of first-order spectra are given in Figures 5.3 and 5.4. The necessity for magnetic equivalence is graphically demonstrated in Figure 5.3, while the requirement that $(\nu_A - \nu_B) \gg J_{AB}$ is portrayed in Figure 5.4. First-order analysis is usually considered applicable (for sets of magnetically equivalent nuclei, of course) when $(\nu_A - \nu_B)/J_{AB} > 7$; however, when $7 < (\nu_A - \nu_B)/J_{AB} < 20$, there is some distortion of intensities from the pattern given in Table 5.1, but the multiplet is still recognizable. The deviation in intensities always occurs in the direction of making the lines near the center of the overall spectrum more intense and those toward the edges less intense.

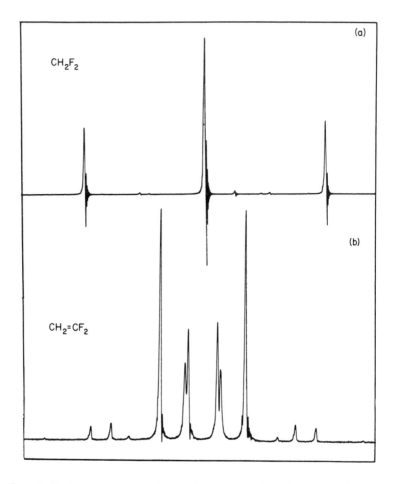

Fig. 5.3   Proton resonance spectra of (a) CH_2F_2 and (b) CH_2=CF_2 at 60 MHz. First-order analysis is applicable in (a) but not in (b). (The very weak lines in (a) and (b) are due to spinning sidebands and to an impurity.)

Figure 5.5 gives an illustration of the repetitive application of first-order analysis. Usually it is convenient to consider the largest coupling first, but it is immaterial to the final result. Since this procedure is widely used, Figure 5.5 should be studied carefully, along with further examples in the problems at the end of this chapter.

5.4 Signs of Coupling Constants

In our discussion of the simple mechanism of electron-coupled spin-spin interactions in Section 5.1, we showed that the state in which two coupled nuclei have antiparallel spin orientations has a lower energy than the one in

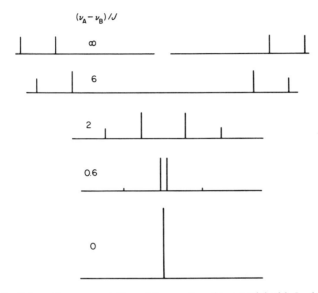

Fig. 5.4   Schematic representation of the spectra of two nuclei with $I = \frac{1}{2}$ as a function of the ratio of chemical shift to spin coupling constant.

which the spins are parallel. Chemical bonding and the interactions of nuclear spins are not always so simple, however, and in some cases the lower energy state is the one in which the spins of the coupled nuclei are parallel. We distinguish between these two situations by referring to the first system as possessing a *positive* coupling constant ($J > 0$) and to the second as having a *negative* coupling constant ($J < 0$).

When the first-order conditions are obeyed, the signs of the coupling constants can never be obtained directly from the spectrum. In more complex cases, however, the *relative* signs of the various coupling constants within the molecule sometimes influence the appearance of the spectrum and hence can be determined from the observed spectrum. We shall discuss this topic in more detail in Chapter 7. Double resonance techniques (Chapter 8) can also be used very effectively to obtain relative signs of coupling constants. The *absolute* signs of J's cannot be found from ordinary high resolution NMR spectra, but there are overwhelming reasons (based on both theory and more sophisticated NMR experiments) for believing that all one-bond ^{13}C—H coupling constants are positive. Absolute values of other coupling constants are usually based on the ^{13}C—H coupling being >0.

The signs of coupling constants are of considerable theoretical importance with regard to chemical bonding and can sometimes be of practical significance

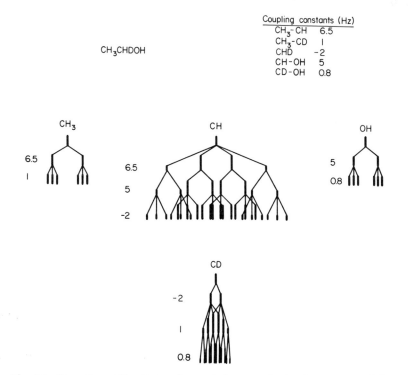

CH$_3$CHDOH

Coupling constants (Hz)

CH$_3$-CH	6.5
CH$_3$-CD	I
CHD	-2
CH-OH	5
CD-OH	0.8

Fig. 5.5   Use of repetitive first-order analysis to synthesize the proton and deuteron spectra of CH$_3$CHDOH. Note that the relative intensities of the lines are carried through each step. (Because of line width effects, the observed spectrum would not show all the lines, but only broad envelopes following the predicted intensity distribution.)

in spectral analysis and in structure elucidation. Further discussion of this point is given in Section 5.7.

5.5 Theory of Spin-Spin Coupling

The general theory of spin-spin coupling is complex, and we shall not treat it in detail. For proton-proton coupling it has been shown that the spin interaction arises principally from the electron spin-electron spin interaction, not from orbital interaction of electrons. This simplifies the theory somewhat. For some other nuclei, orbital interaction may come into play also. We shall summarize a few of the conclusions applicable to spin-spin coupling without going through the details of the theory.

It is found that the interaction depends on the density of electrons at the nucleus. It is well known that only s electrons have density at the nucleus, so we expect a relation between the magnitude of the coupling and the s character of the bond. Such a relation is found, as we shall see in Section 5.7.

The coupling interaction is proportional to the product of magnetogyric ratios of the coupled nuclei. For comparison of the magnitudes of coupling constants between different nuclei, and to compensate for the negative sign introduced in some cases by negative magnetogyric ratios, a *reduced coupling constant* K_{AB} can be defined:

$$K_{AB} = \frac{1}{\gamma_A \gamma_B} J_{AB}. \tag{5.1}$$

One particularly important consequence of the dependence of J on γ is the change in J resulting from deuterium substitution,

$$J_{HX}/J_{DX} = \gamma_H/\gamma_D \approx 6.51. \tag{5.2}$$

The theory of spin coupling is in accord with an interaction of the form $\mathbf{I}_1 \cdot \mathbf{I}_2$, which depends on the orientation of one spin with respect to the other but does *not* depend on the orientation of the spins with respect to the magnetic field.

The theoretical development of the electron-coupled spin-spin interaction has been carried out principally by second-order perturbation theory. The resulting expression contains in the denominator terms involving the excitation energy for an electron going from the ground electronic state to excited triplet electronic states. Exact calculation of coupling constants is virtually impossible with the present limited knowledge of electronic excitation energies and wave functions, but both valence bond and molecular orbital treatments have been applied successfully to small molecules or molecular fragments in predicting the general magnitude of coupling constants and their dependence on various parameters. We shall return to a consideration of some of these predictions and correlations in Section 5.7.

5.6 Some Observed Coupling Constants

Since theory is unable to predict accurate values for coupling constants, our knowledge of the range of coupling constants found for different molecular

Table 5.2

TYPICAL PROTON-PROTON SPIN COUPLING CONSTANTS[a]

Type	J_{HH}(Hz)
H—H	280
![C₂C with two H] (see structure)	−12 to −15
H—C—C—H (free rotation)	7
H—C—C—C—H	0^b
(cyclohexane, axial/equatorial)	ax.-ax. 8–10 ax.-eq. 2–3 eq.-eq. 2–3
(cyclopentane) (cis or trans)	4–5
(cyclobutane) (cis or trans)	8
(cyclopropane) (cis) (trans)	8–10 4–6
H—C—O—H	5
H—C—C—H (with O)	±3
H—C—C—H (with C, O)	8

Type	J_{HH}(Hz)
$\text{H}\diagdown\text{C}=\text{C}\diagup\text{H}$	17
$\diagdown\text{C}=\text{C}\diagup\begin{smallmatrix}\text{H}\\\text{H}\end{smallmatrix}$	0 to ±2
$\text{H}\diagdown\text{C}=\text{C}\diagup\text{H}$	10
$\text{H}-\text{C}\diagdown\text{C}=\text{C}\diagup\text{C}-\text{H}$	1–2
$\diagdown\text{C}=\text{C}\diagup\begin{smallmatrix}\text{C}-\text{H}\\\text{H}\end{smallmatrix}$	7
$\text{H}\diagup\text{C}=\text{C}\diagup\text{C}-\text{H}$	−1.5
$\text{H}\diagdown\text{C}=\text{C}\diagup\text{C}-\text{H}$	−2
$\text{C}=\text{C}-\text{C}=\text{C}$ with H, H below	10
$\text{H}\diagdown\text{C}=\text{C}=\text{C}\diagdown\text{H}$	±1
$-\text{N}=\text{C}\diagup\begin{smallmatrix}\text{H}\\\text{H}\end{smallmatrix}$	7–17
$\text{O}=\text{C}\diagup\begin{smallmatrix}\text{H}\\\text{H}\end{smallmatrix}$	42
$\text{H}-\text{C}-\text{C}\equiv\text{C}-\text{H}$	−2

Table 5.2 —*continued*

Type		J_{HH} (Hz)
H—C—C≡C—C—H		2
	5 mem.	6
	6 mem.	10
	7 mem.	12
	(X = C, O)	0 to ±2
	$J(ortho)$	8
	$J(meta)$	2
	$J(para)$	~0.5
	$J_{(2-3)}$	5
	$J_{(3-4)}$	7.5
	$J_{(2-4)}$	1.8
	$J_{(3-5)}$	1.4
	$J_{(2-5)}$	1
	$J_{(2-6)}$	−0.1
	$J_{(2-3)}$	2
	$J_{(3-4)}$	4
	$J_{(2-4)}$	1
	$J_{(2-5)}$	±1.5
	$J_{(2-3)}$	5
	$J_{(3-4)}$	4
	$J_{(2-4)}$	1
	$J_{(2-5)}$	3

[a] From several sources.[4-8]
[b] J can be several hertz in certain cases; see discussion in text.

Table 5.3

TYPICAL H—X COUPLING CONSTANTS[a]

Type	$|J|$ (Hz)
^{13}C—H (sp^3)	125
(sp^2)	170
(sp)	250
^{13}C—C—H	5
^{13}C—C—C—H	5
$^{15}NH_3$	61
$>^{15}N$—CH_3	1–3
C=^{14}N—CH_3	3
Φ Φ C=^{15}NH	51
	91
^{14}N—C—C—H	2–3
^{14}N—N—C—H	2–4
^{17}O—H	70
H, H C F	45
H—C—C—F	5–20
H—C—C—C—F	5
H (ortho)	8
F (meta)	7
(para)	2

Table 5.3—*continued*

Type	$|J|$ (Hz)
$\underset{H}{\overset{\diagdown}{\nearrow}}C{=}C\overset{F}{\underset{\diagdown}{\diagup}}$	40
$\underset{\diagup}{\overset{H\diagdown}{}}C{=}C\overset{F}{\underset{\diagdown}{}}$	18
$\overset{\diagdown}{\underset{\diagup}{}}C{=}C\overset{F}{\underset{H}{\diagup}}$	80
$H{-}\overset{\overset{\textstyle O}{\|}}{\underset{\underset{\textstyle O}{\|}}{P}}{=}O$	500–700
$H{-}P{\diagdown}$	200
$H{-}\overset{\|}{C}{-}\overset{\|}{P}{=}O$	10
$H{-}\overset{\|}{C}{-}\overset{\|}{C}{-}\overset{\|}{P}{=}O$	<5

---

[a] Data from various sources.[8–11]

systems rests largely on observations and empirical correlation. When a spectrum can be analyzed by first-order procedure, the extraction of the value for J from a multiplet is trivial; in more complex spectra, formidable calculation may be required to find values of J's from the spectra (see Chapter 7).

Table 5.2 lists typical values of proton-proton coupling constants for various molecular species. This tabulation is meant to be illustrative, not exhaustive, with respect to both the types of molecules included and the overall ranges listed.

We have adopted the commonly used notation for coupling constants, in which the number of bonds intervening between the coupled nuclei is given as a superscript and the identity of the coupled nuclei as a subscript (e.g., $^3J_{HH}$ for a coupling between protons on adjacent carbon atoms, sometimes called *vicinal* coupling). The superscript or the subscript, or both, are deleted when there is no ambiguity.

Table 5.4

TYPICAL COUPLING CONSTANTS NOT INVOLVING HYDROGEN[a]

Type	J (Hz)
^{13}C—F	−280 to −350
$-^{13}\overset{\shortmid}{C}-^{13}\overset{\shortmid}{C}-$	35
$-^{13}\overset{\shortmid}{C}-^{13}C\equiv N$	50–55
$>^{13}C=^{13}C<$	70
$-^{13}C\equiv^{13}C-$	170
$^{15}N=^{15}N$	14
$-^{13}\overset{\shortmid}{C}-^{15}N<$	7–8
$-^{13}C\equiv^{15}N$	−17
$>C<^{F}_{F}$	160
$F-\overset{\shortmid}{\underset{\shortmid}{C}}-\overset{\shortmid}{\underset{\shortmid}{C}}-F$	−3 to −20
(benzene with two F substituents)	(*ortho*) −17 to −22 (*meta*) 11 to −10 (*para*) +6 to +14
$_{F}>C=C<^{F}$	−120
$^{F}>C=C<^{F}$	30–40

Table 5.4—*continued*

Type	J (Hz)
$>$P—P$<$	100
O=P—P=O	500
F—P=O	1000

[a] Data from references 8 and 11; also G. A. Gray, private communication.

Proton-proton couplings through single bonds are usually attenuated rapidly, so that generally $^4J < 0.5$, and is usually unobservable. Couplings are stereospecific, as we shall see in Section 5.7, so that certain geometric arrangements of nuclei result in values of ^4J and even ^5J that are observable. Coupling through more than three bonds is called *long-range coupling* and is of considerable interest in stereochemistry.

Generally, couplings are transmitted more effectively through multiple bonds than through single bonds. For example, vicinal couplings for ethane derivatives are usually <10 Hz, while in ethylene derivatives $^3J(cis) \approx 10$ and $^3J(trans) \approx 17$.

In aromatic systems also the coupling is transmitted more effectively than through single-bonded systems. *Ortho* coupling constants (^3J) are generally of the order of 5–8 Hz, *meta* couplings (^4J) are about 1–3 Hz, and *para* couplings (^5J) are quite small, often <0.5 Hz. In general, there is no coupling observed between different rings in fused polycyclic systems, so that such long-range couplings must be <0.5 Hz. Substituents have only small effects on the magnitudes of aromatic couplings, but introduction of hetero atoms can cause significant alterations, as indicated in Table 5.2.

Geminal proton-proton coupling constants (^2J) depend markedly on substituents, as indicated in Table 5.2. The trend of ^2J with substitution has been treated successfully by theory and will be discussed in Section 5.7.

Table 5.3 lists some representative coupling constants between protons and other atoms. ^1J is usually quite large, but other coupling constants cover a wide range. The large value of ^1J for ^{13}C—H often permits the observation of "^{13}C satellites" in a proton resonance spectrum due to proton coupling with the 1.1% ^{13}C present in natural abundance. Such satellites are often of value in determining H—H coupling constants that are otherwise inaccessible (see Section 7.24).

Table 5.4 gives a small illustrative selection of coupling constants not involving protons. Far fewer data are available on such couplings because of the limited amount of work on nuclei other than hydrogen and fluorine.

5.7 Correlation of Coupling Constants with Other Physical Properties

Theory suggests and experiment largely confirms that coupling constants can be related to a number of physical parameters. Among the most important are (1) hybridization, (2) dihedral bond angles, and (3) electronegativity of substituents.

The dependence of J on electron density at the nucleus (Section 5.5) suggests a relation between ^1J and amount of s character in the bond. Such a relation is indeed found for ^{13}C—H couplings in sp, sp^2, and sp^3 hybridized systems, as indicated in Table 5.2. Similar rough correlations are found for other X—H couplings (X = ^{31}P, ^{15}N, ^{119}Sn). In all cases, including ^{13}C—H coupling, however, addition of substituents may well cause large changes in effective nuclear charge, or uneven hybridization in different bonds, so that exact correlations should not be expected. For example, the nominally sp^3 hybridized molecules CH_4, CH_3Cl, CH_2Cl_2, and $CHCl_3$ have values of $J(^{13}C$—H) of 125, 150, 178, and 209 Hz, respectively.[8]

One of the most fruitful theoretical contributions to the interpretation of coupling constants has been the valence bond treatment by Karplus[12] of $^3J_{HH}$ in ethanelike fragments, H_a—C_a—C_b—H_b. The most interesting conclusion is that this coupling depends drastically on the dihedral angle Φ between the H_a—C_a and the C_b—H_b bonds. The calculated results were found to fit approximately the relation

$$^3J = A + B\cos\Phi + C\cos 2\Phi, \tag{5.3}$$

with $A = 4$, $B = -0.5$, and $C = 4.5$ Hz. From empirical studies a better set of parameters, chosen by Bothner-By,[5] is $A = 7$, $B = -1$, and $C = 5$ Hz. Equation 5.3 with the latter set of parameters is plotted in Figure 5.6. It is apparent that large values of J are predicted for *cis* (0°) and *trans* (180°) conformations but small values for *gauche* (60° and 120°) conformations. These predictions have been amply verified, and the Karplus relation is of great practical utility in structure determinations. It must be realized, however, that the Karplus relation contains inherent limitations due to the necessary approximations made in the quantum mechanical treatment, and also that it was derived strictly for ethane. Substitution, especially with strongly electronegative atoms such as oxygen, can cause substantial changes in coupling. Empirical modifications of the Karplus curve to take substituent effects into account have met with some success, but even with modifications one cannot justify use of the relation to determine bond angles to within a few degrees.

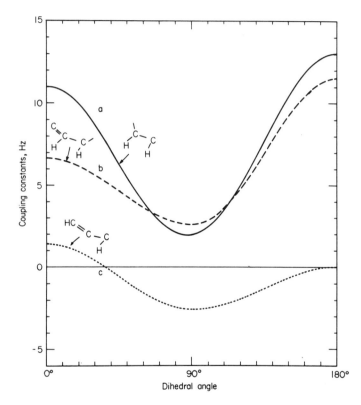

Fig. 5.6   Calculated variation of vicinal and allylic proton-proton coupling constants with dihedral angle between the C—H bonds shown in the figure. Plot[13] based on equations by Bothner-By[5] and Garbisch.[14]

The success of the theoretical treatment of the angular dependence of ^3J in an ethane fragment has served as the rationale for empirical calculations of the angular dependence of $^3J_{ab}$ and $^4J_{ac}$ in the allylic system (III). Plots of

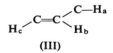

(III)

$^3J_{ab}$ and $^4J_{ac}$ as functions of dihedral angles between C—H$_a$ and C—H$_b$ or C—H$_c$ are given in Figure 5.6. It must be emphasized that these relationships are only approximate, but there is generally rather good agreement with experimental data. While all three curves in Figure 5.6 have a similar angular dependence, the change in sign for ^4J leads to a maximum in $|J|$ near 90°, rather than a minimum as in the two curves for ^3J.

The molecular orbital approach has also been used to calculate proton-proton coupling constants. It has had probably its greatest success in Bothner-By and Pople's treatment of $^2J_{HH}$ in both sp^2 and sp^3 systems.[15] They did not attempt to calculate numerical values for coupling constants, but rather showed the direction and approximate magnitude of the change in $^2J_{HH}$ with change of substituents. The most interesting feature of the theory is that electronegative substituents which remove electrons from the *symmetric* bonding orbital of the CH$_2$ fragment cause increases in $^2J_{HH}$, while substituents that remove electrons from the *antisymmetric* bonding orbital cause decreases in ^2J. The former corresponds to inductive withdrawal of electrons, while the latter arises from hyperconjugation. In some cases the effects add, rather than oppose each other. In formaldehyde, for example, the electronegative oxygen causes an *inductive withdrawal* of electrons from the C—H bonds, thus increasing $^2J_{HH}$; but the two pairs of *nonbonding* electrons of the oxygen are *donated* to the C—H orbitals (hyperconjugation), thus further increasing $^2J_{HH}$. Formaldehyde is predicted, then, to have a large, positive $^2J_{HH}$; the measured value, +42 Hz (see Table 5.2), is the largest H—H coupling constant known, except for the directly bonded protons in the hydrogen molecule.

References

1. N. F. Ramsey and E. M. Purcell, *Phys. Rev.* **85**, 143 (1952).

2. See, for example, J. A. Pople, W. G. Schneider, and H. J. Bernstein, "High Resolution Nuclear Magnetic Resonance," Chapter 6. McGraw-Hill, New York, 1959.

3. See, for example, P. L. Corio, *Chem. Rev.* **60**, 363 (1960).

4. Varian Associates' compilation of coupling constants, distributed at Catholic Univ. NMR Workshop, June, 1967.

5. A. A. Bothner-By, *Advan. Magn. Resonance* **1**, 195 (1965).

6. S. Sternhell, *Rev. Pure Appl. Chem.* **14**, 15 (1964).

7. S. Castellano, C. Sun, and R. Kostelnik, *J. Chem. Phys.* **46**, 327 (1967).

8. J. W. Emsley, J. Feeney, and L. H. Sutcliffe, "High Resolution NMR Spectroscopy." Macmillan (Pergamon), New York, 1966.

9. J. B. Lambert, B. W. Roberts, G. Binsch, and J. D. Roberts, *in* B. Pesce (editor), "Nuclear Magnetic Resonance in Chemistry." Academic Press, New York, 1965.

10. G. Mavel, *Progr. NMR Spectroscopy* **1**, 251 (1966).

11. E. W. Randall and D. G. Gillies, *Progr. NMR Spectroscopy* (to be published).

12. M. Karplus, *J. Chem. Phys.* **30**, 11 (1959); *J. Am. Chem. Soc.* **85**, 2870 (1963).

13. R. J. Highet, personal communication.

14. E. W. Garbisch, Jr., *J. Am. Chem. Soc.* **86**, 5561 (1964).

15. J. A. Pople and A. A. Bothner-By, *J. Chem. Phys.* **42**, 1339 (1965).

Problems

1. The spectrum at 60 MHz from two spin-coupled protons consists of four lines of equal intensity at 72, 80, 350, and 358 Hz, measured with respect to TMS. Predict the spectrum at 100 MHz and state the values of δ (in parts per million) and J.

2. The geminal H—H coupling in CH_4 has been determined as 12.4 Hz (probably negative). Since the spectrum of CH_4 consists of only a single line, how could this figure have been obtained?

3. If $J(^{14}N—H)$ for NH_3 is +40 Hz, what is the sign and magnitude of $J(^{15}N—H)$ in $^{15}NH_3$? Of $J(^{15}N—D)$ in $^{15}ND_3$?

4. Using reduced coupling constants, compare the magnitudes of the X—H coupling in CH_4 (125 Hz) and $^{14}NH_4^+$ (55 Hz).

5. Sketch the ^1H and ^{31}P spectra of $(CH_3O)_3P{=}O$, given that $J_{PH} = 12$ Hz.

6. Sketch the ^1H and $^2H(D)$ spectra of acetone-d_5, given that $^2J_{HD} \approx -2$ Hz. What is $^2J_{HH}$ in acetone?

7. Sketch the spectrum of the CH proton in an isopropyl group, $-CH(CH_3)_2$, assuming that first-order analysis is applicable and that $^3J_{HH} = 6$ Hz. Show that the same result is obtained by (a) considering the CH equally coupled to the six CH_3 protons as though they were a single group of magnetically equivalent nuclei, or by (b) using repetitive first-order analysis with the two CH_3 groups separately.

8. Sketch the ^1H and ^{19}F spectra of CF_3CFH_2, given $^2J_{HF} = 45.5$, $^3J_{HF} = 8.0$, and $^3J_{FF} = 15.5$ Hz.

9. Construct a table analogous to Table 5.1 for coupling to n nuclei of spin 1 for $n = 1$, 2, and 3.

10. Deduce the structures of the molecules giving Spectra 5–10, Appendix B.

Chapter 6

The Use of NMR in Structure Elucidation

Of the many applications of high resolution NMR in all branches of chemistry, the most widespread is its use in the elucidation of the structure of organic and inorganic compounds. With the background that we have presented in the preceding chapters it is now profitable to consider the way in which the NMR spectrum of a new compound might best be approached. We shall find some features of spectra that can be understood only in terms of the additional background developed in the succeeding chapters, but the examples given in this chapter and in the problems at the end demonstrate that in many cases we can obtain valuable structural information with what we have learned thus far.

6.1 A Systematic Approach to the Interpretation of NMR Spectra

In problems of structure elucidation an NMR spectrum may provide useful, even vital data, but it is seldom the sole piece of information available. A knowledge of the source of the compound or its method of synthesis is frequently the single most important fact. In addition, the interpretation of the NMR spectrum is carried out with concurrent knowledge of other physical properties, such as elemental analysis from combustion or mass spectral studies; molecular weight; and the presence or absence of structural features, as indicated by infrared or ultraviolet spectra or by chemical tests. Obviously the procedure used for analyzing the NMR spectrum is highly dependent on such ancillary knowledge. The following procedure is suggested, however, as a systematic method for extracting the information from most NMR spectra of new compounds. This procedure is equally applicable to the assignment of NMR features to given nuclei in the spectrum of a compound of known structure. Since proton resonance has thus far accounted for the vast majority of NMR studies, the procedure is aimed principally at proton NMR spectra, and the examples are drawn from such spectra.

1. Before attempting to interpret an NMR spectrum, it is wise to ascertain whether the spectrum has been obtained under suitable experimental conditions so that it is a meaningful spectrum. The appearance of the line due to TMS (or other reference) should be examined for symmetry and sharpness, as indicated by adequate ringing. Any erratic behavior in the base line or appearance of very broad resonance lines should be noted as possibly indicating the presence of ferromagnetic particles (see Figure 3.11). The trace of the integral should be consistent with proper adjustments of phasing and drift controls (see Figure 3.9). If these criteria are not met, it is usually desirable to rerun the spectrum under better experimental conditions.

It is important to check the calibration of the spectrometer, as indicated by the spectrum. If the TMS line does not appear exactly at zero, a simple additive correction to all observed lines is sufficient, provided that the overall calibration of the sweep width is correct. Often an indication of *gross* errors can be obtained from the observed frequency of solvent lines compared with those in Table 3.1 or other sources. It should be noted, however, that small changes (a few hertz) are often found with different samples due to molecular interactions.

Usually the largest value of H_0 consistent with adequate resolution is used to maximize chemical shifts. Sometimes spectra at two field strengths provide additional information (see Chapter 7).

2. The presence of any known "impurity" lines should be noted. This includes lines due to the solvent itself or to a small amount of undeuterated solvent. If a proton-containing solvent is used, ^{13}C satellites* and spinning sidebands of the solvent peaks may be prominent. Water is often present in solvents, its resonance frequency depending on the extent of hydrogen bonding to the solvent or the sample and on the concentration of water.

3. An examination of the relative areas of the NMR lines or multiplets (resolved or unresolved) is usually the best starting point for the interpretation of the spectrum. One should remember that the accuracy of a single integral trace is seldom better than 2 % of the full scale value, so that the measured area

---

* Proton resonance lines from molecules containing ^{13}C (natural abundance, 1.1%); see Section 7.24 for further details, and Table 5.3 for values of ^{13}C—H coupling constants.

of a small peak in the presence of several larger ones may be appreciably in error. If the total number of protons in the molecule is known, the total area can be equated to it, and the numbers of hydrogen atoms in each portion of the spectrum established. The opposite procedure of assigning the smallest area to one or two protons and comparing other areas to this one is sometimes helpful, but should be used with caution since appreciable error can be introduced in this way. Occasionally lines so broad that they are unobservable in the spectrum itself can be detected in the integral trace.

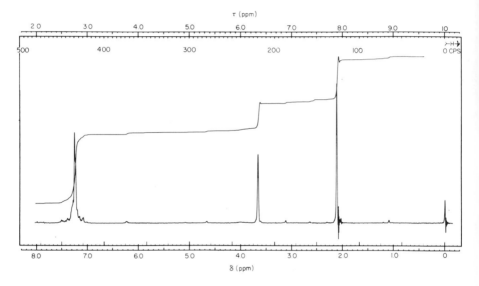

Fig. 6.1 Proton magnetic resonance spectrum (60 MHz) of phenylacetone, $C_6H_5CH_2C(O)CH_3$ in CDCl$_3$.

4. The positions of strong relatively sharp lines should be noted and correlated with expected chemical shifts. This correlation, together with the area measurements, frequently permits the establishment of a number of methyl and methylene groups, aromatic protons (especially in some types of monosubstituted benzene), and in some instances exchangeable protons such as OH and COOH. For example, in Figure 6.1 the line due to three protons at $\delta = 2.10$ is readily identified as a CH$_3$C=O, while that at $\delta = 3.67$ is a methylene group deshielded by nearby substituents. Although the aromatic protons are not precisely equivalent, the differences in their chemical shifts are so small that they give rise to a relatively sharp single line.

Figure 6.2 shows a spectrum typical of a steroid. The protons of the many CH and CH$_2$ groups in the condensed ring system are so nearly chemically equivalent that they give rise to a broad, almost featureless "hump." The

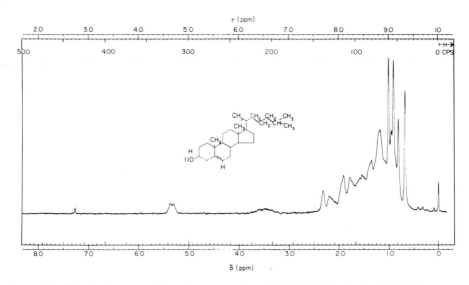

Fig. 6.2 Proton magnetic resonance spectrum (60 MHz) of cholesterol in CDCl₃.

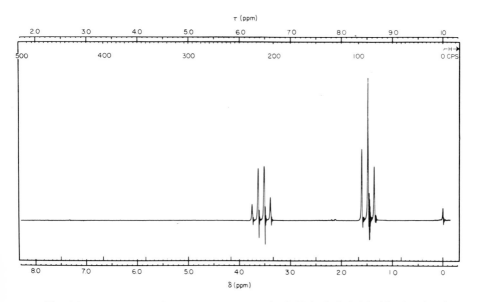

Fig. 6.3 Proton magnetic resonance spectrum (60 MHz) of ethyl chloride, showing the almost first-order splitting of the CH₃ and CH₂ resonances.

angular and side-chain methyl groups, however, show very pronounced sharp lines, the positions of which can provide valuable information on molecular structure (cf. Chapter 4).

5. The approximate centers of all multiplets, broad peaks, and unresolved multiplets should be noted and correlated with functional groups. For example, in Figure 6.2 the presence of the vinyl proton (ca. $\delta = 5.4$ ppm) and the proton adjacent to the 3-hydroxyl group ($\delta = 3.5$ ppm) can be identified. At this stage it is unnecessary to worry about *exact* chemical shifts for complex and unresolved multiplets. The *absence* of lines in characteristic regions often fur-

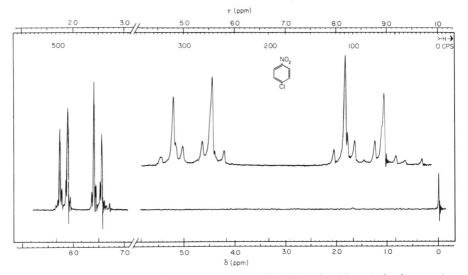

Fig. 6.4 Proton magnetic resonance spectrum (60 MHz) of 1-chloro-4-nitrobenzene in $CDCl_3$. Inset shows spectrum with abscissa scale expanded fivefold.

nishes important data. For example, the molecules whose spectra are given in Figures 6.2 and 6.3 clearly have no aromatic protons.

6. First-order splitting in multiplets should be identified, and values of J deduced directly from the splittings. As noted in Chapter 5, the first-order criterion $(\nu_A - \nu_B) \gg J_{AB}$ often is not strictly obeyed, resulting in a distortion or "slanting" of the expected first-order intensity distribution. This effect can be seen in Figure 6.3; note that the "slanting" of the intensities in one group *always* increases toward the other group with which it is coupled, as we shall see in Chapter 7. The number of components, their relative intensities, the value of J, and the area of the multiplet together provide much valuable information on molecular structure. Commonly occurring, nearly first-order patterns, such as that in Figure 6.3 due to CH_3CH_2X, where X is an electronegative substituent, should be recognized immediately with a little practice.

Other patterns that are actually not first order, such as that due to the magnetically nonequivalent protons in *p*-chloronitrobenzene (Figure 6.4) are also characteristic and should be easily identified. *Para*-substituted benzene rings usually display a pattern characterized by four lines symmetrically placed with a weak, strong, strong, weak intensity relation, and a separation between the outer components of about 8 Hz [approximately $J_{HH}(ortho)$]. There are, however, many less intense lines, as shown in the expanded trace of Figure 6.4. (Spectra of this type are considered in Section 7.22.)

The magnitudes of coupling constants are often definitive in establishing the relative positions of substituents. For example, Figure 6.5 shows that the

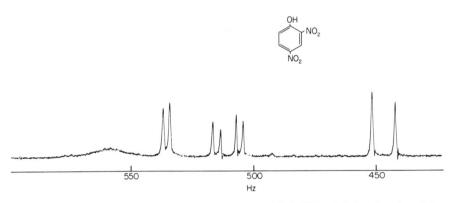

Fig. 6.5 Proton magnetic resonance spectrum (60 MHz) of 2,4-dinitrophenol in CDCl₃, with TMS as internal reference.

three aromatic protons of 2,4-dinitrophenol give rise to a spectrum that is almost first order in appearance. The magnitudes of the splittings suggest that two protons *ortho* to each other give rise to the peaks in the regions of 450 and 510 Hz, and that the latter proton is *meta* to the one resulting in the lines near 530 Hz. From the known effects of electron-withdrawing and electron-donating substituents (Chapter 4) it is clear that the lowest field protons must be adjacent to the NO_2 groups. (Note that the slanting of intensities in this spectrum is in accord with the rule mentioned previously.)

When magnetic nuclei other than protons are present, it should be recalled that some values of J might be as large as many proton chemical shifts. For example, in Figure 6.6, $^2J_{HF} = 48$ Hz, accounting for the widely spaced 1:3:3:1 quartets due to the CH that is coupled to both the fluorine and the adjacent methyl group. Since $^3J_{HF} = 21$ Hz and $^3J_{HH} = 7$ Hz, the CH_3 resonance is a doublet of doublets.

7. Exchangeable protons (OH, NH, or activated CH) can often be

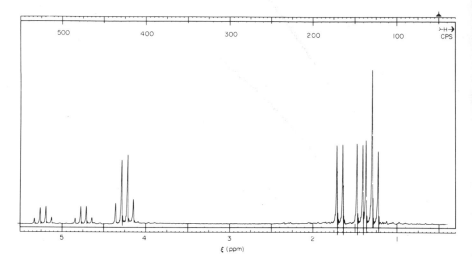

Fig. 6.6   Proton magnetic resonance spectrum (100 MHz) of $CH_3CHFCOOCH_2CH_3$.

identified by addition of a drop of D_2O to the sample (see Section 3.13), and resultant disappearance of peaks.

8. Rerunning the spectrum with the sample dissolved in another solvent is often good practice in order to resolve ambiguities arising from accidental

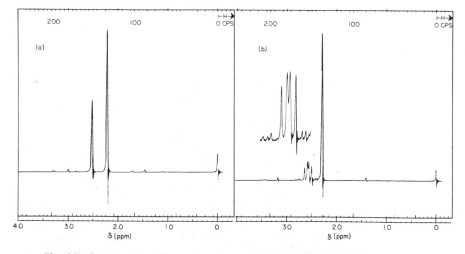

Fig. 6.7   Proton magnetic resonance spectrum (60 MHz) of $(CH_3)_2NCH_2CH_2C\equiv N$ (a) as neat liquid and (b) in $CDCl_3$. Note accidental coincidence of chemical shifts of protons in the two CH_2 groups in (a) and their separation into a complex nonfirst-order multiplet in (b).

coincidence or overlapping of peaks (see Figure 6.7). In addition, specific information on configuration or conformation can sometimes be obtained, as we shall see in Chapter 11.

9. Some complex multiplets (nonfirst-order patterns) can be analyzed by simple procedures that we shall develop in Chapter 7. Frequently, coupling constants (or less often, chemical shifts) derived from such analyses can provide key pieces of information in the elucidation of structure.

10. If there are still ambiguities to be resolved, the technique of spin decoupling is often helpful. By selectively collapsing the splittings of multiplets to single lines, one can often determine unambiguously the origins of certain spin couplings. This important technique will be covered in Chapter 8.

No amount of discussion of the procedure for analyzing spectra can substitute for practice. The collections of spectra in the Varian catalog[1] and in the Sadtler compilation[2] provide some excellent readily available examples that should be studied in detail. In addition, there are a number of spectra of "unknowns" assigned at the end of this chapter. Other NMR books directed at structure elucidation furnish additional suggestions for procedures and many sample spectra.[3-5]

6.2 Spectra of Polymers in Solution

In addition to the extensive work that has been done on correlation of broad line NMR spectra with crystallinity of large polymers, smaller, soluble polymers have been studied by high resolution techniques. Even large polymers of molecular weights around 10^6 can display high resolution NMR spectra (with line widths of the order of 50 Hz) provided there is sufficient segmental motion to average out some of the dipole-dipole interactions (Section 2.6). On the other hand, cross-linked polymers and many biopolymers (large proteins and nucleic acids) that exist in rigid helical conformations have very broad NMR lines.

In some cases the structure elucidation of polymers by NMR is almost identical to that with small molecules except that the greater line widths often preclude the observation of splittings due to spin-spin coupling. One particularly important use of NMR that does not have an exact parallel with small molecules is the determination of stereoregularity (tacticity) of polymers possessing asymmetric centers.[6] The chemical shifts of protons in one monomer unit usually are determined partially by neighboring groups, hence often depend on the optical configuration of adjacent units.* Sequences of two,

* Further discussion of the effect of configuration on chemical shifts will be given in Section 10.6.

three, four, or more units (*dyads*, *triads*, *tetrads*, etc.) may influence chemical shifts. For example, the chemical shift of CH_3 protons in a vinyl polymer (I)

(I)

is strongly dependent on triad sequences. An *isotactic* triad sequence is defined as one in which a monomer unit is flanked by monomer units of the same configuration (e.g., *ddd* or *lll* sequences); a *syndiotactic* triad is one of the form

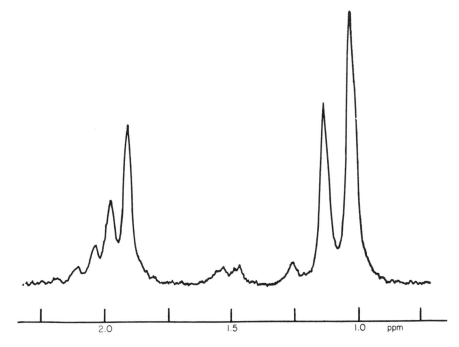

Fig. 6.8   A portion of the proton magnetic resonance spectrum (220 MHz) of poly(α-methyl methacrylate) in *o*-dichlorobenzene at 165°C. Scale is based on an internal reference of hexamethyldisiloxane (Ferguson and Phillips[7]).

dld or *ldl*; and a *heterotactic* triad is one with the random sequences *ddl* or *lld*.

Figure 6.8 shows a portion of the proton resonance spectrum of the vinyl polymer poly(α-methyl methacrylate). The lines at 1.03, 1.14, and 1.27 ppm are assigned to the CH_3 groups in syndiotactic, heterotactic, and isotactic sequences, respectively. Likewise, the CH_2 resonance region near 1.5 and 2 ppm can be assigned to five of the six possible tetrad sequences that influence methylene chemical shifts.[7, 8] Note that the clear separation of peaks is due to the fact that this spectrum was obtained at 220 MHz. At lower frequencies the separations are observable but less well defined.

Useful structural information on biopolymers (proteins, polypeptides, and nucleic acids) is beginning to emerge from proton resonance spectra.[9] Again, it is the higher frequencies and fields, especially those available with superconducting magnets, that permit the spectra to be analyzed.[7] The large line widths in these rigid helical polymers lead to strongly overlapping, often uninterpretable lines at lower frequencies, where chemical shifts are smaller.

References

1. "Varian High Resolution NMR Spectra Catalog," Vols. 1 and 2, Varian Associates, Palo Alto, California, 1963.

2. "Sadtler Standard NMR Spectra," Sadtler Research Laboratories, Philadelphia, Pennsylvania, 1967.

3. R. H. Bible, Jr., "Interpretation of NMR Spectra, An Empirical Approach." Plenum Press, New York, 1965; "Guide to the NMR Empirical Method." Plenum Press, New York, 1967.

4. D. W. Mathieson, "NMR for Organic Chemists." Academic Press, New York, 1967.

5. D. W. Mathieson, "Interpretation of Organic Spectra." Academic Press, New York, 1966.

6. F. A. Bovey and G. V. D. Tiers, *J. Polymer Sci.* **44**, 173 (1960).

7. R. C. Ferguson and W. D. Phillips, *Science* **157**, 257 (1967).

8. An excellent summary of the use of NMR in the determination of polymer configuration is given in F. A. Bovey, "NMR Spectroscopy," Chap. 6, Academic Press, New York, 1968.

9. See, for example, D. H. Meadows, J. L. Markley, J. S. Cohen, and O. Jardetzky, *Proc Nat. Acad. Sci. USA* **58**, 1307 (1967); C. C. McDonald, W. D. Phillips, and J. Lazar, *J. Am. Chem. Soc.* **89**, 4166 (1967); J. A. Ferretti, *Chem. Comm.* p. 1030 (1967).

Problems

1. Determine the structural formulas of the molecules giving Spectra 11–20, Appendix B.

2. Show that for vinyl polymers there are exactly six different tetrad sequences.

3. The proton NMR spectrum of a complex organic molecule has an integral with steps of 6.1, 14.0, 22.0, 28.6, 31.9, 43.0, and 61.7 units on the chart paper. (a) Assume that the smallest peak corresponds to one proton. Compute the number of protons giving rise to each peak and the total number in the molecule. (b) Suppose, alternatively, that evidence is available from mass spectroscopy that there are 44 protons in the molecule. Compute the number of protons causing each peak. How large an experimental error is required for the discrepancy between the results of parts (a) and (b)?

Chapter 7

Analysis of Complex Spectra

Thus far in discussing the various types of splitting patterns found in NMR spectra, we have used only the first-order treatment, which was derived from a qualitative examination of the interactions between nuclei due to polarization of the bonding electrons. The first-order rules regarding number of lines and their relative intensities (Section 5.3) are valid only when chemical shifts are large relative to coupling constants *and* when only groups of magnetically equivalent nuclei are involved.

In this chapter we shall consider a more general treatment of the appearance of complex spectra and of the ways in which nuclei interact with the applied magnetic field and with each other. We shall develop a certain amount of formalism using quantum mechanics, and shall find that there are very simple rules for determining in terms of chemical shifts and coupling constants what a spectrum should look like without any regard to the approximations required by the first-order treatment. The first-order treatment will then follow as a special case. In some situations where first-order treatment is inapplicable, we shall find that simple algebraic equations can be derived for treating the complex spectra. Many of the details of the derivations are omitted, but can be found in the books by Corio,[1] Emsley *et al.*,[2] and Pople *et al.*[3]

7.1 Notation

Our treatment of complex spectra is considerably simplified by restricting ourselves only to nuclei with $I = \frac{1}{2}$. This limitation permits us to cover most of the general principles without tedious algebraic manipulations. In addition, nuclei with $I = \frac{1}{2}$ are studied far more extensively than others.

It will be helpful to use the widely employed system of notation[1-3] in which each nucleus of spin $\frac{1}{2}$ is denoted by some letter of the alphabet: A, B, X, and so forth. We shall choose letters of the alphabet representative of relative chemical shifts; that is, for two nuclei that have a small chemical shift relative to each other, we choose two letters of the alphabet that are close to each other, and for nuclei that have large relative chemical shifts, we use letters from opposite ends of the alphabet. If there are several *magnetically* equivalent nuclei, we denote this fact by a subscript (e.g., A_2X). If there are several nuclei that are *chemically* equivalent, but not magnetically equivalent, we denote this fact by repeating the letter with a prime or a double prime (e.g., AA'X). Nuclei with $I = 0$, as well as those that relax so rapidly that they behave as though they are not magnetic, such as Cl, Br, and I (cf. Section 2.5), are not given any designations. A few examples should suffice to clarify this notation:

(a) $CH_2{=}CCl_2$ A_2
(b) CH_2F_2 A_2X_2
(c) $CH_2{=}CF_2$ AA'XX'
(d) CH_3OH A_3B or A_3X (depending on hydrogen bonding effect on δ_{OH}; see Chapter 11)
(e) $CH_2{=}CHCl$ ABX or ABC

(f)   AA'BB' (assuming no coupling between rings)

(g) $CH_3CH{=}CH_2$ A_3MXY
(h) $^{13}CH_2F_2$ A_2M_2X
(i) $CH_3CH_2NO_2$ A_3X_2

(j)   ABCC'DD'EE'FF'X (for the single conformation shown; see Chapter 10 for effects of rapid interconversion of conformers)

Generally, no significance is attached to the order in which the nuclei are given. For example, in (b) either the hydrogen or fluorine nuclei could be designated A; likewise, (d) could be called an A_3B or AB_3 system. Nuclei with different magnetogyric ratio (e.g., ^1H and ^{13}C) clearly should be denoted by letters far apart in the alphabet, but for those of the same species the notation depends on relative chemical shifts, which are field dependent. When $\delta \gg J$, letters far apart in the alphabet are employed, and even systems that might be classified as, say, ABC are sometimes approximated by, say, ABX. Numerous examples will appear later in this chapter and in the problems at the end of the chapter.

The terminology *weakly coupled* or *strongly coupled* is used to denote nuclei for which $\delta \gg J$ or $\delta \approx J$, respectively. Thus in an ABX system, nuclei A and B are strongly coupled, while A and X are weakly coupled.

7.2 Energy Levels and Transitions in an AX System

Before deriving quantitative expressions for general spin systems, we shall examine qualitatively the energy levels and transitions arising from two nuclei that are not coupled or are only weakly coupled (AX system). We customarily take the static imposed magnetic field to lie along the z axis, and we express the orientation of the z component of nuclear spin, I_z, as α or β for $I_z = \frac{1}{2}$ or $-\frac{1}{2}$, respectively. This notation clearly applies only to nuclei with $I = \frac{1}{2}$. We shall define α and β more precisely in Section 7.4.

When we consider systems containing N nuclei of spin $\frac{1}{2}$ it is convenient to define a quantity F_z as the sum of the z components of all nuclear spins:

$$F_z = (I_z)_1 + (I_z)_2 + \cdots = \sum_{i=1}^{N} (I_z)_i. \tag{7.1}$$

For the AX system we can distinguish four states of spin orientations:

$$
\begin{array}{llll}
(1) & \alpha(A)\,\alpha(X) \equiv \alpha\alpha & F_z = 1; & \\
(2) & \alpha(A)\,\beta(X) \equiv \alpha\beta & 0; & \\
(3) & \beta(A)\,\alpha(X) \equiv \beta\alpha & 0; & \\
(4) & \beta(A)\,\beta(X) \equiv \beta\beta & -1. &
\end{array} \tag{7.2}
$$

The shorter notation $\alpha\alpha$ is often used in place of the notation $\alpha(A)\,\alpha(X)$ when there is no chance of ambiguity. In such cases it is understood that the nuclei are always given in the same order (e.g., A, X in this case).

Case I. No Coupling between A and X. If we consider the imposed magnetic field as lying in the *negative z* direction, so that a β state has lower energy than an α state, the energies of the four states in equation 7.2 will lie in the order given in the center portion of Figure 7.1, provided there is no spin-spin coupling between the nuclei. States (1) and (3) differ in the "flipping" of spin A, as do states (2) and (4). Likewise, states (1) and (2) and states (3) and (4) differ in the spin orientation of X. Thus transitions between the states may be labeled as A or X transitions, and these correspond to the NMR transitions discussed in Chapter 2. (We shall see later that the "double flip" transitions between states (2) and (3) and between states (1) and (4) are forbidden by selection rules.) If we arbitrarily take the resonance frequency of A to be greater than that of X (at constant field), then the energy levels are spaced as indicated in Figure 7.1, and the spectrum consists of two lines, as shown. If magnetic field is held constant, frequency increases to the left; if radio frequency is held constant, magnetic field increases to the right (cf. Section 4.3).

  Case II. Weak Coupling. Suppose there is a coupling $J > 0$ between A and X. Since a positive coupling constant implies that antiparallel spin orientations possess less energy than parallel orientations (cf. Section 5.4), states (2)

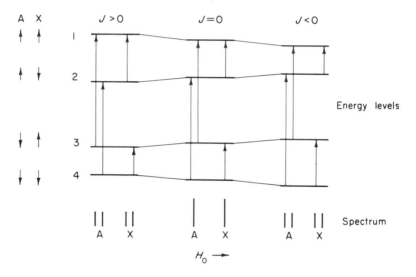

Fig. 7.1   Schematic representation of the energy levels and spectrum of an AX system under different conditions of coupling.

and (3) are lower in energy than they were in the absence of coupling, while states (1) and (4) are higher in energy. This situation is depicted in the left portion of Figure 7.1, but the magnitudes of the changes in energy relative to the separations between levels is exaggerated. The two A transitions no longer have the same energy, and a doublet results in the A portion of the spectrum; a similar doublet appears in the X portion. If $J < 0$, the energy levels change as shown in the right portion of Figure 7.1. Again two doublets appear in the spectrum. In this case the lower-frequency A line results from a transition between states (3) and (1), rather than between states (4) and (2) as in the case where $J > 0$, but there is no *observable* difference in the spectrum with change in the sign of the coupling constant.

  We cannot proceed further with this treatment, either in making it more quantitative or in extending it to strongly coupled nuclei, until we have developed some necessary quantum mechanical background.

7.3 Quantum Mechanical Formalism

A few of the elements of quantum mechanics that are required for the exact treatment of NMR spectra are presented in this section. Standard texts on quantum mechanics, as well as references 1–3, should be consulted for more details.

Provided the rf field is not too large (a requirement met in all high resolution NMR experiments except those involving double resonance; cf. Chapter 8), the state of a nuclear spin system may be described by a steady-state wave function arising from a time-independent Hamiltonian operator $\mathscr{H}$ satisfying the time-independent Schrödinger equation

$$\mathscr{H}\psi = E\psi. \tag{7.3}$$

(E gives the total energy, or energy level, of the system.) The Hamiltonian expresses in quantum mechanical form the potential and kinetic energies of the system. We shall examine in detail the Hamiltonian appropriate to a coupled nuclear spin system in Section 7.5. Before doing so, however, we shall review a general method of obtaining the wave functions and energy levels for any given Hamiltonian.

It is known in general that any wave function ψ may be expressed as a linear combination of some other functions Φ_n,

$$\psi = \sum_n C_n \Phi_n, \tag{7.4}$$

provided the Φ_n form an *orthonormal* and *complete set*. The first requirement is expressed in the integral equation

$$\int \Phi_m^* \Phi_n \, d\tau = \delta_{mn}, \tag{7.5}$$

where Φ_m^* is the complex conjugate of Φ_m, and the Kronecker delta is

$$\delta_{mn} = \begin{cases} 0, & m \neq n, \\ 1, & m = n. \end{cases}$$

The symbol $d\tau$ is used to denote integration over all coordinates of the system. For our purposes, we may completely neglect spatial coordinates and utilize only the x, y, and z components of the nuclear spin or nuclear magnetic moment. We shall not explore the significance of using a complete set except to note that in many quantum mechanical problems the series in equation 7.4 is infinite; in the case of nuclear spin interactions, however, the series contains exactly 2^N terms, where N is the number of nuclei, when the set Φ_n is formed by the simple and natural procedure described in Section 7.4.

If the expression for ψ in equation 7.4 is substituted in equation 7.3, we obtain

$$\mathscr{H} \sum_n C_n \Phi_n = E \sum_n C_n \Phi_n. \qquad (7.6)$$

Multiplying by Φ_m^* and integrating, we get

$$\int \Phi_m^* \mathscr{H} \left(\sum_n C_n \Phi_n \right) d\tau = \int \Phi_m^* E \left(\sum_n C_n \Phi_n \right) d\tau. \qquad (7.7)$$

E and C_n, which are constants, may be removed from the integral, and the order of summing and integrating interchanged:

$$\sum_n C_n \int \Phi_m^* \mathscr{H} \Phi_n \, d\tau = E \sum_n C_n \int \Phi_m^* \Phi_n \, d\tau. \qquad (7.8)$$

If we define

$$\mathscr{H}_{mn} = \int \Phi_m^* \mathscr{H} \Phi_n \, d\tau, \qquad (7.9)$$

and make use of equation 7.5, we obtain

$$\sum_n C_n \mathscr{H}_{mn} = E \sum_n C_n \delta_{mn} \qquad (7.10)$$

or

$$\sum_n C_n (\mathscr{H}_{mn} - E\delta_{mn}) = 0. \qquad (7.11)$$

Equation 7.11 gives a set of 2^N linear, homogeneous equations in the 2^N variables C_n. The necessary and sufficient condition for nontrivial solutions of these equations is that the determinant of the coefficients of the C_n's vanish; that is,

$$|\mathscr{H}_{mn} - E\delta_{mn}| = 0. \qquad (7.12)$$

In expanded form,

$$\begin{vmatrix} \mathscr{H}_{11} - E & \mathscr{H}_{12} & \mathscr{H}_{13} & \cdots \\ \mathscr{H}_{21} & \mathscr{H}_{22} - E & \mathscr{H}_{23} & \cdots \\ \mathscr{H}_{31} & \mathscr{H}_{32} & \mathscr{H}_{33} - E & \cdots \\ \cdots & \cdots & \cdots & \cdots \end{vmatrix} = 0.$$

Equation 7.12 is called the *secular equation*. The quantities $\mathscr{H}_{mn}$ may be arranged in the form of a matrix (the Hamiltonian matrix) and are called *matrix elements*. Our problem, then, reduces to developing expressions for computing these matrix elements, from which the necessary energy levels and wave functions may be calculated.

7.4 Nuclear Spin Basis Functions

In Section 7.2 we found it helpful to denote the spin orientation of a nucleus by the symbol α or β and to use the product of these functions to represent the state of spin orientation of two nuclei. We shall now define α and β more precisely and generalize to more than two nuclei.

The functions α and β must be defined in terms of the quantum mechanical operators corresponding to spin angular momentum: α and β are defined as orthonormal *eigenfunctions* of the z component of spin I_z according to the following equations:

$$I_z \alpha = \tfrac{1}{2}\alpha, \qquad I_z \beta = -\tfrac{1}{2}\beta; \tag{7.13}$$

$$\int \alpha\alpha \, d\tau = \int \beta\beta \, d\tau = 1, \qquad \int \alpha\beta \, d\tau = \int \beta\alpha \, d\tau = 0. \tag{7.14}$$

The properties of spin angular momentum operators have been worked out in detail, principally by analogy with ordinary orbital angular momentum.[1] The results as applied to the functions α and β provide several additional equations involving the x and y components of nuclear spin:

$$
\begin{aligned}
I_x \alpha &= \tfrac{1}{2}\beta, & I_x \beta &= \tfrac{1}{2}\alpha, \\
I_y \alpha &= \tfrac{1}{2}i\beta, & I_y \beta &= -\tfrac{1}{2}i\alpha.
\end{aligned}
\tag{7.15}
$$

Here $i = \sqrt{-1}$. We shall employ these results in calculating matrix elements.

The preceding paragraph defined α and β for a given nucleus. For N nuclei we shall find it most convenient to define the spin state in terms of products of α's or β's for the individual nuclei. With N nuclei of spin $\tfrac{1}{2}$ there are 2^N possible product functions, or 2^N states. For example, two nuclei give the four product functions listed in Section 7.2, which would be designated as $\Phi_1, \ldots, \Phi_4$.

7.5 The Spin Hamiltonian

The Hamiltonian operator may consist of several terms describing the various contributions to the energy of the nuclear spin system. The leading term involves the interaction of each nucleus with the applied magnetic field. Suppose the field H_0 is applied in the negative z direction. We saw in Section 2.2 that the energy of interaction is given by

$$\epsilon = -\mathbf{\mu} \cdot \mathbf{H}_0. \tag{2.10}$$

With H_0 in the negative z direction, this becomes

$$\epsilon = -(\mu_z)(-H_0)$$

$$= \mu_z H_0. \tag{7.16}$$

Substitution of equations 2.1 and 2.2 into equation 7.16 gives

$$\epsilon = \frac{\gamma}{2\pi} hI_z H_0 \quad \text{(ergs)},$$

$$= \frac{\gamma}{2\pi} I_z H_0 \quad \text{(Hz)}. \tag{7.17}$$

(Our later treatment is simplified by expressing the energy in hertz, rather than in ergs, and we shall assume henceforth that all energy terms are expressed in hertz unless otherwise stated.) If I_z is now considered to be a quantum mechanical operator, the expression for the classical interaction energy, equation 7.17, becomes the first term of the Hamiltonian.

Before writing the expression for this part of the Hamiltonian, we must correct for the shielding responsible for the chemical shift. Thus instead of using H_0 we use the field experienced by the nucleus itself, $H_0(1 - \sigma)$. For N nuclei we sum the contributions for each nucleus. The first term in the Hamiltonian is, then,

$$\mathscr{H}^{(0)} = \frac{1}{2\pi} H_0 \sum_{i=1}^{N} \gamma_i(1 - \sigma_i)(I_z)_i. \tag{7.18}$$

This expression shows explicitly that the operator I_z is taken to refer only to one nucleus at a time, that more than one type of nucleus (e.g., ^{1}H and ^{19}F) may be involved, and that the shielding (chemical shift) is taken into account.

As we saw in Section 3.4, a spectrum may be obtained by applying an rf field at a fixed frequency and varying the magnetic field, or by holding the field constant and varying the radio frequency. Our subsequent treatment will be simplified if we adopt the latter approach; the results would be precisely the same if we treated the magnetic field as a variable. To simplify the notation we substitute the Larmor relation, equation 2.9, in equation 7.18 to get

$$\mathscr{H}^{(0)} = \sum_{i=1}^{N} \nu_i(I_z)_i; \tag{7.19}$$

ν_i is the resonance frequency (including the effect of the chemical shift) of the ith nucleus.

Whenever there are electron-coupled spin-spin interactions between two or more of the nuclei, we must add a second term to the Hamiltonian to account for the energy arising from these interactions. Following our discussion in Sections 5.1 and 7.2, the coupling depends only on the relative orientations of the nuclear spins, not on the orientations of the spins with respect to the field. This fact is expressed in the following term:

$$\mathcal{H}^{(1)} = \sum_{i<j} \sum J_{ij} \mathbf{I}_i \cdot \mathbf{I}_j$$
$$= \sum_{i<j} \sum J_{ij} [(I_x)_i(I_x)_j + (I_y)_i(I_y)_j + (I_z)_i(I_z)_j]. \tag{7.20}$$

(The last line is just the expanded form of a vector dot product.) The summation extends over all possible pairs of nuclei, with the notation $i < j$ guaranteeing that each pair is counted only once. For N nuclei the sum includes $\frac{1}{2}N(N-1)$ terms. Thus, for a system of four nuclei there are four terms in $\mathcal{H}^{(0)}$ and six terms in $\mathcal{H}^{(1)}$.

For the types of problems we are treating, where the molecules are tumbling rapidly, the sum of $\mathcal{H}^{(0)}$ and $\mathcal{H}^{(1)}$ is adequate as the complete Hamiltonian. If there are dipole-dipole interactions to be considered, or if there are strong rf fields involved, additional terms must be added. We shall see the effect of a second rf field in Chapter 8, and the effect of dipole interactions in Section 7.25.

7.6 The Two-Spin System without Coupling

We now apply the concepts developed in the preceding sections to the system of just two nuclei, first considering the case where there is no spin coupling between them. In general, when there is no coupling (i.e., $\mathcal{H}^{(1)} = 0$), the form of $\mathcal{H}^{(0)}$ and of the basis functions Φ_n guarantees that the Φ_n are themselves the true wave functions ψ_n. We shall not demonstrate this result in general terms, but it will emerge from the following calculation of energy levels and wave functions for the case of two uncoupled spins.

We shall digress from our usual notation to call the two spins A and B, rather than A and X, since we shall later wish to use some of the present results in treating the coupled AB system. As indicated in Section 7.2, the four product basis functions are

$$\Phi_1 = \alpha_A \alpha_B = \alpha\alpha, \qquad \Phi_2 = \alpha_A \beta_B = \alpha\beta,$$
$$\Phi_3 = \beta_A \alpha_B = \beta\alpha, \qquad \Phi_4 = \beta_A \beta_B = \beta\beta. \tag{7.21}$$

We shall now compute the matrix elements needed for the secular determinant. Since there are four basis functions, the determinant is 4×4 in size, with 16 matrix elements. Many of these will turn out to be zero. For $\mathcal{H}_{11}$ we have, from equations 7.9 and 7.19 (with $\Phi_n^* = \Phi_n$ for the real functions with which we are concerned),

$$\mathcal{H}_{11} = \int \Phi_1 \mathcal{H}^{(0)} \Phi_1 \, d\tau$$

$$= \int \alpha_A \alpha_B [\nu_A (I_z)_A + \nu_B (I_z)_B] \alpha_A \alpha_B \, d\tau$$

$$= \nu_A \int \alpha_A \alpha_B (I_z)_A \alpha_A \alpha_B \, d\tau + \nu_B \int \alpha_A \alpha_B (I_z)_B \alpha_A \alpha_B \, d\tau. \qquad (7.22)$$

The element $d\tau$ refers to spins A and B; thus each of the two integrals in equation 7.22 is really a double integral over $d\tau_A$ and $d\tau_B$. These two spins may be integrated independently:

$$\mathcal{H}_{11} = \nu_A \int \alpha_A (I_z)_A \alpha_A \, d\tau_A \int \alpha_A \alpha_B \, d\tau_B + \nu_B \int \alpha_A \alpha_A \, d\tau_A \int \alpha_B (I_z)_B \alpha_B \, d\tau_B. \qquad (7.23)$$

Using the result of equation 7.13 we obtain

$$\mathcal{H}_{11} = \nu_A (\tfrac{1}{2})(1) + \nu_B (1)(\tfrac{1}{2})$$

$$= \tfrac{1}{2}(\nu_A + \nu_B). \qquad (7.24)$$

By the same procedure, the other three *diagonal* matrix elements (those on the principal diagonal) may be evaluated as

$$\mathcal{H}_{22} = \tfrac{1}{2}(\nu_A - \nu_B),$$

$$\mathcal{H}_{33} = \tfrac{1}{2}(-\nu_A + \nu_B), \qquad (7.25)$$

$$\mathcal{H}_{44} = -\tfrac{1}{2}(\nu_A + \nu_B).$$

In the absence of spin coupling, all *off-diagonal* elements (all those not on the principal diagonal) are zero by virtue of the orthogonality of α and β. This is a general theorem not restricted to the case of two nuclei. We shall illustrate the result for $\mathcal{H}_{12}$:

$$\mathcal{H}_{12} = \int \Phi_1 H^{(0)} \Phi_2 \, d\tau$$

$$= \int \alpha_A \alpha_B [\nu_A (I_z)_A + \nu_B (I_z)_B] \alpha_A \beta_B \, d\tau$$

$$= \nu_A \int \alpha_A (I_z)_A \alpha_A \, d\tau_A \int \alpha_B \beta_B \, d\tau_B + \nu_B \int \alpha_A \alpha_A \, d\tau_A \int \alpha_B (I_z)_B \beta_B \, d\tau_B$$

$$= \nu_A (\tfrac{1}{2})(0) + \nu_B (1)(0). \qquad (7.26)$$

With all off-diagonal elements equal to zero, the secular determinant becomes

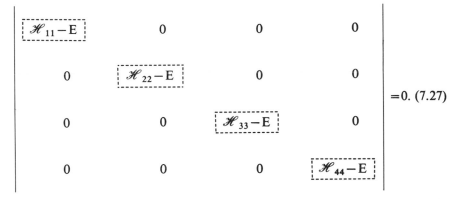

$$\begin{vmatrix} \mathscr{H}_{11}-E & 0 & 0 & 0 \\ 0 & \mathscr{H}_{22}-E & 0 & 0 \\ 0 & 0 & \mathscr{H}_{33}-E & 0 \\ 0 & 0 & 0 & \mathscr{H}_{44}-E \end{vmatrix} = 0. \quad (7.27)$$

Thus the left-hand side of equation 7.27 may be written as the product of four factors and is said to be factored into four 1×1 blocks, as indicated. The four solutions of the equation are, from equations 7.24 and 7.25,

$$\begin{aligned} E_1 &= \mathscr{H}_{11} = \tfrac{1}{2}(\nu_A + \nu_B), \\ E_2 &= \mathscr{H}_{22} = \tfrac{1}{2}(\nu_A - \nu_B), \\ E_3 &= \mathscr{H}_{33} = \tfrac{1}{2}(-\nu_A + \nu_B), \\ E_4 &= \mathscr{H}_{44} = -\tfrac{1}{2}(\nu_A + \nu_B). \end{aligned} \quad (7.28)$$

These energies are easily associated with the four energy levels depicted in Figure 7.1 in our qualitative discussion of the AX system. The allowed transitions, which are also shown in Figure 7.1, correspond to the selection rule $\Delta F_z = \pm 1$ (F_z was defined in equation 7.1). The origin of this selection rule will be taken up later in Section 7.9. It is clear from the values of the energy levels in equation 7.28 that each observed line results from two transitions with precisely the same frequency.

The calculation of the wave function corresponding to each energy level is carried out by evaluating the ratios of the C_n's from equation 7.11 (for each value of E in turn) and substitution of the C_n into equation 7.4.* In this case the calculation is trivial, since for each energy level only one $C_n \neq 0$. Thus

$$\begin{aligned} \psi_1 &= \Phi_1 = \alpha\alpha, & \psi_2 &= \Phi_2 = \alpha\beta, \\ \psi_3 &= \Phi_3 = \beta\alpha, & \psi_4 &= \Phi_4 = \beta\beta. \end{aligned} \quad (7.29)$$

This result, that the true wave functions are identical with the basis product functions, is completely general for any case where there is no spin coupling.

---

* More efficient procedures employing matrix algebra are normally used in practice for finding the *eigenvector* that diagonalizes the Hamiltonian matrix for each *eigenvalue* E_k. There is no difference in the result, and for simple cases the algebra in the scheme used here is not too cumbersome.

It is only the spin coupling interaction, not the chemical shift, that causes the basis functions to *mix*. We shall see in the next section that even with coupling many of the basis functions do not mix.

7.7 Factoring the Secular Equation

Before extending our treatment to two coupled nuclei, it is helpful to consider the conditions that cause zero elements to appear in the secular equation. With this knowledge we can avoid the effort of calculating many of the elements specifically for each case we study; furthermore, the presence of zero elements usually results in the secular determinant being factored into several equations of much smaller order, the solution of which is simpler than that of a high-order equation.

Suppose the basis functions used to construct the secular equation, the Φ_n, are eigenfunctions of some operator F. Consider two of these functions, Φ_m and Φ_n, with eigenvalues f_m and f_n, respectively. Then

$$F\Phi_m = f_m\Phi_m, \qquad F\Phi_n = f_n\Phi_n. \tag{7.30}$$

Suppose further that the operator F commutes with the Hamiltonian:

$$F\mathscr{H} - \mathscr{H}F = 0. \tag{7.31}$$

From these premises it is shown in standard texts on quantum mechanics[4] that

$$(f_m - f_n)\int \Phi_m^* \mathscr{H}\Phi_n \, d\tau = 0,$$

$$(f_m - f_n)\mathscr{H}_{mn} = 0. \tag{7.32}$$

Thus if $f_m \neq f_n$, $\mathscr{H}_{mn} = 0$; that is, if Φ_m and Φ_n have *different* eigenvalues of F, the matrix element connecting them in the secular equation must be zero. (If $f_m = f_n$, nothing can be said from equation 7.32 about the value of $\mathscr{H}_{mn}$.)

There are two types of operators F that are important in the treatment of nuclear spin systems. One is the class of operators describing the symmetry of many molecules. We shall defer a discussion of symmetry until Section 7.12.

The other operator is F_z, which was defined in equation 7.1. Since α and β are eigenfunctions of I_z, the product functions Φ_n are eigenfunctions of F_z with eigenvalues equal to the sum of $+\frac{1}{2}$ for each time an α appears in the product function and $-\frac{1}{2}$ for each time a β appears in the function. By using the well-established commutation rules for angular momentum, it can be shown that F_z and $\mathscr{H}$ commute, so that equation 7.32 is applicable. (We shall not present the details of the proof here.[5]) For example, in the general (coupled) two-spin case, equation 7.2 shows that the four basis functions are classified according to $F_z = 1$, 0, or -1. Only Φ_2 and Φ_3, which have the same value of F_z, can mix. Thus only $\mathscr{H}_{23}$ and $\mathscr{H}_{32}$ might be non-zero; all 10 other off-diagonal elements of the secular equation are zero.

Further factorization of the secular equation according to F_z can sometimes be accomplished to a very high degree of approximation, even when several functions have the same value of F_z. We shall explore this point further in Sections 7.8 and 7.17.

7.8 Two Coupled Spins

We are now in position to complete our calculation of the AB system in general, with no restrictions whatsoever regarding the magnitude of the coupling constant J_{AB}. By virtue of the factoring due to F_z the secular equation is

$$\begin{vmatrix} \mathscr{H}_{11} - E & 0 & 0 & 0 \\ 0 & \mathscr{H}_{22} - E & \mathscr{H}_{23} & 0 \\ 0 & \mathscr{H}_{32} & \mathscr{H}_{33} - E & 0 \\ 0 & 0 & 0 & \mathscr{H}_{44} - E \end{vmatrix} = 0. \qquad (7.33)$$

The secular equation is always symmetric about the principal diagonal; hence $\mathscr{H}_{23} = \mathscr{H}_{32}$. We thus have five matrix elements to evaluate. Since

$$\mathscr{H} = \mathscr{H}^{(0)} + \mathscr{H}^{(1)},$$

we need evaluate only the portion of the matrix elements arising from $\mathscr{H}^{(1)}$ and then merely add the portion evaluated in Section 7.6 from $\mathscr{H}^{(0)}$.

For the first matrix element we find, using equations 7.9 and 7.20,

$$\mathscr{H}_{11}^{(1)} = \int \Phi_1 \mathscr{H}^{(1)} \Phi_1 \, d\tau$$

$$= J_{AB} \int \alpha_A \alpha_B [(I_x)_A (I_x)_B + (I_y)_A (I_y)_B + (I_z)_A (I_z)_B] \alpha_A \alpha_B \, d\tau. \qquad (7.34)$$

As was the case in Section 7.6, the integral in equation 7.34 is really a double integral over the spin coordinates of A and of B. By separating the integrations we obtain

$$\mathscr{H}_{11}^{(1)} = J_{AB} \left[\int \alpha_A (I_x)_A \alpha_A \, d\tau_A \int \alpha_B (I_x)_B \alpha_B \, d\tau_B \right.$$

$$+ \int \alpha_A (I_y)_A \alpha_A \, d\tau_A \int \alpha_B (I_y)_B \alpha_B \, d\tau_B$$

$$\left. + \int \alpha_A (I_z)_A \alpha_A \, d\tau_A \int \alpha_B (I_z)_B \alpha_B \, d\tau_B \right]. \qquad (7.35)$$

Introducing values from equations 7.13, 7.14 and 7.15, we obtain

$$\mathscr{H}_{11}^{(1)} = J_{AB}[0 + 0 + (\tfrac{1}{2})(\tfrac{1}{2})]$$

$$= \tfrac{1}{4}J_{AB}. \tag{7.36}$$

For $\mathscr{H}_{22}$ the equation analogous to equation 7.35 is

$$\mathscr{H}_{22}^{(1)} = J_{AB}\left[\int \alpha I_x \alpha \, d\tau \int \beta I_x \beta \, d\tau + \int \alpha I_y \alpha \, d\tau \int \beta I_y \beta \, d\tau \right.$$

$$\left. + \int \alpha I_z \alpha \, d\tau \int \beta I_z \beta \, d\tau \right]$$

$$= J_{AB}[0 + 0 + (\tfrac{1}{2})(-\tfrac{1}{2})]$$

$$= -\tfrac{1}{4}J_{AB}. \tag{7.37}$$

Similar computations give

$$\mathscr{H}_{33}^{(1)} = -\tfrac{1}{4}J_{AB},$$

$$\mathscr{H}_{44}^{(1)} = \tfrac{1}{4}J_{AB}. \tag{7.38}$$

The lone nonzero off-diagonal element may be evaluated in a similar manner:

$$\mathscr{H}_{23} = \int \Phi_2 \mathscr{H}^{(1)} \Phi_3 \, d\tau$$

$$= J_{AB} \int \alpha_A \beta_B [(I_x)_A (I_x)_B + (I_y)_A (I_y)_B + (I_z)_A (I_z)_B] \beta_A \alpha_B \, d\tau$$

$$= J_{AB}\left[\int \alpha_A (I_x)_A \beta_A \, d\tau_A \int \beta_B (I_x)_B \alpha_B \, d\tau_B \right.$$

$$+ \int \alpha_A (I_y)_A \beta_A \, d\tau_A \int \beta_B (I_y)_B \alpha_B \, d\tau_B$$

$$\left. + \int \alpha_A (I_z)_A \beta_A \, d\tau_A \int \beta_B (I_z)_B \alpha_B \, d\tau_B \right]$$

$$= J_{AB}[(\tfrac{1}{2})(\tfrac{1}{2}) + (\tfrac{1}{2}i)(-\tfrac{1}{2}i) + 0]$$

$$= \tfrac{1}{2}J_{AB}. \tag{7.39}$$

Adding the contribution from $\mathscr{H}^{(0)}$ from equations 7.24 and 7.25, we find that the complete secular equation factors into three equations:

$$[\tfrac{1}{2}(\nu_A + \nu_B) + \tfrac{1}{4}J_{AB} - E] = 0; \tag{7.40}$$

$$\begin{vmatrix} \tfrac{1}{2}(\nu_A - \nu_B) - \tfrac{1}{4}J_{AB} - E & \tfrac{1}{2}J_{AB} \\ \tfrac{1}{2}J_{AB} & \tfrac{1}{2}(-\nu_A + \nu_B) - \tfrac{1}{4}J_{AB} - E \end{vmatrix} = 0; \tag{7.41}$$

$$[-\tfrac{1}{2}(\nu_A + \nu_B) + \tfrac{1}{4}J_{AB} - E] = 0. \tag{7.42}$$

Equations 7.40 and 7.42 immediately give the values of two energy levels, E_1 and E_4. Equation 7.41 is a quadratic equation that is readily solved to give

$$E_2 = \tfrac{1}{2}[(\nu_A - \nu_B)^2 + J_{AB}^2]^{1/2} - \tfrac{1}{4}J_{AB},$$
$$E_3 = -\tfrac{1}{2}[(\nu_A - \nu_B)^2 + J_{AB}^2]^{1/2} - \tfrac{1}{4}J_{AB}. \tag{7.43}$$

The wave functions ψ_1 and ψ_4 are identical with Φ_1 and Φ_4, respectively, as we showed in Section 7.7. The functions ψ_2 and ψ_3 are linear combinations (mixtures) of Φ_2 and Φ_3, the extent of mixing depending on the ratio of $(\nu_A - \nu_B)/J_{AB}$, as shown in the following expressions:*

$$\psi_1 = \Phi_1,$$
$$\psi_2 = \frac{1}{(1 + Q^2)^{1/2}}(\Phi_2 + Q\Phi_3),$$
$$\psi_3 = \frac{1}{(1 + Q^2)^{1/2}}(-Q\Phi_2 + \Phi_3),$$
$$\psi_4 = \Phi_4. \tag{7.44}$$

In equation 7.44 Q is defined as

$$Q = \frac{J}{(\nu_A - \nu_B) + [(\nu_A - \nu_B)^2 + J_{AB}^2]^{1/2}}. \tag{7.45}$$

We shall discuss the spectrum arising from an AB system in detail in Section 7.10.

One point regarding the expressions in equation 7.43 deserves mention at this time: If $(\nu_A - \nu_B) \gg J_{AB}$ (the general AX case), J_{AB}^2 is negligible compared with $(\nu_A - \nu_B)^2$ and may be dropped. The resultant expressions for E_2 and E_3 are then considerably simplified. Note that the same result could have been achieved by dropping the off-diagonal elements $\tfrac{1}{2}J_{AB}$ when the secular equation was written. Dropping such small off-diagonal terms leads to a factorization of the secular equation beyond that given by the factorization according to F_z. This is a general and extremely important procedure, applicable to cases where certain differences in chemical shifts (expressed in hertz) are large compared with the corresponding J's. This is tantamount to a classification of the basis functions, not only according to the total F_z, but also according to $F_z(G)$, where G refers to only strongly coupled nuclei. The definition of $F_z(G)$ and the application to the **ABX** case will be taken up in Section 7.17.

---

* The calculation of the C_n in equation 7.4 is easily carried out by using minors of the secular determinant or by matrix methods. We shall not present the details of the computation.

7.9 Selection Rules and Intensities

We reviewed the basic concepts of absorption of radiation in Section 2.3. We now wish to derive rules governing radiative transitions in systems consisting of N spin-coupled nuclei of spin $\frac{1}{2}$. For such a system we need to consider the interaction between the applied rf field in the x direction and the x component of magnetization, M_x

$$M_x = \frac{1}{2\pi} \sum_{i=1}^{N} \gamma_i (I_x)_i. \tag{7.46}$$

Application of time-dependent perturbation theory leads to an expression which shows that the intensity of a spectral line (transition from state p to state q) is proportional to the *square* of the following matrix element, or integral:

$$M_{pq} \equiv \int \psi_p \sum_{i=1}^{N} \gamma_i (I_x)_i \psi_q \, d\tau$$

$$= \sum_{i=1}^{N} \gamma_i \int \psi_p (I_x)_i \psi_q \, d\tau. \tag{7.47}$$

We recall that each of the ψ's is either one of the basis functions or a linear combination of basis functions. In the former case ψ is merely a product of α's and β's, one for each nucleus. If we examine the form of one of the terms of equation 7.47, say the one for $i = 1$, we find that the integral is really a multiple integral over all nuclear spin coordinates. The integral over nucleus 1, which involves $(I_x)_1$, is zero (cf. equation 7.15) unless nucleus 1 changes its spin state from α to β or from β to α. At the same time the integrals over all nuclei other than nucleus 1 will be different from zero only if there is no change in spin state for each of these nuclei. Thus the only permitted transition has only one nucleus changing its spin state by $\Delta I_z = \pm 1$.

In general, where ψ is a linear combination of basis functions, the requirement for an allowed transition is less stringent, for the I_x operator for each of the strongly coupled nuclei may contribute to a given transition. Even so, the results of the previous paragraph may readily be generalized to give a selection rule $\Delta F_z = \pm 1$. When the system may be divided into sets of strongly coupled nuclei, with only weak coupling between sets, we define $F_z(G)$ for each set, and the more restrictive selection rules $\Delta F_z(G) = \pm 1$ must be obeyed for each G.

7.10 The AB Spectrum

We found in Section 7.2 that the values of F_z for the two-spin system are $+1, 0, 0,$ and -1 for states (1), (2), (3), and (4), respectively. Thus the selection rule $\Delta F_z = \pm 1$ forbids transitions between states (2) and (3) and between states (1) and (4). There are then four allowed transitions: (3) $\rightarrow$ (1), (4) $\rightarrow$ (2), (4) $\rightarrow$ (3), and (2) $\rightarrow$ (1); but the selection rule itself gives no indication of the relative probabilities of these transitions or the intensities of the corresponding spectral lines. However, by using the expressions derived in Section 7.8 for the energy levels and wave functions, we can calculate the frequencies and relative intensities of the four lines of the AB spectrum.

We denote by $T_{p \rightarrow q}$ the frequency of the transition from state p to state q and by $M_{p \rightarrow q}$ the matrix element of M_x (equation 7.47). The relative intensities of the spectral lines are thus proportional to $(M_{p \rightarrow q})^2$. From equations 7.40–7.43 we obtain

$$l_1 = T_{3 \rightarrow 1} = \tfrac{1}{2}(\nu_A + \nu_B) + \tfrac{1}{2}[(\nu_A - \nu_B)^2 + J^2]^{1/2} + \tfrac{1}{2}J,$$

$$l_2 = T_{4 \rightarrow 2} = \tfrac{1}{2}(\nu_A + \nu_B) + \tfrac{1}{2}[(\nu_A - \nu_B)^2 + J^2]^{1/2} - \tfrac{1}{2}J,$$

$$l_3 = T_{2 \rightarrow 1} = \tfrac{1}{2}(\nu_A + \nu_B) - \tfrac{1}{2}[(\nu_A - \nu_B)^2 + J^2]^{1/2} + \tfrac{1}{2}J,$$

$$l_4 = T_{4 \rightarrow 3} = \tfrac{1}{2}(\nu_A + \nu_B) - \tfrac{1}{2}[(\nu_A - \nu_B)^2 + J^2]^{1/2} - \tfrac{1}{2}J.$$

$$(7.48)$$

We have dropped the subscript for J since there is one coupling constant involved and have introduced the expressions l_i as a convenient notation for the frequencies of the lines. It is apparent that lines 1 and 2 are always separated by J, as are lines 3 and 4. Thus the value of J may be extracted immediately from an AB spectrum. If J^2 is negligible relative to $(\nu_A - \nu_B)^2$, then the average of l_1 and l_2 immediately gives ν_A, and the average of l_3 and l_4 gives ν_B. In general, however, the calculation of ν_A and ν_B for an AB spectrum requires slightly more effort. The separation between l_1 and l_3 gives $[(\nu_A - \nu_B)^2 + J^2]^{1/2}$, and since J has already been found, $|\nu_A - \nu_B|$ may be calculated. The sum of l_2 and l_3 gives $\nu_A + \nu_B$, so that ν_A and ν_B may be calculated.

To find the relative intensities of the four AB lines we use the wave functions from equation 7.44 to evaluate the matrix elements defined by equation 7.47. (Since we are interested in the case involving only a single nuclear species, we can drop γ from this equation.)

$$M_{2 \rightarrow 1} = \int \psi_1 [(I_x)_A + (I_x)_B] \psi_2 \, d\tau$$

$$= \frac{1}{(1 + Q^2)^{1/2}} \int \alpha\alpha [(I_x)_A + (I_x)_B](\alpha\beta + Q\beta\alpha) \, d\tau$$

$$= \frac{1}{(1+Q^2)^{1/2}} \left\{ \int \alpha\alpha(I_x)_A \, \alpha\beta \, d\tau + Q \int \alpha\alpha(I_x)_A \, \beta\alpha \, d\tau \right.$$

$$\left. + \int \alpha\alpha(I_x)_B \, \alpha\beta \, d\tau + Q \int \alpha\alpha(I_x)_B \, \beta\alpha \, d\tau \right\}$$

$$= \frac{1}{(1+Q^2)^{1/2}} \left\{ \alpha(I_x)_A \, \alpha \, d\tau_A \int \alpha\beta \, d\tau_B + Q \int \alpha(I_x)_A \, \beta \, d\tau_A \int \alpha\alpha \, d\tau_B \right.$$

$$\left. + \int \alpha\alpha \, d\tau_A \int \alpha(I_x)_B \, \beta \, d\tau_B + Q \int \alpha\beta \, d\tau_A \int \alpha(I_x)_B \, \alpha \, d\tau_B \right\}$$

$$= \frac{1}{(1+Q^2)^{1/2}} \{ 0 + \tfrac{1}{2}Q + \tfrac{1}{2} + 0 \}$$

$$= \frac{1+Q}{2(1+Q^2)^{1/2}}. \tag{7.49}$$

Similar calculations show that

$$M_{4\to 2} = M_{2\to 1},$$

$$M_{4\to 3} = M_{3\to 1} = \frac{1-Q}{2(1+Q^2)^{1/2}}. \tag{7.50}$$

The relative intensities of the lines are proportional to the $(M_{p\to q})^2$

$$M_{4\to 2}^2 = M_{2\to 1}^2 = \frac{(1+Q)^2}{4(1+Q^2)} = \frac{1}{4}\left[1 + \frac{2Q}{1+Q^2} \right],$$

$$M_{4\to 3}^2 = M_{3\to 1}^2 = \frac{(1-Q)^2}{4(1+Q^2)} = \frac{1}{4}\left[1 - \frac{2Q}{1+Q^2} \right]. \tag{7.51}$$

In order to simplify the expressions, we introduce the notation

$$2C \equiv [(\nu_A - \nu_B)^2 + J^2]^{1/2}. \tag{7.52}$$

Table 7.1 and Figure 7.2 give the frequencies of the lines in terms of C. By using equations 7.45 and 7.52, the relative intensities of the lines given in equation 7.51 may be expressed in terms of C and J, and are listed in Table 7.1.*

* One convenient way of transforming from the intensity expressions in terms of Q to those in terms of C and J is by defining

$$\sin\theta \equiv Q/(1+Q^2)^{1/2}.$$

Expressions for $\cos\theta$ and $\sin 2\theta$ are easily obtained from trigonometric identities, and the expressions of equation 7.51 reduce to $\frac{1}{4}(1 \pm \sin 2\theta)$. Relative intensities are often expressed in this way for the AB system,[2,3] and we shall use a similar notation in treating the ABX spectrum. Note that the angle θ has no physical significance.

From Table 7.1 and Figure 7.2 it is evident that an AB spectrum consists of four lines with a symmetric weak, strong, strong, weak intensity distribution.

Table 7.1

TRANSITIONS, FREQUENCIES, AND RELATIVE INTENSITIES FOR THE AB SYSTEM

Line	Transition	Frequency (Hz)[a]	Relative intensity
1	$T_{3\rightarrow1}$	$C+\frac{1}{2}J$	$1-\dfrac{J}{2C}$
2	$T_{4\rightarrow2}$	$C-\frac{1}{2}J$	$1+\dfrac{J}{2C}$
3	$T_{2\rightarrow1}$	$-C+\frac{1}{2}J$	$1+\dfrac{J}{2C}$
4	$T_{4\rightarrow3}$	$-C-\frac{1}{2}J$	$1-\dfrac{J}{2C}$

[a] Referred to the center of the four-line pattern, $\frac{1}{2}(\nu_A+\nu_B)$.

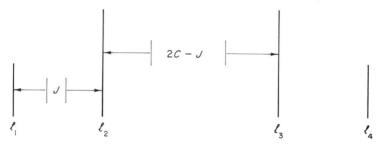

Fig. 7.2 Schematic representation of an AB spectrum.

$$|J| = |l_1 - l_2| = |l_3 - l_4|,$$
$$|\nu_A - \nu_B| = [(l_1 - l_4)(l_2 - l_3)]^{1/2}.$$

The separation between the outer lines in either half of the spectrum is equal to J. The value of $|\nu_A - \nu_B|$ is easily found from the separation between the outer and the inner lines, for equation 7.52 may be rewritten

$$(\nu_A - \nu_B)^2 = 4C^2 - J^2,$$
$$|\nu_A - \nu_B| = [4C^2 - J^2]^{1/2}$$
$$= [(2C - J)(2C + J)]^{1/2}$$
$$= [(l_2 - l_3)(l_1 - l_4)]^{1/2}. \tag{7.53}$$

From Table 7.1 we see that the ratio of the *intensities* of the inner to the outer lines is

$$\frac{I(\text{inner})}{I(\text{outer})} = \frac{2C + J}{2C - J} = \frac{l_1 - l_4}{l_2 - l_3}. \tag{7.54}$$

Thus the intensities must accord with the frequencies of a set of four lines if they constitute an AB pattern.

The appearance of an AB spectrum is determined entirely by the ratio $J/(\nu_A - \nu_B)$, as was shown in Figure 5.4. Note that the analysis of an AB spectrum gives only $|J|$ and $|\nu_A - \nu_B|$; we cannot determine from the spectrum itself the sign of J or which nucleus, A or B, is more shielded.

7.11 Spectral Contributions from Equivalent Nuclei

Let us examine the AB spectrum when $\nu_A = \nu_B$ (i.e., an A_2 system). From equations 7.40–7.43 the energy levels are

$$E_1 = \nu_A + \tfrac{1}{4}J, \qquad E_2 = \tfrac{1}{4}J,$$
$$E_3 = -\tfrac{3}{4}J, \qquad E_4 = -\nu_A + \tfrac{1}{4}J. \tag{7.55}$$

In principle, from the four allowed transitions we should be able to find the value of J. From equation 7.52, however, we find that $2C = J$. Table 7.1 shows, then, that two lines, l_2 and l_3, coincide at ν_A, while l_1 and l_4 have zero intensity.

The foregoing example is just one illustration of the lack of splitting due to spin coupling in spectra where certain types of equivalence exist among the nuclei. We shall state without proof an extremely important NMR theorem and its corollary:

1. The spectrum arising from a system of nuclear spins that includes one or more sets of *magnetically* equivalent nuclei is independent of the spin coupling between nuclei within a magnetically equivalent set. For example, the spectrum of an A_3B system does not in any way depend on J_{AA}, but the spectrum of an AA'BB' spectrum is a function of $J_{AA'}$. The proof of this theorem depends on commutation properties of angular momentum operators.[6]

2. A molecule in which *all* coupled nuclei have the same chemical shift gives a spectrum consisting of a single line. For example, CH_4, which has four magnetically equivalent protons, gives a single proton resonance line; but CH_3D does not, since here one of the set of coupled nuclei clearly has a

"chemical shift" different from the rest. This corollary does not depend on the reason for the chemical equivalence, which may result from molecular symmetry or from an accidental equivalence in shielding. When *all* coupled nuclei in a molecule are chemically equivalent, they are also magnetically equivalent, since they are equally coupled ($J = 0$) to all *other* nuclei.

7.12 Symmetry of Wave Functions

The presence of symmetry in a molecule imposes severe restrictions on many chemical and spectral properties. Often the existence of symmetry permits considerable simplification in the analysis of NMR spectra.

We speak of a *symmetry operation* $\mathscr{R}$ as an operation which when applied to a molecule leaves it in a configuration that is *physically indistinguishable* from the original configuration. With regard to wave functions, it is ψ^2 that corresponds to a physically measurable quantity, not ψ itself. Hence we require that

$$\mathscr{R}\psi^2 = \psi^2. \tag{7.56}$$

For a nondegenerate wave function, which is to remain normalized, equation 7.56 is valid *only* if the new ψ following the symmetry operation is either equal to the original ψ or is its negative:

$$\mathscr{R}\psi = +\psi \quad \text{or} \quad -\psi. \tag{7.57}$$

A function that is unchanged by the operation is said to be *symmetric*; one changed into its negative is *antisymmetric*.

Let us now consider the application of this concept to a two-spin system, where the two spins are chemically equivalent (not necessarily magnetically equivalent) by virtue of their positions in a symmetric molecule. (Such nuclei are said to be *symmetrically equivalent*.) We shall designate the spins by the subscripts a and b, but this does not imply any difference between them. Following the procedure of Section 7.6, we can write four basis functions for this system:

$$
\begin{aligned}
\Phi_1 &= \alpha_a \alpha_b \quad &\text{symmetric,} \\
\Phi_2 &= \alpha_a \beta_b \quad &\text{asymmetric,} \\
\Phi_3 &= \beta_a \alpha_b \quad &\text{asymmetric,} \\
\Phi_4 &= \beta_a \beta_b \quad &\text{symmetric.}
\end{aligned}
\tag{7.58}
$$

If we perform the symmetry operation of interchanging these two identical nuclei, Φ_1 and Φ_4 will clearly be unchanged; hence we label them as symmetric functions. However, Φ_2 and Φ_3 are neither symmetric nor antisymmetric, since

$$\mathcal{R}\Phi_2 \equiv \mathcal{R}\alpha_a\beta_b = \alpha_b\beta_a = \beta_a\alpha_b \equiv \Phi_3,$$

$$\mathcal{R}\Phi_2 \neq \Phi_2 \quad \text{or} \quad -\Phi_2; \tag{7.59}$$

Φ_2 and Φ_3 have been labeled as *asymmetric*. They are not in themselves acceptable wave functions. We may, if we wish, use them as basis functions in a calculation involving the secular equation, and we shall ultimately obtain the correct solution to the problem. However, the calculations are greatly simplified by selecting in place of Φ_2 and Φ_3 two functions that have the proper symmetry and yet maintain the desirable properties of product basis functions. For the two-spin system this can be accomplished easily by selecting functions that are the sum and difference of Φ_2 and Φ_3:

$$\Phi_2' = \frac{1}{\sqrt{2}}(\alpha_a\beta_b + \beta_a\alpha_b) \qquad \text{symmetric};$$

$$\Phi_3' = \frac{1}{\sqrt{2}}(\alpha_a\beta_b - \beta_a\alpha_b) \qquad \text{antisymmetric}. \tag{7.60}$$

The factor $1/\sqrt{2}$ maintains the normalization condition.

We know from Section 7.3 that the true wave functions $\psi_1, \ldots, \psi_4$ are linear combinations of the basis functions. If we begin with symmetrized functions, such as Φ_2' and Φ_3', then each of the ψ's can be formed exclusively from symmetric functions or exclusively from antisymmetric functions. Stated another way, *functions of different symmetry do not mix*. The result is that, like the situation with F_z, many off-diagonal elements of the secular equation must be zero, and the equation factors into several equations of lower order. We shall study an example of this factoring in Section 7.15, when we consider the A_2B system.

Simplification of the spectrum itself also results from the presence of symmetry, since transitions are permitted *only* between two symmetric or two antisymmetric states. We shall see in Section 7.15 that there is often a considerable reduction in the number of NMR lines.

For the two-spin system the only symmetry operation is the interchange of the two nuclei, and the correct linear combinations, Φ_2' and Φ_3', could be constructed by inspection. When three or more symmetrically equivalent nuclei are present, the symmetry operations consist of various permutations of the nuclei. The correct symmetrized functions can be determined systematically only by application of results from group theory. We shall not present the details of this procedure, but in Section 7.16 we shall use functions derived in this way for the A_3B system.

7.13 Summary of Rules for Calculating Spectra

In Sections 7.8 and 7.10 we derived in considerable detail the expressions for the secular equation and the transitions of the AB system. It is apparent that the calculation of each element in the secular equation from the general theory would become very tedious for systems of three or more nuclei. Fortunately, general rules have been derived to simplify the calculation.[3] We shall not derive these expressions, but we present the rules in a concise form to illustrate the simplicity of the calculation.

1. The calculation always begins with the writing of the 2^N simple product functions (e.g., $\alpha\alpha\beta\alpha$, etc.). In the absence of symmetry these serve as the basis functions.

2. If symmetry is present, suitable linear combinations of the product functions are used as basis functions Φ_n. Normally, group theory is used as an aid to selecting appropriate linear combinations.

3. The diagonal matrix elements of the Hamiltonian (or the secular equation) are

$$\mathscr{H}_{mm} = \sum_{i=1}^{N} v_i[(I_z)_i]_m + \tfrac{1}{4}\sum_{i<j}\sum J_{ij}T_{ij}, \tag{7.61}$$

where

$$[(I_z)_i]_m = \begin{cases} +\tfrac{1}{2} & \text{if nucleus } i \text{ has spin } \alpha \text{ in } \Phi_m, \\ -\tfrac{1}{2} & \text{if nucleus } i \text{ has spin } \beta \text{ in } \Phi_m; \end{cases}$$

and

$$T_{ij} = \begin{cases} +1 & \text{if spins } i \text{ and } j \text{ are parallel in } \Phi_m, \\ -1 & \text{if spins } i \text{ and } j \text{ are antiparallel in } \Phi_m. \end{cases}$$

For example, if $\Phi_m = \alpha_1\,\alpha_2\,\beta_3\,\alpha_4$, then

$$\mathscr{H}_{mm} = \tfrac{1}{2}(v_1 + v_2 - v_3 + v_4) + \tfrac{1}{4}(J_{12} - J_{13} + J_{14} - J_{23} + J_{24} - J_{34}).$$

4. The off-diagonal matrix elements are

$$\mathscr{H}_{mn} = \tfrac{1}{2}UJ_{ij} \tag{7.62}$$

where

$$U = \begin{cases} 1 & \text{if } \Phi_m \text{ and } \Phi_n \text{ differ } only \text{ in the interchange of the spins of } i \text{ and } j, \\ 0 & \text{otherwise.} \end{cases}$$

For example, if $\Phi_m = \alpha_1 \alpha_2 \beta_3 \alpha_4$ and $\Phi_n = \alpha_1 \beta_2 \alpha_3 \alpha_4$, then $\mathscr{H}_{mn} = \frac{1}{2}J_{23}$. But if $\Phi_m = \alpha_1 \alpha_2 \beta_3 \beta_4$ and $\Phi_n = \beta_1 \beta_2 \alpha_3 \alpha_4$, then $\mathscr{H}_{mn} = 0$.

5. Matrix elements involving basis functions that are linear combinations of product functions are evaluated by expansion, that is, as the sum of several integrals. For example, if Φ'_2 and Φ'_3 are the functions of equation 7.60, then

$$\mathscr{H}_{2'3'} = \frac{1}{2}\left(\int \alpha\beta \mathscr{H} \alpha\beta \, d\tau + \int \alpha\beta \mathscr{H} \beta\alpha \, d\tau + \int \beta\alpha \mathscr{H} \alpha\beta \, d\tau + \int \beta\alpha \mathscr{H} \beta\alpha \, d\tau \right).$$

6. Many matrix elements need not be evaluated since the secular equation factors according to (a) symmetry; (b) F_z; and (c) $F_z(G)$, to a high degree of approximation.

7. The energy levels are found as the solutions to the secular equation by treating each factor separately.

8. The frequencies of the spectral lines are calculated as differences between energy levels according to the selection rules for symmetry, F_z and $F_z(G)$.

9. The wave functions are found either from the original 2^N linear equations or as the eigenvectors that diagonalize the Hamiltonian matrix.

10. The intensities of the spectral lines are found from equation 7.47.

When the application of step 6 results in factors no larger than 2×2, the equations may be solved readily and algebraic expressions derived for the frequencies and intensities of the spectral lines in terms of ν's and J's. The AB case served as an example of this procedure. Most other simple systems have been treated in this way;[1-3] we shall consider several of them in succeeding sections.

When factors larger than 2×2 are present in the factored secular equation, general algebraic solutions are not possible, and the analysis of each spectrum must be carried out individually, usually by a trial and error procedure. First, assumed values of ν's and J's are used with the foregoing rules to calculate a spectrum, which is compared with an experimentally determined spectrum. The trial values of ν and J are then altered systematically until a suitable fit is obtained. This process is clearly adaptable to a high-speed digital computer, which can be programmed to carry out steps 1–10 for each choice of trial parameters and to check for best agreement between calculated and experimental spectra according to a least squares criterion.* We shall consider an example of this procedure in the following section.

* Of the many computer programs available, probably the two most widely used general iterative-type programs are those described by Castellano and Bothner-By[7] and Swalen and Reilly.[7] The procedures used to relate calculated and observed frequencies differ between the two programs. The latter is more easily adapted to employ information derived from double resonance studies (see Chapter 8). Simpler, noniterative programs are often used to obtain approximations to observed spectra or to investigate the variation of particular parameters on the appearance of spectra.

7.14 The Three-Spin System: ABC

Let us now consider the general three-spin system with no restrictions regarding relative sizes of chemical shifts and coupling constants. Such ABC systems are frequently found, for example, among vinyl compounds, tri-substituted aromatics, and disubstituted pyridines. There are 2^3 basis functions

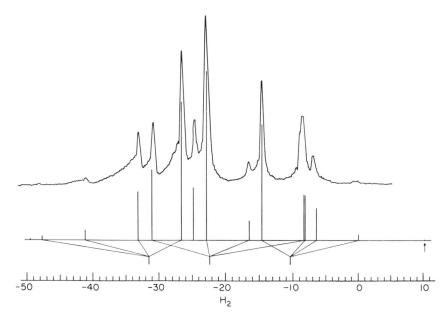

Fig. 7.3 Proton resonance spectrum (40 MHz) of the vinyl group of methyl acrylate. The calculated line positions and calculated chemical shifts of the three protons are indicated (Castellano and Waugh[8]).

that can be formed as products without regard to symmetry considerations. These can be classified into four sets according to the values of F_z:

$$
\begin{aligned}
&\Phi_1 = \alpha\alpha\alpha, && F_z = \tfrac{3}{2}; \\
&\Phi_2 = \alpha\alpha\beta, \quad \Phi_3 = \alpha\beta\alpha, \quad \Phi_4 = \beta\alpha\alpha, && F_z = \tfrac{1}{2}; \\
&\Phi_5 = \beta\beta\alpha, \quad \Phi_6 = \beta\alpha\beta, \quad \Phi_7 = \alpha\beta\beta, && F_z = -\tfrac{1}{2}; \\
&\Phi_8 = \beta\beta\beta, && F_z = -\tfrac{3}{2}.
\end{aligned}
\tag{7.63}
$$

Application of the selection rule $\Delta F_z = \pm 1$ shows that there are 15 allowed transitions.

Because the functions for $F_z = \frac{1}{2}$ and $-\frac{1}{2}$ lead to cubic equations, it is not possible to express the transition energies in simple algebraic form as functions of the six parameters ν_A, ν_B, ν_C, J_{AB}, J_{AC}, and J_{BC}. Hence, an analysis of an ABC spectrum must be carried out for each case individually, using an iterative procedure such as that mentioned in the preceding section. Often the ABC spectrum may be roughly approximated as an ABX spectrum and analyzed by procedures we shall discuss in Section 7.17. The parameters thus obtained can be used as initial guesses for the iterative treatment of the ABC system. In favorable cases excellent agreement between observed and calculated spectra may be obtained, as indicated in Figure 7.3. One must be extremely careful in using iterative computer analyses for ABC and other complex systems since the values of the parameters selected to provide the "best" agreement with the experimental frequencies may not be unique. In fact, if the criteria of agreement for both frequencies and intensities are not sufficiently stringent, these parameters may not even represent one correct solution. Double resonance techniques (Chapter 8) provide valuable additional information that can be used in such analyses. The use of computers in spectral analysis has been reviewed.[9]

For the ABC system, alternative mathematical treatments have been developed which provide all possible sets of parameters consistent with the observed spectrum.[8, 10] The complexity of the mathematics virtually limits its application to the three-spin case. Further details on the analysis of ABC spectra can be found elsewhere.[2]

7.15 The A_2B System

When two of three strongly coupled nuclei are magnetically equivalent, the presence of symmetry results in considerable simplification of the calculation. In the first place, the spectrum is now determined by only two chemical shifts, ν_A and ν_B, and one coupling constant, J_{AB}. We saw in Section 7.11 that the appearance of the spectrum does not depend on J_{AA}, and there is no way that this parameter can be derived from the observed spectrum.*

Each of the eight basis functions is now formed as the product of the spin function of B with one of the symmetrized functions given in equations 7.58 and 7.60. These basis functions are given in Table 7.2.

* J_{AA} might be determined, however, from studies of an isotopic derivative (Chapter 5) or from oriented molecules (Section 7.25).

As with the ABC case, the basis functions divide into four sets according to F_z, with 1, 3, 3, and 1 functions in each set. However, of the three functions in the set with $F_z = \frac{1}{2}$ or $-\frac{1}{2}$, two are symmetric and one antisymmetric. Hence each of the two 3×3 blocks of the secular equation factors into a 2×2 block

Table 7.2

BASIS FUNCTIONS FOR THE A₂B SYSTEM

Function	A₂	B	F_z	Symmetry
Φ_1	$\alpha\alpha$	α	$\frac{3}{2}$	s
Φ_2	$(1/\sqrt{2})(\alpha\beta + \beta\alpha)$	α	$\frac{1}{2}$	s
Φ_3	$(1/\sqrt{2})(\alpha\beta - \beta\alpha)$	α	$\frac{1}{2}$	a
Φ_4	$\beta\beta$	α	$-\frac{1}{2}$	s
Φ_5	$\alpha\alpha$	β	$\frac{1}{2}$	s
Φ_6	$(1/\sqrt{2})(\alpha\beta + \beta\alpha)$	β	$-\frac{1}{2}$	s
Φ_7	$(1/\sqrt{2})(\alpha\beta - \beta\alpha)$	β	$-\frac{1}{2}$	a
Φ_8	$\beta\beta$	β	$-\frac{3}{2}$	s

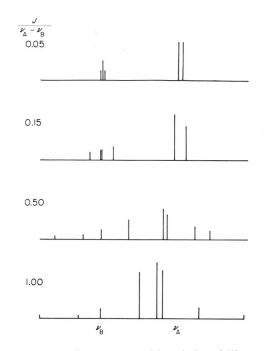

Fig. 7.4 Computed A₂B spectra with variation of $J/(\nu_A - \nu_B)$.

and a 1×1 block. Algebraic solutions are thus possible. Furthermore, the presence of symmetry reduces the number of allowed transitions from 15 to 9, since no transitions are allowed between states of different symmetry.

The computation of transition frequencies and intensities can be carried out according to the rules of Section 7.13. We shall not reproduce the expressions thus derived, but rather we can illustrate the behavior of the spectrum in Figure 7.4. It may be noted from this figure that the frequency of line 3

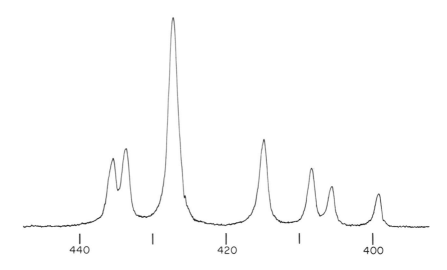

Fig. 7.5 Spectrum of the aromatic protons of 2,6-di-*tert*-butylphenol in $CDCl_3$, an example of an A_2B spectrum.

always gives ν_B. (This is the single transition allowed between the antisymmetric states ψ_3 and ψ_7.) The value of ν_A may also be found readily; it is the average of the frequencies of lines 5 and 7. From the detailed expressions for the line frequencies it is easily shown[1] that

$$J = \tfrac{1}{3}|l_1 - l_4 + l_6 - l_8|,$$

where the l's are the line frequencies.

Alternatively, the ratio of $|J/(\nu_A - \nu_B)|$, and hence the value of $|J|$, may be determined by use of Table 7.3. The frequencies of all lines are listed, for various ratios of $|J/(\nu_A - \nu_B)|$, relative to ν_B as zero with $\nu_A - \nu_B = 1.00$. One need only divide the observed line frequencies (measured relative to line 3 as zero) by the observed value of $(\nu_A - \nu_B)$ and find from Table 7.3 the value of $J/(\nu_A - \nu_B)$ that best reproduces the experimental frequencies and intensities. Sometimes for analysis of an A_2B spectrum it is helpful to plot the frequencies in Table 7.3 versus $J/(\nu_A - \nu_B)$, and superimpose the observed spectrum.

For convenience, the lines are listed in Table 7.3 as A or B lines, depending on their behavior at $J = 0$. Line 9, a so-called *combination* line, involves the simultaneous "flipping" of all three nuclei. It is forbidden in the limits $J = 0$

Table 7.3

FREQUENCIES AND RELATIVE INTENSITIES FOR THE A$_2$B SYSTEM[a,b]

J		B				A			Comb.
$(\nu_A - \nu_B)$	1	2	3	4	5	6	7	8	9
0	0	0	0	0	1.000	1.000	1.000	1.000	2.000
	(1.00)	(1.00)	(1.00)	(1.00)	(2.00)	(2.00)	(2.00)	(2.00)	(0.00)
0.1	−0.105	0.010	0	0.095	0.950	0.955	1.050	1.055	2.010
	(0.82)	(0.97)	(1.00)	(1.21)	(2.21)	(2.18)	(1.82)	(1.79)	(0.00)
0.2	−0.218	−0.040	0	0.178	0.904	0.918	1.096	1.122	2.040
	(0.66)	(0.89)	(1.00)	(1.45)	(2.46)	(2.34)	(1.66)	(1.55)	(0.00)
0.3	−0.338	−0.088	0	0.250	0.862	0.889	1.138	1.200	2.088
	(0.54)	(0.78)	(1.00)	(1.68)	(2.68)	(2.46)	(1.54)	(1.32)	(0.00)
0.4	−0.463	−0.153	0	0.310	0.827	0.863	1.173	1.290	2.153
	(0.44)	(0.65)	(1.00)	(1.91)	(2.90)	(2.56)	(1.44)	(1.09)	(0.00)
0.5	−0.593	−0.233	0	0.360	0.797	0.843	1.202	1.390	2.233
	(0.37)	(0.53)	(1.00)	(2.11)	(3.10)	(2.63)	(1.36)	(0.89)	(0.01)
0.6	−0.726	−0.326	0	0.400	0.774	0.826	1.226	1.500	2.326
	(0.31)	(0.43)	(1.00)	(2.27)	(3.26)	(2.69)	(1.30)	(0.73)	(0.01)
0.7	−0.862	−0.429	0	0.433	0.755	0.812	1.245	1.617	2.429
	(0.26)	(0.34)	(1.00)	(2.41)	(3.40)	(2.74)	(1.25)	(0.59)	(0.01)
0.8	−1.000	−0.540	0	0.460	0.740	0.800	1.260	1.740	2.540
	(0.22)	(0.28)	(1.00)	(2.52)	(3.50)	(2.78)	(1.21)	(0.48)	(0.01)
0.9	−1.140	−0.658	0	0.481	0.728	0.790	1.271	1.868	2.658
	(0.19)	(0.22)	(1.00)	(2.60)	(3.59)	(2.81)	(1.18)	(0.40)	(0.01)
1.0	−1.280	−0.781	0	0.500	0.719	0.781	1.281	2.000	2.781
	(0.17)	(0.18)	(1.00)	(2.67)	(3.65)	(2.83)	(1.15)	(0.33)	(0.01)
2.0	−2.732	−2.146	0	0.586	0.682	0.732	1.318	3.414	4.146
	(0.06)	(0.04)	(1.00)	(2.91)	(3.90)	(2.94)	(1.05)	(0.09)	(0.01)

[a] Frequencies are given relative to $\nu_B = 0$, with $(\nu_A - \nu_B) = 1.00$. Relative intensities are listed in parentheses below the line frequencies.
[b] From Corio.[1]

and $\nu_A - \nu_B = 0$ and has only low intensity in other cases. An example of an A$_2$B spectrum is shown in Figure 7.5.

The sign of J cannot be determined from the spectrum, but, unlike the AB case, it *is* possible simply from the areas under the lines to determine which nucleus, A or B, is more shielded.

7.16 The A_3B System; Subspectral Analysis

The symmetry inherent in this four-spin system can be employed to simplify the treatment. The 16th-order secular determinant factors by symmetry and F_z into blocks no larger than 2×2, so that again algebraic solution is possible. Here too the appearance of the spectrum depends entirely on the ratio $J_{AB}/(\nu_A - \nu_B)$, and the analysis of an A_3B spectrum can be carried out using a table analogous to that used for the A_2B system (see, e.g., Corio[1]).

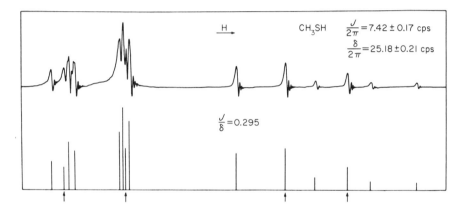

Fig. 7.6 Application of subspectral analysis to the proton resonance spectrum of methyl mercaptan (40 MHz). The calculated spectrum is shown for $J/(\nu_A - \nu_B) = 0.295$ with the ab subspectrum indicated. Spectrum and analysis from Corio.[1]

An alternative procedure for analyzing an A_3B spectrum, as well as many more complex spectra, is the method of *subspectral analysis*.[11] Many complex spectra can be shown to contain one or more simpler subspectra, which may be analyzed separately provided the observed spectral lines can be properly assigned to the correct subspectra. For example, the A_3B spectrum is composed of an ab subspectrum (small letters are used to denote subspectra), as well as other lines not belonging to a subspectrum of a simpler system. However, since both the A_3B spectrum and the ab subspectrum are determined completely by the parameters $(\nu_A - \nu_B)$ and J_{AB}, analysis of the ab subspectrum provides all the information that could be extracted from the more complex A_3B spectrum. An example of this analysis is shown in Figure 7.6. The essential point, of course, is the selection of the lines belonging to the ab subspectrum. This must be done in accordance with the spacing and intensity relationships given in Section 7.10.

The method of subspectral analysis has its greatest utility with more complex spectra, such as ABB'XX'. A discussion of such applications is beyond the scope of this book, but is given in a recent review article.[11]

7.17 The ABX System

Intermediate in complexity between the AMX system, which can be analyzed by first-order procedures, and the completely strongly coupled ABC system, which must be treated by individual computer-aided analysis, is the ABX system. The presence of one nucleus only weakly coupled to the others permits factoring of the secular equation so that algebraic solutions are possible. We shall summarize the results of the solution of the secular equation and shall devote considerable attention to the application of the resulting equations to the analysis of observed ABX spectra. There are two reasons for this emphasis on ABX spectra: First, ABX spectra occur frequently, for example in trisubstituted aromatics and in vinyl systems. Second, the ABX system is the simplest one in which many important concepts common to more complex systems can be demonstrated. These include the effects of the signs of coupling constants and the "deceptive simplicity" often found in complex spectra.

The basis functions for the ABX system are just those used in equation 7.63 for the general three-spin system. However, because $(\nu_A - \nu_X)$ and $(\nu_B - \nu_X)$ are much larger than J_{AX} and J_{BX}, we can define an F_z for the AB nuclei separately from F_z for the X nucleus (cf. Section 7.8). The basis functions classified in this way are given in Table 7.4. Of the three functions with $F_z = \frac{1}{2}$,

Table 7.4

BASIS FUNCTIONS FOR THE ABX SYSTEM

Function	AB	X	$F_z(AB)$	$F_z(X)$	F_z
Φ_1	$\alpha\alpha$	α	1	$\frac{1}{2}$	$\frac{3}{2}$
Φ_2	$\alpha\alpha$	β	1	$-\frac{1}{2}$	$\frac{1}{2}$
Φ_3	$\alpha\beta$	α	0	$\frac{1}{2}$	$\frac{1}{2}$
Φ_4	$\beta\alpha$	α	0	$\frac{1}{2}$	$\frac{1}{2}$
Φ_5	$\beta\beta$	α	-1	$\frac{1}{2}$	$-\frac{1}{2}$
Φ_6	$\beta\alpha$	β	0	$-\frac{1}{2}$	$-\frac{1}{2}$
Φ_7	$\alpha\beta$	β	0	$-\frac{1}{2}$	$-\frac{1}{2}$
Φ_8	$\beta\beta$	β	-1	$-\frac{1}{2}$	$-\frac{3}{2}$

Φ_3 and Φ_4 have the same values of $F_z(AB)$ and $F_z(X)$, but Φ_2 is in a separate class and does not mix with Φ_3 and Φ_4. Thus the 3×3 block of the secular equation factors into a 2×2 block and a 1×1 block. Analogous factoring occurs for the 3×3 block arising from the three functions with $F_z = -\frac{1}{2}$.

The computation of the matrix elements, the solution of the factors of the secular equation, and the calculation of the transition frequencies and intensities are readily carried out using the procedure outlined in Section 7.13. The results are summarized in Table 7.5 in terms of the following commonly employed [2,3] notation.

$$2D_+ \cos 2\theta_+ = (\nu_A - \nu_B) + \tfrac{1}{2}(J_{AX} - J_{BX}); \tag{7.64a}$$

$$2D_+ \sin 2\theta_+ = J_{AB}; \tag{7.64b}$$

$$2D_- \cos 2\theta_- = (\nu_A - \nu_B) - \tfrac{1}{2}(J_{AX} - J_{BX}); \tag{7.64c}$$

$$2D_- \sin 2\theta_- = J_{AB}; \tag{7.64d}$$

$$\nu_{AB} = \tfrac{1}{2}(\nu_A + \nu_B). \tag{7.65}$$

Table 7.5

ABX SPECTRUM: FREQUENCIES AND RELATIVE INTENSITIES[a,b]

Line	Origin	Energy	Relative intensity
1	B	$\nu_{AB} + \tfrac{1}{4}(-2J_{AB} - J_{AX} - J_{BX}) - D_-$	$1 - \sin 2\theta_-$
2	B	$\nu_{AB} + \tfrac{1}{4}(-2J_{AB} + J_{AX} + J_{BX}) - D_+$	$1 - \sin 2\theta_+$
3	B	$\nu_{AB} + \tfrac{1}{4}(2J_{AB} - J_{AX} - J_{BX}) - D_-$	$1 + \sin 2\theta_-$
4	B	$\nu_{AB} + \tfrac{1}{4}(2J_{AB} + J_{AX} + J_{BX}) - D_+$	$1 + \sin 2\theta_+$
5	A	$\nu_{AB} + \tfrac{1}{4}(-2J_{AB} - J_{AX} - J_{BX}) + D_-$	$1 + \sin 2\theta_-$
6	A	$\nu_{AB} + \tfrac{1}{4}(-2J_{AB} + J_{AX} + J_{BX}) + D_+$	$1 + \sin 2\theta_+$
7	A	$\nu_{AB} + \tfrac{1}{4}(2J_{AB} - J_{AX} - J_{BX}) + D_-$	$1 - \sin 2\theta_-$
8	A	$\nu_{AB} + \tfrac{1}{4}(2J_{AB} + J_{AX} + J_{BX}) + D_+$	$1 - \sin 2\theta_+$
9	X	$\nu_X - \tfrac{1}{2}(J_{AX} + J_{BX})$	1
10	X	$\nu_X + D_+ - D_-$	$\cos^2(\theta_+ - \theta_-)$
11	X	$\nu_X - D_+ + D_-$	$\cos^2(\theta_+ - \theta_-)$
12	X	$\nu_X + \tfrac{1}{2}(J_{AX} + J_{BX})$	1
13	Comb.	$2\nu_{AB} - \nu_X$	0
14	Comb. (X)	$\nu_X - D_+ - D_-$	$\sin^2(\theta_+ - \theta_-)$
15	Comb. (X)	$\nu_X + D_+ + D_-$	$\sin^2(\theta_+ - \theta_-)$

[a] Pople et al. (Ref. 3).
[b] See equations 7.64 and 7.65 for definition of terms.

The four quantities D_+, D_-, θ_+, and θ_- are *defined* by equations 7.64; D_+ and D_- are analogous to the quantity C utilized in the analysis of the AB spectrum (cf. equations 7.52), as we shall see below. The angles θ_+ and θ_- are analogous to the quantity θ mentioned in the AB analysis in Section 7.10. They have *no* physical significance and merely provide a convenient way of expressing the relations of the spectral parameters to the intensities of the spectral lines.

There are certain limitations that we shall impose on the quantities defined in equations 7.64; D_+ and D_- are defined as *positive* quantities. There are, in principle, no restrictions on θ_+ and θ_-, but we shall see later that they can be limited without affecting the observed spectrum. Without any loss of generality we shall always label the nuclei so that

$$\nu_A \geqslant \nu_B. \tag{7.66}$$

If the right-hand side of one or more of equations 7.64 is negative, no inconsistencies result, since θ_+ and θ_- can assume values such that the sine

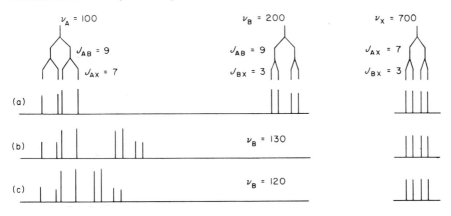

Fig. 7.7 Computed ABX spectra as a function of only one changing parameter, ν_B.

and/or cosine factor is negative. By squaring equations 7.64a and 7.64b (or equations 7.64c and 7.64d), adding, and taking the square root, we obtain

$$2D_+ = \{[(\nu_A - \nu_B) + \tfrac{1}{2}(J_{AX} - J_{BX})]^2 + J_{AB}^2\}^{1/2},$$
$$2D_- = \{[(\nu_A - \nu_B) - \tfrac{1}{2}(J_{AX} - J_{BX})]^2 + J_{AB}^2\}^{1/2}. \tag{7.67}$$

Equations 7.67 show the analogy between D_+ and C used in the AB analysis. Note, however, that where $(\nu_A - \nu_B)$ appeared in the expression for the AB case, equations 7.67 contain $[(\nu_A - \nu_B) \pm \tfrac{1}{2}(J_{AX} - J_{BX})]$, which serve as "effective chemical shifts." We shall refer later to the concept of "effective Larmor frequencies" and effective chemical shifts.

A better appreciation of the significance of the expressions in Table 7.5 may be obtained from an examination of some calculated ABX spectra. Figure 7.7 shows ABX spectra computed for the parameters shown. All parameters remain constant through the series except ν_B. The spectrum in

Figure 7.7a may be analyzed approximately as a first-order AMX case, as shown. The frequencies calculated from the first-order treatment are nearly identical with those found in the ABX calculation, while the intensities are only slightly in error. As $(\nu_A - \nu_B)$ decreases (Figure 7.7b), there is a greater departure from the first-order calculation. In Figure 7.7c the lines originating with nucleus A and those originating with nucleus B can still be recognized by comparison with the spectrum in Figure 7.7b; but the wave functions are now mixtures of A and B functions, and the transitions cannot strictly be called A or B transitions. The labeling "A" or "B" in the second column of Table 7.5 is convenient but is strictly applicable only in the limiting case of large $(\nu_A - \nu_B)$. The "combination" transition 13 involves simultaneous flipping of all spins and is forbidden in the ABX case. Transitions 14 and 15 also involve change in spin of all nuclei, but may have considerable intensity when $(\nu_A - \nu_B)$ is small. They appear in the X region and are discussed with the four X lines.

7.18 Analysis of an ABX Spectrum

The "complete" analysis of an ABX spectrum would require the determination from the spectrum of nine quantities: the three chemical shifts ν_A, ν_B, and ν_X; the magnitudes of the three coupling constants $|J_{AB}|$, $|J_{AX}|$, and $|J_{BX}|$; and the signs of the coupling constants. As we shall see, some of these quantities cannot be determined.

From Table 7.5 and Figure 7.8 it is apparent that the X lines are *symmetrically* arranged about ν_X, so that ν_X is immediately determined. It is seen from Table 7.5 that the average of the frequencies of all eight AB lines gives $\nu_{AB} = \frac{1}{2}(\nu_A + \nu_B)$; a determination of ν_A and ν_B then requires only the additional value of $(\nu_A - \nu_B)$ (see below).

Consideration of Table 7.5 shows that a change in sign of J_{AB} has no effect on either the observed frequencies or intensities. The AB lines would have different labels (e.g., lines 1 and 3 would be interchanged), but no *observable* change would take place.

Likewise, the absolute signs of J_{AX} and J_{BX} cannot be determined. Examination of equation 7.67 shows that a change in sign of *both* J_{AX} and J_{BX} corresponds to an interchange of D_+ and D_-. Interchange of these quantities and of the signs of J_{AX} and J_{BX} in Table 7.5 shows that the spectrum is again unchanged in both frequency and intensity. A change in sign of only *one* of these two coupling constants may well change some features in the spectrum, so that it is often possible to determine the *relative* signs of J_{AX} and J_{BX}. This point will be explored later.

Figure 7.8 shows that the AB portion of the spectrum may be divided into two AB-type quartets, or subspectra, which we shall designate as $(ab)_+$ and $(ab)_-$. From the expressions for the line frequencies in Table 7.5, we see that such a division may always be made. The difference in frequency between lines 1 and 3, lines 2 and 4, lines 5 and 7, and lines 6 and 8 is equal to J_{AB}. As indicated in Figure 7.8, the difference between the first and third lines of each quartet (between lines 2 and 6 and between lines 1 and 5), gives $2D_+$

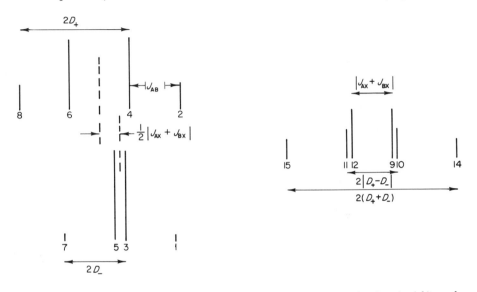

Fig. 7.8 Schematic representation of a typical ABX spectrum, showing the $(ab)_+$ and $(ab)_-$ quartets and the parameters that may be extracted readily from the spectrum. The numbering of the lines applies to the case $\nu_A > \nu_B$ and $J_{AX} > J_{BX} > 0$.

and $2D_-$, respectively, so that the effective chemical shifts for the $(ab)_+$ and $(ab)_-$ subspectra are

$$\delta_+ = (\nu_A - \nu_B) + \tfrac{1}{2}(J_{AX} - J_{BX}),$$
$$\delta_- = (\nu_A - \nu_B) - \tfrac{1}{2}(J_{AX} - J_{BX}),$$
(7.68)

. as pointed out previously. The relative intensities are also correct for AB spectra. The centers of the quartets are separated by $\tfrac{1}{2}|J_{AX} + J_{BX}|$ (difference between the average of lines 3 and 5 and the average of lines 4 and 6). The absolute value symbol is used since we cannot know the labeling of the observed lines.

We have no way of telling a priori which of the two quartets to associate with $(ab)_+$ and which with $(ab)_-$. The later calculations will be considerably simplified if we arbitrarily choose

$$D_+ > D_-. \qquad (7.69)$$

From equation 7.67 this choice is equivalent to taking the quantities $(\nu_A - \nu_B)$ and $(J_{AX} - J_{BX})$ to be of the same sign. This relation, together with our previous choice of $\nu_A > \nu_B$ (equation 7.66), requires* that

$$J_{AX} > J_{BX}. \qquad (7.70)$$

The X portion of the spectrum (Figure 7.8 and Table 7.5) consists of three pairs of lines symmetrically placed around ν_X. The two strongest lines (9 and 12) are separated by $|J_{AX} + J_{BX}|$, which is just twice the separation of the centers of the $(ab)_+$ and $(ab)_-$ quartets. A pair of lines (10 and 11) is separated by $2(D_+ - D_-)$, while another pair (14 and 15) is separated by $2(D_+ + D_-)$. Lines 14 and 15 must lie outside lines 10 and 11, but the relation to lines 9 and 12 is variable. Frequently lines 14 and 15 (the combination lines) have so little intensity that they are not observed; that is, $\sin^2(\theta_+ - \theta_-) \approx 0$. In that case $\cos^2(\theta_+ - \theta_-) \approx 1$ by trigonometric identity, so that lines 10 and 11 are essentially equal in intensity to lines 9 and 12. In some cases the converse occurs, with lines 10 and 11 virtually disappearing and lines 14 and 15 becoming intense.

The analysis of an ABX spectrum to extract the magnitudes of the three chemical shifts and the three coupling constants is in principle straightforward, but in practice a number of ambiguities can occur. We shall summarize insofar as possible a general approach to the analysis of an ABX spectrum and indicate the limitations that might occur in practical examples.

1. The starting point for analysis is usually the identification of the two quartets $(ab)_+$ and $(ab)_-$; J_{AB} can usually be found with no difficulty. The association of the left and right halves of the quartets can often be done in two ways consistent with the frequencies but *usually* only in one way that is consistent with AB intensity relations. Sometimes, however, there is ambiguity in this selection, partly because of experimental inaccuracies or overlapping lines. For the present we shall assume that an unequivocal selection of the $(ab)_+$ and $(ab)_-$ quartets can be made. In Section 7.19 we shall examine the consequences of an incorrect selection of the two quartets.

---

* This requirement may appear to impose an unacceptable restriction, since physically there is no reason why J_{AX} might not be smaller in magnitude than J_{BX}. However, if we recall that both J_{AX} and J_{BX} could be negative or both positive with no *observable* change in the spectrum, then we note that a *mathematical* solution of, for example, $J_{AX} = -3$ and $J_{BX} = -10$ meets the requirement that $J_{AX} > J_{BX}$, yet is physically indistinguishable from the solution $J_{AX} = +3$ and $J_{BX} = +10$. (If $D_+ = D_-$, then $J_{AX} = J_{BX}$, and the magnitudes of both are immediately found from the known value of $|J_{AX} + J_{BX}|$.)

2. The centers of the $(ab)_+$ and $(ab)_-$ quartets are separated by $\frac{1}{2}|J_{AX}+J_{BX}|$, so this quantity is now readily determined.

3. Turning to the X region, we can now identify lines 9 and 12, since they are separated by $|J_{AX}+J_{BX}|$, and thus confirm the value of this quantity.

4. D_+ and D_- can be found from the $(ab)_+$ and $(ab)_-$ quartets, and the values checked by the separations in the X region. (In accordance with our assumption (equation 7.69), D_+ is taken to be the larger of these two quantities.) Sometimes overlap of lines renders the values obtained from one or the other region of the spectrum less accurate.

5. By squaring, rearranging, and taking square roots in equation 7.67, we obtain the relations

$$\delta_+ = (\nu_A - \nu_B) + \tfrac{1}{2}(J_{AX} - J_{BX}) = \pm[4D_+^2 - J_{AB}^2]^{1/2} \equiv \pm 2M,$$
$$\delta_- = (\nu_A - \nu_B) - \tfrac{1}{2}(J_{AX} - J_{BX}) = \pm[4D_-^2 - J_{AB}^2]^{1/2} \equiv \pm 2N; \tag{7.71}$$

M and N are defined as *positive* numbers by the relations at the right of equation 7.71. Mathematically, the following four solutions result from the possible choices of sign in equations 7.71:

	①	②	③	④
$\nu_A \quad \nu_B$	$M + N$	$M - N$	$-M + N$	$-M - N;$
$\tfrac{1}{2}(J_{AX} - J_{BX})$	$M - N$	$M + N$	$-M - N$	$-M + N.$

From the restrictions expressed in equations 7.66 and 7.70, both $(\nu_A - \nu_B)$ and $(J_{AX} - J_{BX})$ must be positive; hence solutions ③ and ④ can be disregarded. But since $M > N$, as a result of $D_+ > D_-$ (equation 7.69), ① and ② are both valid so far as our present equations are concerned. Thus one of the two quantities $(M + N)$ and $(M - N)$ gives $(\nu_A - \nu_B)$, but we cannot tell at this point which one. The resolution of this ambiguity requires a consideration of the intensity distribution in the X region.

6. The relative intensities of the X lines depend on the angles θ_+ and θ_-, as shown in Table 7.5. Equation 7.64 defined these angles with no restrictions on their magnitudes. For ease of calculation, however, we shall restrict θ_+ to lie between $0°$ and $45°$ and θ_- to lie between $0°$ and $90°$; that is, $0° \leqslant 2\theta_+ \leqslant 90°$, and $0° \leqslant 2\theta_- \leqslant 180°$. This restriction is equivalent to requiring that J_{AB} be positive, but as we have seen, the entire spectrum is independent of the sign of J_{AB}. The restriction is also consistent with our choices of $\nu_A > \nu_B$ and $J_{AX} > J_{BX}$.

From the values already found for J_{AB}, $2D_+$, and $2D_-$, the values of $\sin 2\theta_+$ and $\sin 2\theta_-$ can be calculated from equations 7.64b and 7.64d. As indicated in Figure 7.9, there are two values of the angle $2\theta_-$, r and $(180° - r)$, consistent with this value of $\sin 2\theta_-$. The two angles correspond to positive and negative values of $\cos 2\theta_-$, hence, from equations 7.64a and 7.64c, to interchange of $(\nu_A - \nu_B)$ and $\frac{1}{2}(J_{AX} - J_{BX})$. Thus each of the two possible values of $2\theta_-$ is associated with one of the two possible solutions in paragraph 5. Since M and N are positive, solution ① gives $(\nu_A - \nu_B) > \frac{1}{2}(J_{AX} - J_{BX})$, and thus must have a value of $\cos 2\theta_- > 0$, or $0° \leqslant 2\theta_- < 90°$. Solution ② has $90° < 2\theta_- \leqslant 180°$.

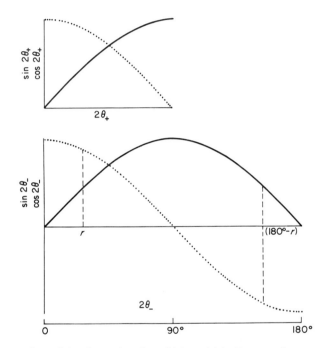

Fig. 7.9 Plots of the sine and cosine of $2\theta_+$ and $2\theta_-$. In general, two values of $2\theta_-$, r and $(180° - r)$, are consistent with the value of $\sin 2\theta_-$ found from the spectrum.

From the two possible values of $2\theta_-$, two values of $(\theta_+ - \theta_-)$ can be calculated, leading in general to quite different ratios of the intensities of lines 10 and 11 relative to lines 14 and 15. If one of the calculated intensity ratios is inconsistent with the observed intensities, then that value of θ_- and the corresponding solution ① or ② can be discarded. Sometimes the difference in intensity distribution between the two solutions is too small to permit an unequivocal decision as to the correct solution, but usually the distinction is clear.

    7. With the correct value of $(\nu_A - \nu_B)$ selected, the previously determined value of $(\nu_A + \nu_B)$ can be used to find ν_A and ν_B.

    8. From the correctly chosen value of $\frac{1}{2}(J_{AX} - J_{BX})$ and the previously

determined value of $|J_{AX} + J_{BX}|$, J_{AX} and J_{BX} can be found. The question arises whether $(J_{AX} + J_{BX})$ is positive or negative. It was pointed out in Section 7.18 that a change in sign of this sum does not affect the observed spectrum, since it corresponds merely to an interchange of D_+ and D_-. However, at this point in the calculation it is extremely important to recognize the distinction, since we have already for purposes of calculation made a choice in the values of D_+ and D_-. A choice in the sign of $(J_{AX} + J_{BX})$ that is inconsistent with the values of D_+ and D_- will cause an interchange in the calculated values of J_{AX}

Table 7.6

PROCEDURE FOR THE ANALYSIS OF AN ABX SPECTRUM

1. Identify the two ab quartets on the basis of frequency and intensity relations. Note the value of J_{AB}.
2. Find the value of $\frac{1}{2}|J_{AX} + J_{BX}|$ from the separation of the centers of the two ab quartets.
3. Check the value of $|J_{AX} + J_{BX}|$ from the separation of the two strongest X lines, and identify lines 9 and 12 (see Figure 7.8).
4. Find $2D_+$ and $2D_-$ from the separations of the first and third lines in the (ab)$_+$ and (ab)$_-$ quartets. Choose $2D_+$ as the larger. Check the values of $2D_+$ and $2D_-$ from the separations of lines in the X region and identify lines 10, 11, 14, and 15 (see Figure 7.8).
5. Calculate M and N, where

$$2M = (4D_+^2 - J_{AB}^2)^{1/2}; \qquad 2N = (4D_-^2 - J_{AB}^2)^{1/2}.$$

The two solutions for $(v_A - v_B)$ and $\frac{1}{2}(J_{AX} - J_{BX})$ are

	①	②
$v_A - v_B$	$M + N$	$M - N$
$\frac{1}{2}(J_{AX} - J_{BX})$	$M - N$	$M + N$

6. Find the value of $2\theta_+$, where $0 \leqslant 2\theta_+ \leqslant 90°$, from the relation

$$\sin 2\theta_+ = J_{AB}/2D_+.$$

Find the *two* possible values of $2\theta_-$, where $0 \leqslant 2\theta_- \leqslant 180°$, from the relation

$$\sin 2\theta_- = J_{AB}/2D_-.$$

Calculate the two possible values of $\sin(\theta_+ - \theta_-)$ and $\cos(\theta_+ - \theta_-)$ and from Table 7.5 compute the intensities of the X lines for each solution. If the smaller value of θ_- $(0°–45°)$ gives X intensities consistent with the observed spectrum, while the larger value $(45°–90°)$ does not, then choose solution ① as the correct solution. If the converse is true, choose solution ②.
7. Find $\frac{1}{2}(v_A + v_B)$, which is the average of the centers of the (ab)$_+$ and (ab)$_-$ quartets, or equivalently, the average of the frequencies of all eight AB lines. From this value and the correct value of $(v_A - v_B)$ determined in steps 5 and 6, calculate v_A and v_B.
8. Assign to the sum $\frac{1}{2}(J_{AX} + J_{BX})$, for which the absolute value was found in step 2, a positive sign if the (ab)$_+$ quartet is centered at a higher frequency than the (ab)$_-$ quartet, or a negative sign if the reverse order is true. From this value and the correct value of $\frac{1}{2}(J_{AX} - J_{BX})$ determined in steps 5 and 6, calculate J_{AX} and J_{BX}.

and J_{BX}, which will not fit the observed spectrum. An examination of Table 7.5 shows that the expressions for the lines of the $(ab)_+$ quartet (characterized by D_+) always contain $(J_{AX} + J_{BX})$, while the expressions for the $(ab)_-$ quartet contain $(-J_{AX} - J_{BX})$. Thus the $(ab)_+$ quartet will be centered at a higher frequency than the $(ab)_-$ quartet if the sum $(J_{AX} + J_{BX})$ is positive, but at a lower frequency if the sum is negative. Hence the sign of this sum may be chosen unambiguously from the appearance of the spectrum.

Table 7.6 summarizes the procedure suggested in the foregoing paragraphs for the analysis of an ABX spectrum. The numbered steps in the table correspond to the paragraphs in this section.

7.19 Relative Signs of J_{AX} and J_{BX} in an ABX Spectrum

The analysis discussed in the previous section *should* lead unambiguously to the correct set of parameters needed to describe an observed ABX spectrum. But the solution derived in this way is in some instances not unique. In this section and the following one we shall investigate these ambiguities and the conditions responsible for them.

From the procedure of Section 7.18 we derive numerical values for J_{AX} and J_{BX}. Since these numbers are signed, we know the relative signs of these two coupling constants (same or opposite). We know the spectrum would be unchanged if the signs of *both* J's were changed. However, in some cases, we shall see that the spectrum may be virtually unchanged if the sign of only *one* of the J's is changed. In an AMX spectrum, which is just an ABX spectrum with a very large value of $(\nu_A - \nu_B)$ relative to J_{AB}, first-order analysis applies, and a change in sign of one or more coupling constants leaves the observed spectrum completely unchanged, as indicated at the top of Figure 7.10.* However, as $(\nu_A - \nu_B)/J_{AB}$ decreases, the spectrum becomes progressively more dependent on the relative signs of J_{AX} and J_{BX}, as illustrated in Figure 7.10.

It is apparent from Figure 7.10 that a change in sign of J_{BX} for large $(\nu_A - \nu_B)/J_{AB}$ merely interchanges pairs of lines. In analyzing a spectrum, then, the choice of the wrong relative signs for the J's is associated with an incorrect choice of the $(ab)_+$ and $(ab)_-$ quartets. If the left half of $(ab)_+$ is mistakenly associated with the right half of $(ab)_-$ and vice versa, the centers of the two quartets thus selected are separated by $(D_+ - D_-)$, not $\frac{1}{2}|J_{AX} + J_{BX}|$. The X region may be of no help in rectifying this misassignment, since it is

---

* The relative signs of the J's can be determined by double resonance, as pointed out in Section 8.7.

sometimes impossible to distinguish between lines 9 and 12, separated by $|J_{AX} + J_{BX}|$, and lines 10 and 11, separated by $2(D_+ - D_-)$. If all six X lines are observed, the intensities will permit the distinction, since lines 9 and 12 are then the most intense. The correct assignment of the $(ab)_+$ and $(ab)_-$ quartets can be checked in principle by the relative intensities of the AB lines

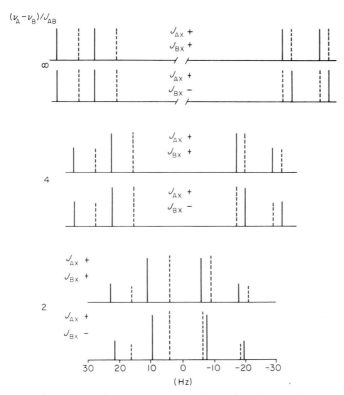

Fig. 7.10   The effect of changing the sign of J_{BX} on the AB part of an ABX spectrum. Solid lines: $(ab)_+$ subspectrum; dashed lines: $(ab)_-$ subspectrum. Parameters: $J_{AB} = 12$, $J_{AX} = 7$, $J_{BX} = \pm 3$ Hz; $(\nu_A - \nu_B)/J_{AB}$ indicated in figure.

where each of the two quartets is typical of an AB-type system. However, the distinction may not be clear if either (a) the line intensities are perturbed because the X nucleus has a chemical shift that is not infinitely far removed from those of A and B, or (b) $(\nu_A - \nu_B)/J_{AB}$ is large enough so that the lines behave more like an AM pair than an AB pair. Generally, values of $(\nu_A - \nu_B)/J_{AB} < 2$ cause little difficulty. It should be noted that an incorrect assignment of $(ab)_+$ and $(ab)_-$ leads only to a reversal of one of the signs of J_{AX} or J_{BX} in the case of large $(\nu_A - \nu_B)/J_{AB}$, but can actually lead to the calculation of slightly different magnitudes of these J's as well, if $(\nu_A - \nu_B)/J_{AB} < {\sim}2$.

We have seen that the AB region of the spectrum is in general compatible with two distinct solutions, even when the $(ab)_+$ and $(ab)_-$ quartets have been correctly assigned. The general appearance of the AB region can, however, sometimes give information on the relative signs of J_{AX} and J_{BX}.[12] If the $(ab)_+$

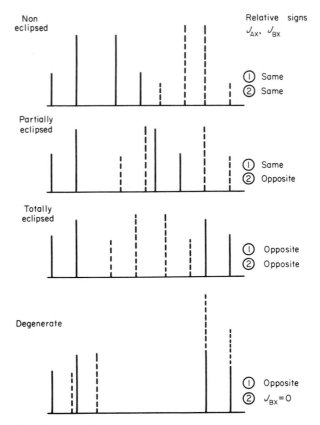

Fig. 7.11 Possible general patterns in the AB region of an ABX spectrum. Relative signs of J_{AX} and J_{BX} are given for the two solutions consistent with the spectrum in the AB region. In the totally eclipsed case the "dashed" subspectrum is contained between the first and fourth lines of the "solid" subspectrum but need not lie entirely between the second and third lines as in the illustration.

and $(ab)_-$ quartets are completely noneclipsed, as indicated in Figure 7.11, then *both* possible solutions have J's with like signs. In the most general case, with partially overlapping quartets, one solution has J's of the same signs, while the other has J's of opposite signs. When one quartet lies completely inside the other, both solutions give J's of opposite signs. One final case depicted in Figure 7.11 is the "degenerate" spectrum arising when two pairs of lines accidentally overlap. The degenerate case pictured could arise from $J_{BX} = 0$ or from the J's of opposite signs with all parameters having certain ratios. Other types of degeneracy in line positions in ABX spectra can occur; one example will be considered in the next section.

7.20 ABX Patterns; Deceptively Simple Spectra

Our analysis of an ABX spectrum was based on the assumption that all eight AB lines and either four or six X lines are observed. Frequently, however, some of the lines coincide, creating a spectrum whose appearance is not that of a typical ABX pattern. For example, Figure 7.12 shows calculated ABX

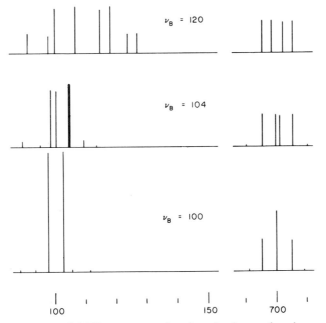

Fig. 7.12 Computed ABX spectra as a function of only one changing parameter, ν_B. The spectrum at the bottom is an AA'X (deceptively simple) spectrum.

spectra as a function of only one changing parameter, ν_B. The spectrum at the top, which is the same as that at the bottom of Figure 7.7, is readily recognized as an ABX pattern. As ν_B approaches ν_A, the appearance changes drastically, and when $\nu_B = \nu_A$, the AB region appears to be simply a doublet, while the X region is a 1:2:1 triplet. Actually there are other weak lines, as indicated, but in a practical case these would be lost in noise.

This spectrum is an excellent example of what have been termed "deceptively simple spectra." If one were confronted with such a spectrum and did not realize that it is a special case of ABX (actually AA'X, since the chemical shifts of A and B are equal), the doublet and triplet might mistakenly be interpreted as the components of a first-order A_2X spectrum, with $J_{AX} = 5$ Hz. Actually, the observed splitting is the average of J_{AX} and $J_{A'X}$. Deceptively simple spectra are widespread and are, of course, not limited to ABX systems;

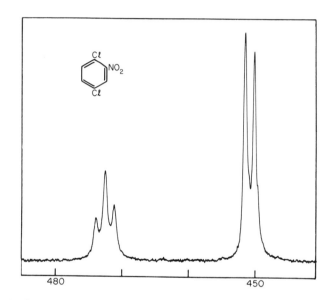

Fig. 7.13 Proton resonance spectrum (60 MHz) of 2,5-dichloronitrobenzene in $CDCl_3$. The low field triplet is due to H_6 and the doublet to H_3 and H_4, which are fortuitously chemically equivalent. The observed splitting of 1.6 Hz is about what would be expected as the average of $J(meta)$ (3 Hz) and $J(para)$ (0).

misinterpretations must be guarded against. An example of an AA'X deceptively simple spectrum is shown in Figure 7.13. Note that the AA'X spectrum is independent of the value of $J_{AA'}$, which in this example is $J(ortho)$, usually about 8 Hz.

Other pronounced departures from the "classical" ABX pattern occur for specific values of certain parameters. As pointed out in Section 7.17, the effective chemical shifts of the $(ab)_+$ and $(ab)_-$ quartets are $[(\nu_A - \nu_B) + \frac{1}{2}(J_{AX} - J_{BX})]$ and $[(\nu_A - \nu_B) - \frac{1}{2}(J_{AX} - J_{BX})]$, respectively. If one of these quantities is zero for particular values of the ν's and the J's, the corresponding ab subspectrum degenerates to a single line, while the other ab subspectrum remains a typical AB-type quartet.

Because of the many ways in which degeneracies or near degeneracies in line positions can occur, it is not possible to give a systematic treatment. The best ways of resolving degeneracy or deceptive simplicity are to obtain the spectrum at a different applied field or in another solvent (see Section 7.24).

7.21 "Virtual Coupling"

The ABX system provides a convenient framework for introducing the concept (actually poorly named) of *virtual coupling*. Consider the ABX system in the molecular fragment (I):

$$
\begin{array}{ccc}
R & R & R \\
| & | & | \\
R-C-C-C-OR \\
| & | & | \\
H_A & H_B & H_X
\end{array}
$$

(I)

The exact nature of the substituents is not important; it is only necessary that they contain no protons that couple with the three shown. Furthermore, let us assume that the R's are such that we have the chemical shift parameters given in Figure 7.14. If we assume that there is free rotation of the C—C bonds, then the couplings J_{AB} and J_{BX} should be nearly equal and each of the order of 7 or 8 Hz. J_{AX}, on the other hand, should be nearly zero. If we direct our attention only to the X portion of the spectrum (as might often happen in a complex molecule where the A and B portion would be overlapped by other aliphatic protons), we might well be tempted to treat the X portion of the spectrum by simple first-order analysis since $(\nu_B - \nu_X) \gg J_{BX}$. First-order analysis would then predict a simple doublet of approximately equal intensities with a splitting of 8 Hz. If, however, we recognize that this is really an ABX system and treat it accordingly, the X portion of the spectrum has 6 lines, as shown in Figure 7.14. The two most intense lines are again separated by 8 Hz, but the other lines are quite significant in intensity.

Since the ABX calculation is certainly correct, the first-order approximation must be wrong in this case. In fact, the first-order calculation will always fail in circumstances of this sort where the proton in question (X) is coupled to one of a set of strongly coupled nuclei (i.e., a set in which J is greater than the chemical shift difference in hertz). In these circumstances we sometimes say that the X proton will "behave" as though it were coupled to both A and B, whereas in fact it is coupled to only one of the two. This *apparent but not real coupling* has been termed virtual coupling. It is important to note that virtual coupling is *not* a new and different phenomenon. It is merely a way of expressing the fact that first-order analysis is not applicable in this type of situation, and as a result the *splittings* observed in the spectrum are not necessarily equivalent to the magnitudes of certain J's.

The term virtual coupling is usually reserved for those nonfirst-order situations where a hasty examination might lead one to infer incorrectly that first-order rules are applicable. Such cases often occur in symmetric molecules

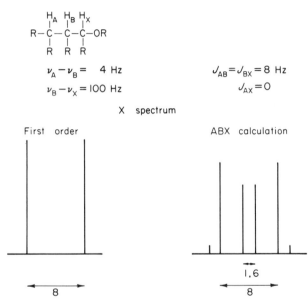

$$\nu_A - \nu_B = \quad 4 \text{ Hz} \qquad\qquad J_{AB} = J_{BX} = 8 \text{ Hz}$$
$$\nu_B - \nu_X = 100 \text{ Hz} \qquad\qquad J_{AX} = 0$$

X   spectrum

First   order   ABX   calculation

1.6

8   8

Fig. 7.14   Calculated spectrum for H_X in the molecular fragment shown, with the parameters as indicated.

where one might confuse chemical and magnetic equivalence. Two examples of systems other than ABX may help emphasize the types of circumstances where virtual coupling can occur. Figure 7.15a shows the spectrum of 1,4-dibromobutane in which the protons attached to carbons 2 and 3 are chemically but not magnetically equivalent. They are coupled to each other with a coupling constant $J_{23} \approx 7 \text{ Hz}$ (a typical average value for such vicinal coupling); since $(\nu_2 - \nu_3) = 0$, the four protons on C_2 and C_3 behave as a strongly coupled group. The result, as shown in spectrum a, Figure 7.15, is that the protons on C_1 and C_4 give rise not to a simple triplet, as might be expected from first-order analysis, but to the complex low field multiplet shown. The multiplet for the protons on C_2 and C_3 is likewise complex. This situation can be contrasted with that in 1,5-dibromopentane (Figure 7.15b). In this case the chemical shifts of the protons on C_2 and C_3 are different; for $J \approx 7 \text{ Hz}, J_{23}/(\nu_2 - \nu_3) \approx 0.3,$

so the C_2 and C_3 protons are not strongly coupled. The C_1 and C_5 protons thus give a first-order triplet. Protons on C_2 and C_4 are, of course, chemically equivalent, but $J_{24} \approx 0$, so these are not strongly coupled.

Another interesting example of virtual coupling is shown in Figure 7.16.

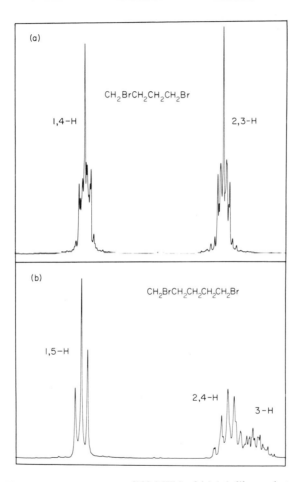

Fig. 7.15 Proton resonance spectra (100 MHz) of (a) 1,4-dibromobutane and (b) 1,5-dibromopentane. Virtual coupling occurs in (a) but not in (b).

The spectrum of 2,5-dimethylquinone (a) is readily interpreted by first-order analysis; that of 2,6-dimethylquinone (b) shows additional splittings caused by the virtual coupling of the C_2 methyl protons with C_5H, and by symmetry of the C_6 methyl with C_3H. In the latter molecule the protons on C_3 and C_5 are coupled by about 2 Hz, and their chemical equivalence results in a large value of J/δ. In 2,5-dimethylquinone, however, protons on C_3 and C_6 are apparently not coupled; at least, any coupling between them is too small to permit observable effects with the available resolution.

Often the effect of virtual coupling is merely to bring about an apparent broadening of peaks when many lines fall close together. The possibility of

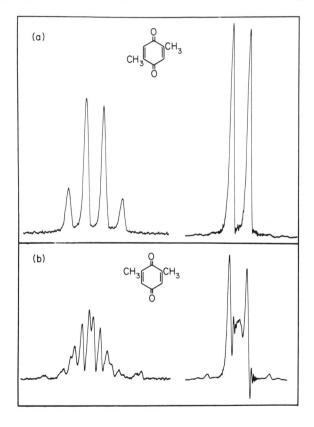

Fig. 7.16   Proton resonance spectra (60 MHz) of (a) 2,5-dimethylquinone and (b) 2,6-dimethylquinone, showing the effect of virtual coupling in (b).

virtual coupling should always be suspected when there are two or more strongly coupled nuclei that are chemically but not magnetically equivalent.

7.22 The AA′BB′ and AA′XX′ Systems

These four-spin systems are characterized by two chemical shifts and four coupling constants, $J_{AA'}$, $J_{BB'}$, J_{AB}, and $J_{AB'}$. The last two are not equal, leading to magnetic nonequivalence.

The calculation of the energy levels and transitions is considerably simplified by inclusion of the symmetry of the system. As we saw in Section 7.12, the four basic symmetry functions for two equivalent nuclei can easily be constructed to be either symmetric or antisymmetric with respect to interchange of the nuclei. The 16 basis functions for the AA'BB' system are the products of the four symmetrized AA' functions (equations 7.58 and 7.60)

Table 7.7

AA'XX' SPECTRUM: FREQUENCIES AND RELATIVE INTENSITIES OF THE A PROTON[a]

Line	Frequency relative to ν_A	Relative intensity
1	$\frac{1}{2}N$	1
2	$\frac{1}{2}N$	1
3	$-\frac{1}{2}N$	1
4	$-\frac{1}{2}N$	1
5	$P + \frac{1}{2}K$	$1 - K/2P$
6	$P - \frac{1}{2}K$	$1 + K/2P$
7	$-P + \frac{1}{2}K$	$1 + K/2P$
8	$-P - \frac{1}{2}K$	$1 - K/2P$
9	$R + \frac{1}{2}M$	$1 - M/2R$
10	$R - \frac{1}{2}M$	$1 + M/2R$
11	$-R + \frac{1}{2}M$	$1 + M/2R$
12	$-R - \frac{1}{2}M$	$1 - M/2R$

[a] $K = J_{AA'} + J_{XX'}$, $L = J_{AX} - J_{AX'}$, $M = J_{AA'} - J_{XX'}$, $N = J_{AX} + J_{AX'}$, $2P = (K^2 + L^2)^{1/2}$, $2R = (M^2 + L^2)^{1/2}$.

with the four identical symmetrized BB' functions. The resultant secular determinant factors according to symmetry and F_z into two 1×1, five 2×2, and one 4×4 blocks. There are 28 transitions allowed by symmetry and the selection rule $\Delta F_z = \pm 1$, but four of these are combination transitions and are normally too weak to be observed. The remaining transitions are symmetrically arranged around the average of the A and B chemical shifts, $\frac{1}{2}(\nu_A + \nu_B)$.

Because of the presence of the 4×4 block in the Hamiltonian, explicit algebraic expressions for only 12 of the 24 expected transitions can be obtained. As a result, the analysis of an AA'BB' spectrum is usually tedious and requires a trial and error procedure aided by a computer. Even if this analysis is accomplished, there are some ambiguities in the signs and assignments of coupling constants. Probably the best method for complete analysis of an AA'BB' spectrum is by means of double resonance techniques (see Section

8.8). We shall discuss some special AA'BB' cases after we have taken up the AA'XX' system.

As in the ABX case, the larger chemical shift difference found in the AA'XX' system permits the definition of $F_z(A)$ and $F_z(X)$. As a result, the Hamiltonian factors into twelve 1×1 and two 2×2 blocks. As in the AA'BB' system, there are 24 allowed transitions of significant intensity, again arranged symmetrically around the frequency $\frac{1}{2}(\nu_A + \nu_X)$. Table 7.7 gives the frequencies

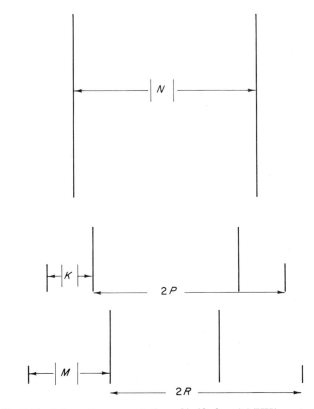

Fig. 7.17   Schematic representation of half of an AA'XX' spectrum.

and intensities of the A transitions, and Figure 7.17 depicts the half-spectrum schematically. (The X spectrum would be identical and furnishes no additional information.) It is apparent that the A spectrum is also symmetric about its midpoint, which is ν_A. In Table 7.7 the frequencies are given in terms of the parameters K, L, M, N, P, and R defined in the table. Lines 1 and 2 always coincide, as do lines 3 and 4. Thus the half-spectrum has only 10 lines.

The analysis of an AA'XX' spectrum is straightforward, but a number of ambiguities occur because of the symmetry of the spectrum. The chemical shifts ν_A and ν_X are of course easily determined as the midpoints of the respective half-spectra. The two strongest lines in the half-spectrum are separated by $|N|$. The remaining lines can be shown to arise from two ab subspectra characterized by "coupling constants" of K and M, respectively; P and R are defined by analogy to C in equation 7.52. Table 7.7 and Figure 7.17 show that the frequencies and intensity ratios conform to the AB pattern. The values of $|K|$ and $|M|$ are easily found from the subspectra, but cannot be distinguished from each other; $|L|$ is easily calculated from the spectral line separations and the value of either $|K|$ or $|M|$ already found (cf. Figure 7.2). The relative signs of J_{AX} and $J_{AX'}$ can be determined by noting whether $|N|$ is larger or smaller than $|L|$. Since K and M cannot be distinguished, we cannot ascertain the relative signs of $J_{AA'}$ and $J_{XX'}$. And finally, there is no way from the spectrum alone that we can decide which of the calculated pair is $J_{AA'}$ and which is $J_{XX'}$. The same ambiguity exists with J_{AX} and $J_{AX'}$. Often the coupling constants can be assigned to the proper nuclei on the basis of analogy to other systems. For example, the spectrum of 1,1-difluoroethylene in Figure 5.3 is an AA'XX' spectrum, which has been analyzed to give the absolute values $J_{HH'} = 4.8$, $J_{FF'} = 36.4$, $J_{HF}(cis) = 0.7$, $J_{HF}(trans) = 33.9$ Hz.[13] The assignments were readily made by analogy (see Tables 5.3 and 5.4).

As $(\nu_A - \nu_X)$ becomes smaller and the system converts to an AA'BB' system, the lines toward the center of the complete spectrum grow in intensity, while those toward the outside diminish in intensity (cf. AX $\rightarrow$ AB, Figure 5.4). We shall describe two commonly encountered AA'BB' patterns.

One situation occurs when $|J_{AB}|$ is much greater than $|J_{AA'}|$, $|J_{BB'}|$, and $|J_{AB'}|$, as in p-disubstituted benzenes (cf. Table 5.2) (II). The dominance of

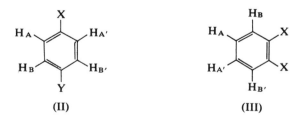

(II)   (III)

one coupling constant causes the spectrum to resemble roughly an AB quartet, but closer examination reveals several smaller peaks, which may be used in analyzing the spectrum. One example was given in Figure 6.4, and many others are included among the spectra in Appendix B.

A different relation among the coupling constants, $|J_{AB}| \gg |J_{AB'}|$ and simultaneously $|J_{AA'}| \gg |J_{BB'}|$, occurs, for example, in symmetrically o-disubstituted benzenes (III). In this case the spectrum is complex, with lines frequently tending to appear as very closely spaced doublets, as shown in Figure 7.18. Many other AA′BB′ patterns are possible, depending on the relations among the various parameters.

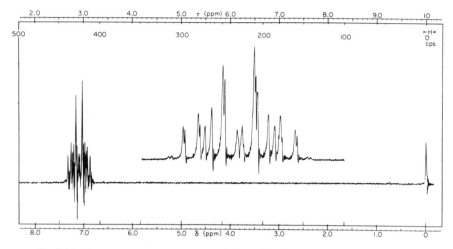

Fig. 7.18   Proton resonance spectrum (60 MHz) of *ortho*-dichlorobenzene, one type of AA′BB′ spectrum.

7.23 Other Complex Spectra

A large number of spin systems have been studied in detail and are discussed elsewhere. Those involving groups of magnetically equivalent nuclei, such as $A_m B_n X_p$, can usually be treated algebraically,[1,2] while others possessing fewer spins, such as ABXY, can be treated analytically only in certain limiting cases.[14]

7.24 Aids in the Analysis of Complex Spectra

Variation of H_0. A number of procedures are available to simplify the analysis of complex spectra. Probably the most useful is observation of the spectrum of two or more values of the applied magnetic field. A spectrum that defies analysis at one field may be simplified greatly at higher field. The present general availability of proton resonance spectrometers operating at 60 and at 100 MHz and the increasing number of instruments operating above 200 MHz make field-dependent studies feasible. The field dependence is sometimes turned to advantage in another way by deliberately reducing the field to convert a first-order spectrum that is independent of certain parameters, such as signs of J's, to a more complex pattern from which the desired information can be extracted by iterative computer-aided analysis.[15]

Isotopic Substitution. Isotopic substitution, especially involving the specific interchange of magnetic and nonmagnetic nuclei, frequently aids analysis of complex spectra. Deuterium substitution is most common, with the smaller magnetogyric ratio of deuterium rendering many spin couplings negligibly small. If necessary, the deuterium coupling effects can be eliminated by spin decoupling (see Chapter 8). ^{15}N substitution is occasionally used to avoid the broadening effects of the quadrupole containing ^{14}N.

^{13}C *Satellites.* One particularly useful isotopic substitution that is always available in organic molecules involves ^{13}C. This isotope is present at a natural abundance of 1.1 %. ^{13}C has a spin of $\frac{1}{2}$, and as we saw in Chapter 5, $^{1}J(^{13}C—H)$ is normally 100–200 Hz. Hence a resonance line from a proton attached to a carbon atom (^{12}C) will be accompanied by weak ^{13}C satellites symmetrically placed about it at a frequency separation of $\frac{1}{2}J(^{13}C—H)$.* For example, the proton resonance of chloroform in Figure 7.19a shows ^{13}C satellites (or ^{13}C sidebands).

When the molecule in question contains more than one carbon atom, the ^{13}C satellites often become much more complex. Consider, for example, the molecule $CHCl_2CHCl_2$, the proton resonance of which is shown in Figure 7.19b. The ordinary spectrum is a single line because of the magnetic equivalence of the two protons. On the other hand, the approximately 2.2 % of the molecules that contain one ^{13}C and one ^{12}C have protons that are not magnetically equivalent. In fact, the proton resonance spectrum of these molecules should be an ABX spectrum in which $\nu_A \approx \nu_B$. The ABX analysis is also shown in Figure 7.19. Note that because $(\nu_A - \nu_B) \approx 0$ and $J_{AX} \gg J_{BX}$, the protons behave as though the effective chemical shift of H_A is about 91 Hz ($\frac{1}{2}J_{AX}$) away from H_B. Since this value is much greater than J_{AB} (3 Hz), the A—B coupling can then be interpreted to a high degree of approximation on a first-order basis. This is a general result with ^{13}C satellites since $^{1}J(^{13}C—H)$ normally is much greater than $^{2}J(^{13}C—H)$ and $^{3}J(H—H)$.

With the recent marked improvement in NMR sensitivity (see Section 3.5) so that ^{13}C satellites may be readily observed, this technique has become a

---

* The position of the satellites about the main peak is usually not quite symmetric because of a small isotope effect on the chemical shift.

powerful tool in determining H—H coupling constants in symmetric molecules where this coupling normally leads to no observable splitting.

The phenomena discussed here are not, of course, restricted to ^{13}C. Other

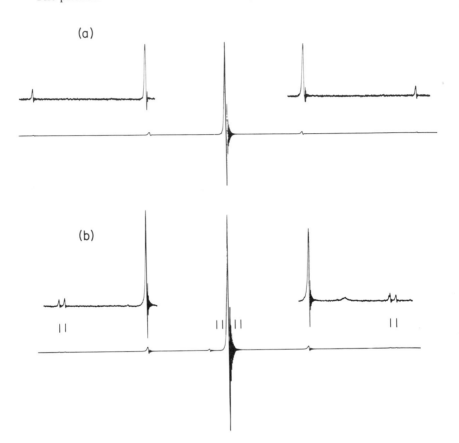

Fig. 7.19   Proton resonance spectra (60 MHz) showing ^{13}C satellites. (a) CHCl$_3$; (b) CHCl$_2$CHCl$_2$, with the AB portion of an ABX simulation of the spectrum. The sharp lines close to the main resonance in each case are spinning sidebands; the ^{13}C satellites are near the edges of the figure. The satellites shown in the simulated spectrum are obscured by the strong central peak; their positions are estimated and cannot be determined from the observed spectrum.

magnetic nuclei present at low abundance with the principal isotope of $I = 0$ display similar spectra. ^{29}Si, ^{199}Hg, and ^{183}W are among the best known.

Double Quantum Transitions. When very high rf power is used in scanning a spectrum, it is possible that two quanta of the *same* frequency will be absorbed to produce flipping of two coupled spins. These "double quantum transitions" appear as sharp lines under conditions where the normal spectrum is almost completely saturated, as indicated in Figure 7.20. Theory shows that from the frequencies of the double quantum lines we can often obtain information on coupling constants that differs from the information obtainable from the ordinary spectrum. For example, in the ABC system the double quantum spectrum, together with the ordinary spectrum, provides enough information to determine from the frequencies the relative signs of all three J's.[16] Double

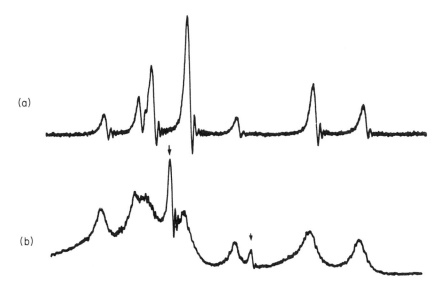

(a)

(b)

Fig. 7.20 Proton resonance spectrum (60 MHz) of 2-fluoro-4,6-dichlorophenol. (a) Spectrum with small H_1, showing AB portion of an ABX spectrum (from the aromatic protons and fluorine). (b) Spectrum with larger H_1, showing double quantum transitions (arrows) at the centers of the $(ab)_+$ and $(ab)_-$ quartets (Corio[1]).

quantum transitions occur for only a narrow range of rf power. They are sometimes observed inadvertently when a normal scan is conducted with excess rf power.

Double resonance and *solvent effects* may be useful aids to analysis. They are discussed in Chapters 8 and 11, respectively.

7.25 Use of Liquid Crystals as Solvents

Liquid crystals are known to form a partially ordered structure, but with more intermolecular motion than exists in ordinary crystals. Small anisotropic molecules dissolved in liquid crystals experience partial orientation and thus do not achieve complete cancellation of direct dipole-dipole interactions (see Section 2.6). The spectrum is dependent on both these dipole couplings and ordinary spin couplings, including those that normally would not appear because of magnetic equivalence. In addition, the anisotropy in the chemical shifts is sometimes manifested. The result is that the spectrum becomes extremely complex but can be analyzed to provide information on these

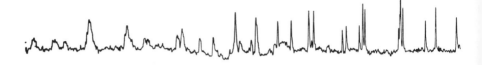

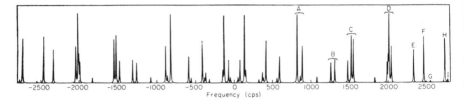

Fig. 7.21 Top: Fluorine resonance spectrum (56.4 MHz) of hexafluorobenzene dissolved in the liquid crystal nematic phase of p,p'-di-n-hexyloxyazoxybenzene at 58°C. Bottom: Computer-simulated spectrum with parameters as follows: Dipole-dipole interactions, $D(ortho) = -1452.67$; $D(meta) = -271.56$; $D(para) = -194.15$; spin-spin couplings, $J(ortho) = -22$; $J(meta) = -4$; $J(para) = +6$ Hz (Snyder and Anderson[17]).

anisotropies and dipole interactions unobtainable in other ways. For example, the spectrum of hexafluorobenzene, which is a single line in ordinary solvents, is shown in Figure 7.21. This spectrum has been completely analyzed to yield the signs and magnitudes of all J's, as well as the values of the dipole couplings. Since the latter interactions vary inversely with the cube of internuclear distance, the results provide a sensitive measure of molecular geometry in solution.

References

1. P. L. Corio, "Structure of High Resolution NMR Spectra." Academic Press, New York, 1966.

2. J. W. Emsley, J. Feeney, and L. H. Sutcliffe, "High Resolution NMR Spectroscopy," Chapter 8. Macmillan (Pergamon), New York, 1965.

3. J. A. Pople, W. G. Schneider, and H. J. Bernstein, "High Resolution NMR," Chapter 6. McGraw-Hill, New York, 1959.

4. See, for example, H. Eyring, J. Walter, and G. E. Kimball, "Quantum Chemistry," p. 37. Wiley, New York, 1944.

5. See, for example, reference 3, p. 105.

6. See reference 1, p. 172.

7. S. Castellano and A. A. Bothner-By, *J. Chem. Phys.* **41**, 3863 (1964); J. D. Swalen and C. A. Reilly, *J. Chem. Phys.* **37**, 21 (1962).

8. S. Castellano and J. S. Waugh, *J. Chem. Phys.* **34**, 295 (1961).

9. J. D. Swalen, *Progr. NMR Spectroscopy* **1**, 205 (1966).

10. J. S. Waugh and S. Castellano, *J. Chem. Phys.* **35**, 1900 (1961).

11. P. Diehl, R. K. Harris, and R. G. Jones, *Progr. NMR Spectroscopy* **3**, 1 (1967).

12. P. Diehl, personal communication.

13. G. W. Flynn and J. D. Baldeschwieler, *J. Chem. Phys.* **38**, 226 (1963).

14. For a summary of systems treated in the literature, see reference 2, pp. 661–663.

15. W. B. Moniz and E. Lustig, *J. Chem. Phys.* **46**, 366 (1967).

16. See, for example, reference 2, pp. 453–455.

17. L. C. Snyder and E. W. Anderson, *J. Chem. Phys.* **42**, 3336 (1965).

Problems

1. Describe the following spin systems as AB, etc.: $CH_2{=}CHF$; PF_3; cubane; $CH_3CHOHCH_3$; H_2; chlorobenzene; *n*-propane.

2. Show that for N coupled nuclei there are $\frac{1}{2}N(N-1)$ coupling constants.

3. Verify that ψ_2 in equation 7.44 gives the value of E_2 in equation 7.43.

4. Which of the following spectra result from AB systems? Spectra are listed as: frequency (relative intensity).
   (a) 100 (1), 108 (2.3), 120 (2.3), 128 (1).
   (b) 100 (1), 104 (2.4), 113 (2.4), 120 (1).
   (c) 100 (1), 110 (4), 114 (4), 124 (1).
   (d) 100 (1), 107 (15), 108 (15), 115 (1).

5. The following quartet appears as part of a rich NMR spectrum: 100 (1), 108 (3), 116 (3), 124 (1). (a) Give *two* possible explanations of its origin. (b) By what experiment could this ambiguity be resolved? (c) Predict the frequencies and relative intensities in each case.

6. Find ν_A and ν_B from each of the following AB spectra: (a) 117, 123, 142, 148; (b) 206, 215, 217, 226.

7. Verify the nonmixing of basis functions of different symmetry for $\Phi_{2'}$ and $\Phi_{3'}$ (equation 7.60) by calculating $\mathscr{H}_{2'3'}$.

8. Use the ABC basis functions in equation 7.63, the rules of Section 7.13, and the theorem on factoring of the secular equation according to F_z to construct the Hamiltonian matrix for the ABC system.

9. Analyze the spectrum in Figure 7.5 to obtain ν_A, ν_B, and J_{AB}.

10. Derive equations 7.67 from equations 7.64.

11. Show from Table 7.5 that a change in sign of J_{AB} leads to the same spectrum (both frequencies and intensities).

12. Show from Table 7.5 that the centers of the $(ab)_+$ and $(ab)_-$ quartets are separated by $\frac{1}{2}|J_{AX} + J_{BX}|$.

13. Use the procedure of Table 7.6 to analyze the spectra in Figure 7.7b, c.

14. Use the procedure of Table 7.6 to analyze the spectrum in Figure 7.10b. Make the calculation both for the "correct" ab subspectra and for the subspectra "incorrectly" assigned.

15. In which of the following molecules is virtual coupling likely to appear?

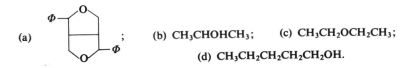

(a)   ;   (b) $CH_3CHOHCH_3$;   (c) $CH_3CH_2OCH_2CH_3$;

(d) $CH_3CH_2CH_2CH_2CH_2OH$.

16. Determine the structural formulas of compounds in Spectra 21 and 22, Appendix B. Analyze the ABX portions of the spectra by the procedure of Table 7.6.

17. Analyze the AA′XX′ spectra 23 and 24, Appendix B. From the values of the coupling constants deduce the correct isomeric structure of each compound (cf. Figure 5.3).

18. Determine the structures of the molecules giving Spectra 25–30, Appendix B.

19. Use the procedure of Table 7.6 to analyze the ABX patterns in Spectra 25 and 26, Appendix B. Could first-order analysis be used for these spectra? Why?

20. Determine all six coupling constants in the molecule giving Spectrum 27, Appendix B.

21. Account for the appearance of Spectrum 28, Appendix B, by a modified first-order analysis.

Chapter 8

Theory and Application of Double Resonance

Our discussion of NMR thus far has dealt with the situation in which the sample is subjected to only one radio-frequency field, namely, that needed to observe the resonance. We now wish to consider the effects of applying simultaneously two (or more) rf fields at different frequencies, one used to observe resonance and the other(s) to perturb the nuclear spin system. This procedure is generally called nuclear magnetic *double resonance*, abbreviated as NMDR, or *multiple resonance* if two or more perturbing fields are employed. We shall see that if the perturbing field is sufficiently strong and is applied at the resonant frequency of one of a pair of spin-coupled nuclei, the other nucleus behaves in its NMR as though it were no longer coupled. This technique, *spin decoupling*, is a powerful tool in unraveling the spectra of many complex molecules. On the other hand, if the strength of the perturbing field is rather small, additional splittings and/or changes in relative intensities of lines may occur. These branches of double resonance, *spin tickling* and *nuclear Overhauser effects*, are also, as we shall see, of great value in unraveling complex spectra.

8.1 Notation and Terminology

We shall continue to use the notation already employed, in which H_0 denotes the large applied magnetic field, which is taken to be along the z axis, while H_1 denotes the radio-frequency field, which can be thought of as rotating in the xy plane at a frequency v_1 in the same direction in which the nuclei precess. We now denote by H_2 the second rf field, also rotating in the xy plane in the same direction as H_1, but with frequency v_2.

If the frequencies v_1 and v_2 are both near the Larmor frequency of one type of nucleus (e.g., the proton), so that they differ only by an audio frequency (from a few hertz to a few thousand hertz), we speak of *homonuclear* double resonance (or homonuclear decoupling or tickling). If v_1 and v_2 differ by a radio frequency (e.g., 60 MHz for ^1H and 24.3 MHz for ^{31}P), then we speak of *heteronuclear* double resonance. In the heteronuclear case, a commonly used notation lists first the nucleus that is observed at frequency v_1 followed, in brackets, by the nucleus that is irradiated at frequency v_2; for example, $^1H\{^{19}F\}$.

8.2 Experimental Techniques

The apparatus used for double resonance studies is essentially that used in ordinary single resonance experiments with the additional provision for supplying to the transmitter coil of the probe the second radio frequency at the desired power level. The procedures normally used are quite different for homonuclear and heteronuclear double resonance.

For heteronuclear double resonance the second radio frequency is generally supplied by a second stable rf oscillator operating at frequency v_2. This oscillator must be tunable over the range of resonance frequencies (chemical shifts) expected for the nucleus to be irradiated. Commercial units of moderate stability are available that cover a range of several kilohertz around a crystal-controlled frequency. Probably the most satisfactory source of the second rf field is a frequency synthesizer, which can be set to better than 0.1 Hz over a range of many megahertz and maintained constant to about 0.01 Hz. Most heteronuclear experiments that have been performed to date rely on adequate short-term stability of the two rf oscillators. For many uses, however, normal stability of two crystal-controlled oscillators is insufficient, and the two rf sources must be locked together, with both frequencies ultimately derived from a single crystal.

Since two different rf frequencies are applied to the sample, the transmitter coil in the probe must be tuned to accept both frequencies. Such double tuning is a relatively simple electronic problem, and commercial tuning adapters are available.

We have pointed out in previous chapters that an NMR spectrum may be scanned by varying H_0 while holding v_1 constant (field sweep) or by varying

v_1 while holding H_0 constant (frequency sweep). For single resonance studies, both procedures produce identical spectra, but this is not true for double resonance, as we shall see in Section 8.3. We can easily recognize the difference between the two types of sweep in an A{X} experiment. In a frequency sweep H_0 is constant so that the Larmor frequency of X, v_X, is also constant. Hence v_2 may be fixed so that $v_2 = v_X$ or so that $(v_2 - v_X)$ is any desired value. In a field sweep, however, v_X will be swept past v_2 as the field is swept. In general, the frequency sweep method provides a "cleaner" arrangement, but many instruments (especially external lock systems) are limited to field sweep capabilities only.

There is a second type of frequency sweep method possible in double resonance studies. This method requires that H_0 be maintained constant and that v_1 be held constant at a value exactly on one of the A resonance lines. Frequency v_2 is then swept in the vicinity of v_X and perturbations in the A spectrum are recorded. This technique has been called INDOR (internuclear double resonance).[1] We shall see some examples of the use of INDOR in Section 8.6. It is apparent that v_1 can be maintained precisely on one of the spectral lines of A only if a very good field/frequency control is used (usually an internal lock; see Section 3.4).

In principle, *homo*nuclear double resonance can be accomplished by the use of two rf oscillators or frequency synthesizers locked together, and such studies have been carried out.[2] Usually, however, the experimental arrangement is simpler and less costly if the methods of audio modulation described in Section 3.3 are employed. For example, in proton resonance at 60 MHz an audio frequency v_1' ($\sim$2000 Hz) is often applied to modulate the radio frequency or, equivalently, the magnetic field. The resonance signal is then phase detected at v_1', so that the NMR is carried out at a frequency of (60 MHz $\pm v_1'$), depending on whether the upper or lower sideband is used. If an additional audio signal at frequency v_2' is used for the modulation but not the detection, the nuclei experience the observing frequency $v_1 = 60$ MHz $\pm v_1'$, as well as the frequency $v_2 = 60$ MHz $\pm v_2'$. The modulation indices of the frequencies v_1' and v_2' can be adjusted to obtain the desired power level in each sideband.

As in the case of heteronuclear double resonance, there are three types of sweep possible. The ordinary frequency sweep, usually obtained by varying v_1' while holding H_0, v_2', and the 60-MHz frequency (or whatever the nominal resonance frequency of A is) constant, is the simplest to comprehend and normally gives the most easily interpretable results. The situation is exactly the same as in the heteronuclear case. The other frequency sweep, in which v_2' is varied while H_0, v_1', and the 60 MHz are held constant, is also exactly the same as in the heteronuclear case. Field sweep, in which H_0 is varied while all frequencies remain constant, brings v_X and v_2 into coincidence only at one point in the scan. In the homonuclear case, it is often convenient to think of a field sweep as though the field were held constant while both v_1' and v_2' move across the spectrum at a constant separation $(v_1' - v_2')$. If two coupled nuclei are separated in chemical shift by $(v_1' - v_2')$, one of the pair will be irradiated by field H_2 while the second is being observed. We shall see examples of spin decoupling experiments carried out in this way in Section 8.4.

8.3 Theory of Double Resonance

The general theory of double resonance is quite complex and is far beyond the scope of this book. We shall concentrate merely on indicating the general approach and discussing some of the most important results.

In our general consideration of complex spectra in Chapter 7 we found, in Section 7.5, that the Hamiltonian could be written as the sum of two parts,

$$\mathcal{H} = \mathcal{H}^{(0)} + \mathcal{H}^{(1)}.$$

$\mathcal{H}^{(0)}$ refers to the interaction of the nuclei with the magnetic field H_0, while $\mathcal{H}^{(1)}$ takes account of spin-spin coupling between the nuclei. The effect of the rf field H_1, used to observe resonance, was introduced as a time-dependent perturbation after the equation had been solved with the above Hamiltonian.

In our consideration of double resonance phenomena we can still introduce H_1 as a time-dependent perturbation, since it is a weak field. However, we cannot validly treat H_2 in a similar manner because the energy of interaction between H_2 and the nuclear spin system is often of the same magnitude as, or even greater than, the energy of interaction (coupling) between nuclei. Hence the effect of H_2 must be included by adding an extra term to the Hamiltonian:

$$\mathcal{H}(v_2\,t) = \mathcal{H}^{(0)} + \mathcal{H}^{(1)} + \mathcal{H}^{(2)}(v_2\,t). \tag{8.1}$$

We have noted specifically that since $\mathcal{H}^{(2)}$ is a periodic function of time, the total Hamiltonian will also vary periodically. Fortunately, a general theorem by Larmor (mentioned in Section 2.2) shows that the effect of a magnetic field on a set of spins is equivalent to subjecting the spins to a rotating coordinate system. By using the Larmor theorem and making a simple transformation of coordinates from the fixed laboratory frame of reference to a frame of reference rotating at v_2, the frequency of the time-dependent portion of $\mathcal{H}$, we can convert $\mathcal{H}$ to a time-independent $\mathcal{H}_R$:

$$\mathcal{H}_R = \mathcal{H}_R^{(0)} + \mathcal{H}^{(1)} + \mathcal{H}_R^{(2)}$$

$$= \sum_i (v_i - v_2)(I_z)_i + \sum_{i<j}\sum J_{ij}\,\mathbf{I}_i\cdot\mathbf{I}_j - \frac{1}{2\pi}\sum_i \gamma_i\,H_2(I_x)_i. \tag{8.2}$$

(H_0 is still taken along the negative z axis, while H_2 is along the positive x axis.) From comparison of equation 8.2 with equations 7.17 and 7.18, it is apparent that the effects of transforming to the rotating frame is to cause all chemical shifts to be measured relative to v_2 (i.e., $(v_i - v_2)$ appears instead of

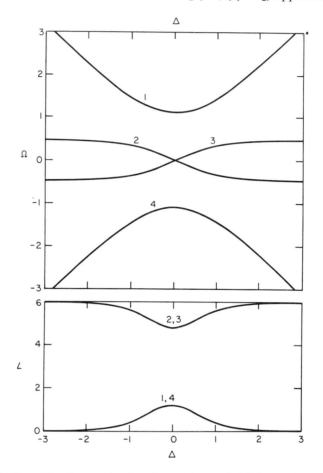

Fig. 8.1 Transition frequencies Ω and transition probabilities L of the A resonance in an AX system plotted against the offset parameter Δ for an irradiation field strength $\gamma H_2/2\pi = J$. See text for definitions of symbols. Based on the plots by Anderson and Free-man.[4]

v_i in the first term) and to introduce an interaction term between H_2 and the x component of each spin.

The diagonalization of $\mathcal{H}_R$ is a considerably harder task than its ordinary counterpart in the absence of the second rf field. The solution has been carried out in different ways, depending on the relative values of the parameters involved.[3] One particularly important case is that where $|v_i - v_j| \gg J_{ij}$ for all i and j. This situation often occurs for heteronuclear double resonance; it also occurs in those cases of homonuclear double resonance that would be simply analyzed by first order in the absence of H_2. The solution for this case

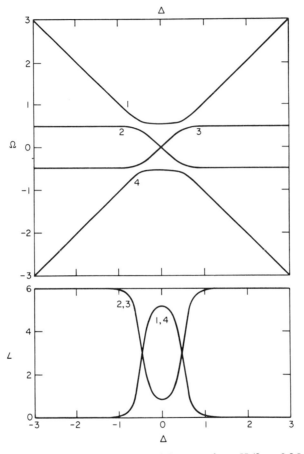

Fig. 8.2   Plot analogous to Figure 8.1 except that $\gamma H_2/2\pi = 0.2J$.

of weakly coupled nuclei has been obtained[4] and can be expressed conveniently in graphical form, as indicated in Figures 8.1 and 8.2 for the AX system. These curves give the frequencies and relative intensities of the A lines in an A{X} experiment. The curves are given in terms of the dimensionless parameters Δ and Ω, defined as

$$\Delta \equiv (v_2 - v_X)/J,$$
$$\Omega \equiv (v_1 - v_A)/J.$$

(8.3)

Figures 8.1 and 8.2 refer to different values of the perturbing field H_2. It is convenient to measure H_2 in terms of the equivalent frequency from the Larmor relation, $\gamma H_2/2\pi$. The "offset parameter" Δ measures the difference between the frequency of the perturbing field and the resonance frequency of X. A frequency sweep corresponds to a vertical line through the upper portion of the figures at the appropriate value of Δ. A field sweep corresponds

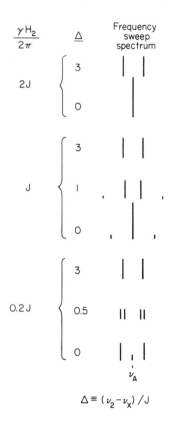

Fig. 8.3   Schematic spectra expected for the A resonance of an AX system when a second rf field is applied near the resonance frequency of X. See text for definition of symbols. Based on plots of Freeman and Whiffen.[5]

to a cut through the figure by a line with a slope $|\gamma_A/\gamma_X|$ (slope of unity for homonuclear double resonance), with an intercept Δ' at $\Omega = 0$, where

$$\Delta' = [(\nu_A - \nu_X) - (\nu_1 - \nu_2)]/J. \tag{8.4}$$

An INDOR experiment is represented by a horizontal line at the appropriate value of Ω provided ν_2 is swept at an extremely slow rate. A spectral transition occurs at each intersection of the "sweep line" with one of the curves in the upper portion of the figures. The intensity of each line can be read from the lower portions of the figures at the value of Δ where the line appears.

Figure 8.3 shows several schematic spectra that would be obtained in an A{X} experiment for an AX system. When $\Delta > 3$, there is no observable effect; but as ν_2 approaches ν_X, changes in line frequency and intensity occur. For $\gamma H_2/2\pi > 2J$ the A doublet collapses to a singlet at ν_A when $\nu_2 = \nu_X$. This is *spin decoupling*.* When systems of more than two nuclei are studied (e.g., A_nX), the collapse of the spectrum to a single line is incomplete, and "residual splittings" are observed even with a large value of the perturbing (decoupling) field H_2. The splittings are reduced in spacing, however, by $2\pi J/\gamma_X H_2$.[4]

Figure 8.3 also shows an interesting effect in the frequency sweep spectrum with $\gamma_X H_2/2\pi = 0.2J$ and $\Delta = 0.5J$; that is, a weak perturbing field applied exactly at the frequency of *one* of the two X lines. This is an example of *tickling*. We see that each of the A lines splits into a very closely spaced doublet. We shall discuss tickling in more detail in Section 8.8.

The results in Figures 8.1–8.3 were obtained with the assumption that all J's are negligible relative to $|\nu_A - \nu_X|$. In many cases of homonuclear double resonance this condition is not satisfied. The results of Figures 8.1–8.3 are still valid approximately for moderate chemical shift differences, except that optimum decoupling occurs not when $\nu_2 = \nu_X$, but when

$$(\nu_1 - \nu_2) = (\nu_A - \nu_X) - \frac{(\gamma H_2/2\pi)^2}{2(\nu_A - \nu_X)}. \tag{8.5}$$

Equation 8.5 results from the presence of two effects: first, the additional field strength arising from H_2, which increases the Larmor frequency of A; and second, the effect of the nonnegligible J in altering the effective fields seen by the nuclei in the rotating frame of reference.[4] For accurate measurements of chemical shifts by homonuclear spin decoupling (see Section 8.5) the value of H_2 must be determined[2] and the correction of equation 8.5 applied.

Our discussion of the theory of NMDR began with the observation that H_2 may be large enough so that it cannot be treated merely as a perturbation. In some cases, however, use is made of a rather weak H_2 so that the effects we have considered can be ignored. In this application H_2 is used not to alter energy levels, but to bring about changes in populations of the levels. This technique is called the *nuclear Overhauser effect* (by analogy to a similar effect found by Overhauser[6] for interactions between electrons and nuclei). The

---

* An often quoted qualitative "explanation" for spin decoupling is that the high power in H_2 causes such rapid transitions among the X nuclei that the energy of the A nucleus responds only to the average X energy, which is zero. Hence the A energy levels behave as though the X nucleus were not coupled to A. This rationalization for the observed phenomenon clearly does not account for the effects shown in Figure 8.3 for weaker perturbing fields. It also is inadequate in explaining completely the observations in strong fields when an A_nX system is considered.

theory of the nuclear Overhauser effect is complex and depends upon relaxation mechanisms. We shall not take up the theory, but shall discuss briefly the use of this effect in structure elucidation (Section 8.4).

We have described several types of double resonance experiments, which depend upon the strength of the perturbing field H_2. Table 8.1 summarizes these branches of NMDR, giving for each type the typical effect on NMR lines. All four kinds of study can be carried out with either homonuclear or heteronuclear double resonance. We shall now investigate some of the applications of NMDR.

Table 8.1

Types of Double Resonance

$\gamma H_2/2\pi$ (Hz)	Designation	Typical effect
$>2J\,^a$	Spin decoupling	Collapse of multiplets
$\sim J$	Selective spin decoupling	Partial collapse of multiplets
$\sim \nu_{1/2}{}^b \ll J$	Spin tickling	Splitting of lines
$< \nu_{1/2}$	Nuclear Overhauser effect	Change in area under line

^{a} J is the spin-spin coupling constant between the irradiated and observed nuclei.
^{b} $\nu_{1/2}$ is the width at half-maximum intensity of the irradiated line.

8.4 Structure Elucidation

Spin decoupling has proved to be an invaluable tool in the elucidation of the structures of many complex molecules. Often a knowledge of which protons in a molecule are spin coupled to each other can provide a piece of information that makes possible an unequivocal structural assignment. A typical example of this use of spin decoupling is given in Figure 8.4. In this case the structure of an unknown molecule was restricted by other data to two possibilities, I and II. In each case the olefinic proton would be expected to have a chemical shift in the vicinity of 700 Hz (7.0 ppm) from TMS and to be split approximately into a triplet by coupling to the adjacent CH_2 protons and to be further split by the four-bond coupling through the double bond. In structure I, the CH_2 to which the olefinic proton is coupled would be expected to resonate near 2.5 ppm since it is adjacent to a doubly bonded carbon, while in structure II it would appear at much lower field since it is adjacent to both a double-bonded carbon and oxygen. The decoupling experiment shown in Figure 8.4c demonstrates clearly that the CH_2 resonates near 2.5 ppm and hence rules out structure II.

Spin tickling is also beginning to find application in problems of structure elucidation. Adjustment of parameters, particularly the strength of H_2, is generally more difficult for tickling studies, so that the less demanding technique of spin decoupling is usually preferred. Tickling has the advantage, however, of causing only slight perturbations, which are less likely to interfere

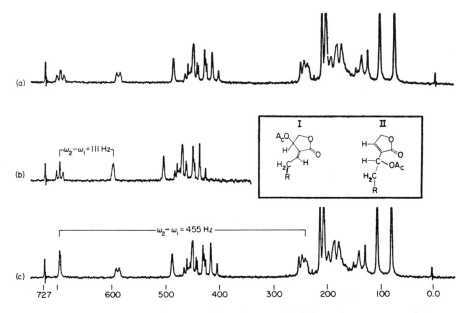

Fig. 8.4 Use of spin decoupling in structure elucidation of an unsaturated lactone, I or II. (a) Single resonance proton NMR spectrum at 100 MHz. (b) Field sweep double resonance spectrum with irradiation field 111 Hz to the high field side of the observing frequency. (c) Field sweep double resonance spectrum with H_2 455 Hz to the high field side of the observing frequency (Shoolery[7]).

with the recording of the spectrum or with the maintenance of an internal lock signal. In general, the high power needed for complete spin decoupling precludes the irradiation at frequencies much less than 40 Hz from the observing frequency, but in tickling, closer approach to the observing frequency is possible.

The nuclear Overhauser effect also has great potential in the elucidation of the structures of certain complex molecules. First the Boltzmann distribution of one type of proton is disrupted by application of a field H_2 that is strong enough to partially saturate the system but not strong enough to cause tickling or decoupling effects. If the saturated proton interacts via a dipole-dipole mechanism with another proton, the second proton will experience a disruption of its Boltzmann distribution, hence a change in the intensity of its resonance line. The utility in structure determination lies in the fact that dipole-dipole interactions vary inversely with the cube of distance between the dipoles, so that information on spatial orientation of the nuclei might be extracted in favorable cases. So far, only limited use has been made of the technique.[8] Either very accurate measurements must be made of line intensities so as to assess the magnitude of changes with imposition of H_2, or circuitry must be used that permits the direct measurement of the *changes* in the spectrum with H_2, rather than the spectrum itself.[9]

8.5 Location of "Hidden" Lines

Removal of splittings by spin decoupling often permits the observation of resonances that would otherwise be undetectable. One increasingly popular use of this technique is in ^{13}C resonance, where signal/noise ratio is usually poor due to the somewhat poor sensitivity of this nucleus and to its low abundance (1.1 %). Most ^{13}C resonance lines are split into multiplets by spin coupling to protons one, two, or three bonds away, hence are frequently undetectable because of low signal/noise for each component of the multiplet. A $^{13}C\{H\}$ double resonance can collapse many multiplets. The ^{13}C signal resulting from the coalescence of the multiplets is usually further enhanced by the presence of the nuclear Overhauser effect as a by-product of the decoupling. Since several protons with different chemical shifts might be coupled to a given ^{13}C, it is often desirable to decouple over a range of proton frequencies. This can be accomplished by the use of two or more proton frequencies, each with a substantial amount of power, since the effective range[3] of frequencies perturbed by H_2 is

$$\nu_2 \pm \frac{\gamma H_2}{2\pi}.$$ 　　　　　(8.6)

Complete decoupling over the entire range of proton chemical shifts is not possible with this procedure, for the amount of power required would damage the probe. Probably the best method for decoupling over a range of frequencies is the use of a "noise box," which generates rf over a wide frequency range.[10]

In the proton resonance spectra of complex molecules one often encounters the situation where a multiplet is hidden under other peaks, so that an accurate measurement of the chemical shift of the proton in question is impossible from the single resonance spectrum. In some cases spin decoupling may be used to collapse the multiplet and permit the observation of the collapsed line above interfering peaks. In other instances it is better to turn the experiment around and to irradiate in the vicinity of the overlapping peaks and to observe optimum decoupling of the other portion of the spin multiplet, which may be in a clear region of the spectrum. The latter procedure is also useful when a resonance is unobservable, not because of overlapping peaks, but because it is inherently broad due to coupling with a nucleus, such as ^{14}N, which relaxes rapidly. (We shall discuss this process in more detail in Chapter 9.)

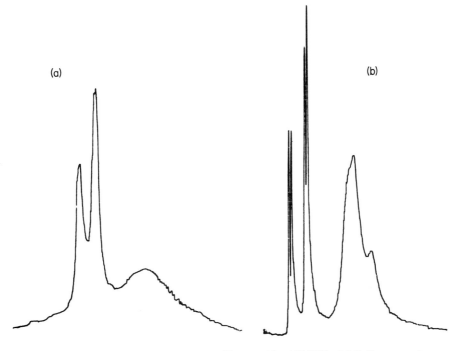

Fig. 8.5 Proton resonance spectrum of formamide at 60 MHz. (a) Ordinary spectrum; (b) ^{14}N decoupled by $\nu_2 \approx 4.3$ MHz.

The broadening effect of ^{14}N on the resonance of a proton coupled to it may alternatively be eliminated directly by decoupling the ^{14}N. An illustration of heteronuclear decoupling to sharpen proton resonance lines is given in Figure 8.5.

8.6 Determination of Chemical Shifts

When nuclei A and X are coupled, it is sometimes preferable to determine the spectrum of X, or at least its chemical shift, by a double resonance experiment, rather than by direct study of X. This situation occurs principally when

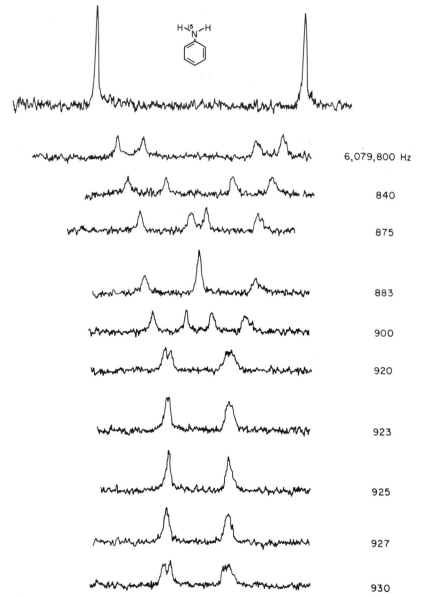

Fig. 8.6 Determination of the chemical shift of ^{15}N in $C_6H_5\,^{15}NH_2$ dissolved in dimethyl sulfoxide-d_6 at a concentration of 0.1 M. Top: Single resonance frequency sweep spectrum at 60 MHz. Others: Double resonance frequency sweep spectra with ν_2 as indicated and $\gamma_N H_2/2\pi \approx 80$ Hz ($^1J(^{15}N$—H)). For this A_2X system the A{X} double resonance experiment gives a closely spaced doublet at the optimum decoupling frequency, as shown by curves analogous to those in Figure 8.1.[4]

A is a nucleus of high sensitivity, such as ^{1}H or ^{19}F, while X is a nucleus of low sensitivity. For example, Figure 8.6 shows the $^{1}H\{^{15}N\}$ spectrum of aniline-^{15}N, where the ^{15}N chemical shift is determined by the frequency for optimum decoupling (6.079925 MHz in a field H_0 where TMS, which is used as an internal lock, resonates at 59.998168 MHz). Since the sensitivity of ^{15}N is only 0.001 as great as that of the proton, it is apparent that ^{15}N data on this compound at a concentration of 0.1 M could have been obtained in a direct ^{15}N resonance measurement only by *extensive* use of time-averaging procedures.

The decoupling experiment just discussed suffers from two disadvantages: First, a subjective judgment is required as to the pattern for the "best" decoupling; second, the technique does not lend itself to time-averaging procedures for further signal enhancement. Both of these shortcomings are

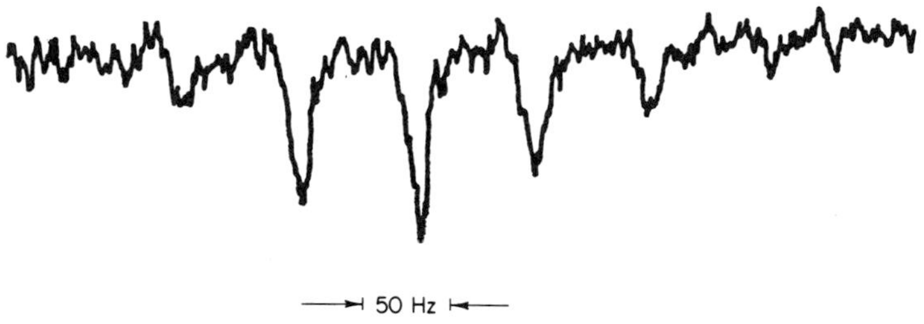

——⊢ 50 Hz ⊢——

Fig. 8.7 Use of internuclear double resonance (INDOR) to study the ^{29}Si resonance spectrum of SiF_3 $^{29}SiF_2SiF_3$ by monitoring the intensity of one of the ^{19}F lines while weakly irradiating in the vicinity of the ^{29}Si frequency (Johannesen[11]).

avoided in the elegant INDOR technique, where a rather weak perturbing field can be swept in the vicinity expected for the resonance of X, while the magnetic field and observation frequency are held rigidly fixed at one of the peaks in the A spectrum. As ν_2 passes in turn through the X lines, a change in intensity or frequency of the A line may occur, leading to a vertical movement of the recorder pen. Figure 8.7 shows a clear example of an INDOR spectrum, which in this case resembles an inverted X (^{29}Si) single resonance spectrum. The sweep rate of ν_2 must be kept very low to avoid transient effects, and in more complex spin systems the observed pattern may not be simply a replica of the X spectrum.

In the determination of chemical shifts by double resonance, careful consideration must be given to the exact manner in which the measurements are made, since this will affect the comparability of measurements for different substances. If the field H_0 is locked to the basic A frequency by means of an internal lock system employing an internal reference, such as TMS, then the

X decoupling frequencies for two or more compounds will be directly representative of the X chemical shifts in those compounds. On the other hand, if the magnetic field is swept, so that the value of H_0 when the double resonance is made is that required for resonance of the A nucleus, then a correction for the chemical shift of A in the different compounds must be made in order to obtain chemical shifts of X. With careful attention to such details, one can make very accurate chemical shift determinations in various nuclei, and in principle they could all ultimately be referred to TMS.

8.7 Relative Signs of Coupling Constants

Double resonance usually provides the best means of determining relative signs of coupling constants. In a weakly coupled (first-order) system it is, in fact, the only simple method of obtaining this information. We can illustrate the reasoning behind the use of double resonance by considering the weakly coupled AMX system. We know that the ordinary spectrum appears to be the same if any one of the signs of the three J's is changed. However, as we saw in Figure 7.10, a change in sign of one J actually interchanges pairs of lines. Double resonance serves as a probe of these line positions.

From a simple consideration of the origin of the lines in an AMX spectrum we can write the following expressions for the frequencies of the four A, the four M, and the four X lines:

$$\nu(A_i) = \nu_A + J_{AM} m_M + J_{AX} m_X;$$

$$\nu(M_i) = \nu_M + J_{AM} m_A + J_{MX} m_X; \qquad (8.7)$$

$$\nu(X_i) = \nu_X + J_{AX} m_A + J_{MX} m_M.$$

The small m's can independently assume the values $+\frac{1}{2}$ or $-\frac{1}{2}$ to account for all 12 lines. The index i runs from 1 to 4 and denotes the four A, four M, and four X lines in order of increasing frequency, that is, in the order in which they appear in the spectrum. For example, if both J_{AM} and J_{AX} are positive (and if γ's are positive), line A_1 arises from a "flip" of the A spin, while spins M and X remain oriented with the field (i.e., $m_M = m_X = -\frac{1}{2}$).

Suppose we wish to determine the relative signs of J_{AX} and J_{MX}. The experiment is most easily carried out and the situation most easily explained if J_{AX} and J_{MX} are both somewhat larger than the third coupling constant, J_{AM}. Figure 8.8 has been drawn for this situation, and in the following discussion we shall assume that this is the case. We must focus our attention on the A and M parts of the spectrum. Lines A_1 and A_2 differ only in the value of m_M assigned to them; they have the same value of m_X and may be said to correspond to the same X state. Identical statements may be made about the pairs of lines A_3 and A_4, M_1 and M_2, and M_3 and M_4. If J_{AX} and J_{MX} are both positive, then the low-frequency pair of A lines, A_1 and A_2, arise from the $-\frac{1}{2}$ X state, and the low-frequency pair of M lines, M_1 and M_2, also arise from the $-\frac{1}{2}$ X state. The high-frequency pairs in each case then, of course, arise from the $+\frac{1}{2}$ X state. If both J_{AX} and J_{MX} are negative, the $-\frac{1}{2}$ X state gives rise to the higher-frequency pair in *both* A and M spectra. If, however, J_{AX} and J_{MX} have opposite signs, then the $-\frac{1}{2}$ X state is responsible for the low-frequency pair in one case and the high-frequency pair in the other.

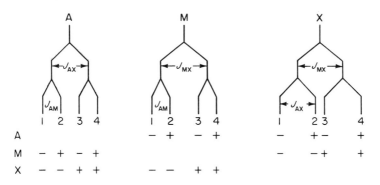

Fig. 8.8   Schematic representation of an AMX spectrum. Spin states ($+\frac{1}{2}$ or $-\frac{1}{2}$) are denoted by + or − signs. The situation depicted is that with all three J's positive.

By adjusting the strength of H_2 so that

$$|J_{AM}| < \frac{\gamma H_2}{2\pi} < |J_{AX}|, |J_{MX}| \tag{8.8}$$

and placing ν_2 at the average frequency of M_3 and M_4, we can obtain *selective decoupling* of only half the molecules—those with a specific X state, either $+\frac{1}{2}$ or $-\frac{1}{2}$. By observing the collapse of either the upper or lower pair of A lines, we can infer that J_{AX} and J_{MX} have the same or opposite signs, respectively. An example of this procedure is shown in Figure 8.9.

If the value of H_2 can be limited according to equation 8.8, the decoupling covers only a limited range of frequencies and produces the type of selective decoupling illustrated in Figure 8.9. If J_{AM} is not appreciably smaller than the other J's, the selective decoupling experiment can often be carried out anyway, but the collapse of a portion of the spectrum will not be so clear. For example, $^1H\{^{14}N\}$ selective decoupling experiment in ethyl isonitrile has been carried out to determine the relative signs of several J's, even though the spectral lines from the various ^{14}N states overlap considerably. The situation is depicted in

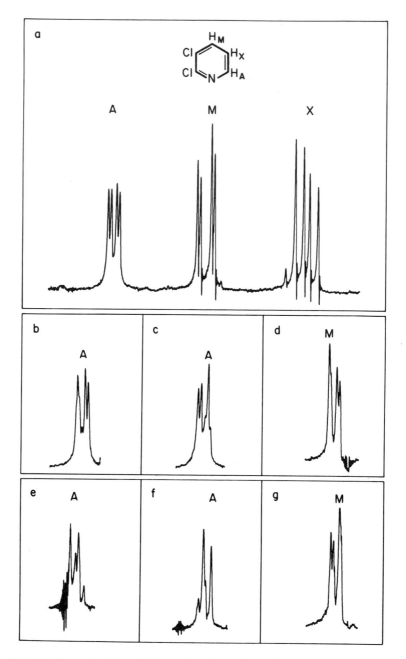

Fig. 8.9 Determination of the relative signs of coupling constants in 2,3-dichloro-pyridine at 100 MHz. (a) Unperturbed spectrum; (b)–(g) selectively decoupled portions of spectrum with decoupling frequency centered as follows: (b) lines M_1 and M_2, (c) M_3 and M_4, (d) A_1 and A_2, (e) X_3 and X_4, (f) X_1 and X_2, (g) A_3 and A_4. See Fig. 8.8 for numbering of lines. (The beat pattern seen in some spectra results from unwanted 60 Hz modulation.)

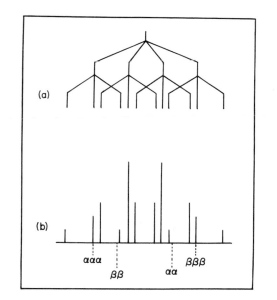

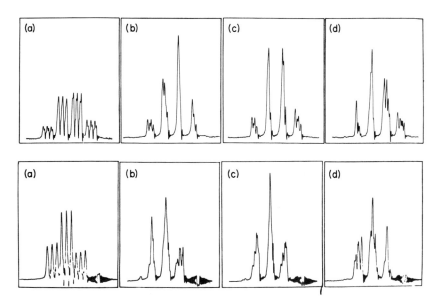

Fig. 8.10 Top: Schematic representation of the ^{14}N spectrum of CH_3CH_2NC, indicating the "centers of gravity" of the two extreme CH_3 spin states ($\alpha\alpha\alpha$ and $\beta\beta\beta$) and of the extreme spin states of the CH_2 protons ($\alpha\alpha$ and $\beta\beta$). Bottom: Frequency sweep *proton* NMR spectra of the CH_2 and CH_3 groups under identical irradiation conditions. (a) Ordinary spectrum; (b) $\nu_2 = 4.334476$ MHz; (c) $\nu_2 = 4.334479$ MHz; (d) $\nu_2 = 4.334481$ MHz. The beat pattern is a spinning sideband of the TMS lock signal. (J. A. Ferretti and L. Paolillo, unpublished results.)

Figure 8.10. The upper portion of the figure shows (a) the first-order splitting expected for the ^{14}N spectrum due to coupling with the CH$_3$ protons ($|^3J|$ = 2.43 Hz) and the CH$_2$ protons ($|^2J|$ = 1.98 Hz); and (b) the resultant ^{14}N spectrum with the "centers of gravity" of the extreme CH$_3$ spin states indicated by $\alpha\alpha\alpha$ and $\beta\beta\beta$ and the centers of gravity of the extreme CH$_2$ spin states by $\alpha\alpha$ and $\beta\beta$. The situation shown is for ^2J and ^3J of opposite signs; if they had the same sign, $\alpha\alpha$ and $\beta\beta$ would be interchanged. The bottom portion of Figure 8.10 shows the effect on the CH$_2$ and CH$_3$ signals, respectively, of irradiating near the ^{14}N frequency, with ν_2 increasing from (b) to (d). Note that the left-hand portion of the CH$_3$ multiplet and the right-hand portion of the CH$_2$ multiplet undergo partial decoupling at the same time, as expected for the labeling of spin states as given. Thus ^2J and ^3J have opposite signs.

Spin tickling may also be used for the determination of the relative signs of J's. This technique is particularly valuable with strongly coupled spin systems. Since the sign determination is only one aspect of a general analysis, we shall defer a discussion of this application to the next section.

8.8 Determination of Energy Level Arrangements

The analysis of a complex spectrum to obtain chemical shifts and coupling constants is often a perplexing problem when it involves a strongly coupled system, such as ABC or AA'BB'. The basic problem is that the observed frequencies are not related directly to the chemical shifts and coupling constants, but represent only differences in the energy levels. If a complete and accurate energy level diagram can be constructed from the observed spectrum, the determination of the chemical shifts and coupling constants can be carried out rapidly and reliably by an iterative computer program. Spin tickling and other double resonance techniques are extremely valuable in constructing such an energy level diagram.

In building up an energy level diagram, we shall rely on *connected transitions*, which are spectral transitions with an energy level in common. Two cases may be distinguished: If the common level lies between the other levels involved in the transitions, the transitions are said to constitute a *progressive* pair; if the common level is higher or lower than both of the other levels, the transitions form a *regressive* pair.

We saw in Figure 8.3 that irradiation with a weak H_2 of one of the X lines in an AX system caused each of the A lines to split into a closely spaced doublet. A more careful analysis of the energy levels involved in an AX or an AB system (Figure 8.11) shows that transitions A$_1$ and A$_2$ have no energy level in common, but that A_1 and B_1 form a regressive pair, while A_1 and B_2 constitute a progressive pair. It has been shown that a weak irradiation of one of a pair of connected transitions causes the other to split, the two components of the split peak being extremely sharp for a regressive pair of transitions but rather broad for a progressive pair.[12] Transitions not connected to the irradi-

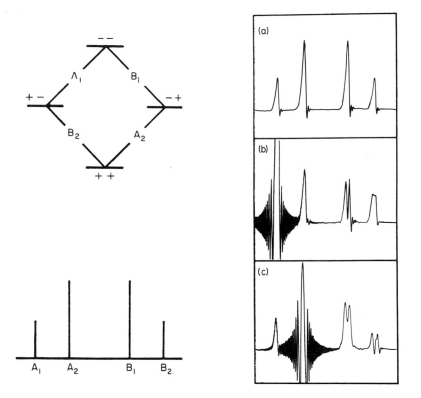

Fig. 8.11 Left: Energy level pattern, transitions, and spectrum (schematic) for an AB system. Right: Proton NMR spectrum (frequency sweep) for 2-bromo-5-chlorothiophene (a) unperturbed, (b) with ν_2 centered at line A_1, and (c) with ν_2 at line A_2. The beat pattern results from the passage of ν_1 through ν_2 during the scan (Freeman and Anderson[12]).

ated one are unaffected by the tickling irradiation. These points are clearly demonstrated for an AB system in Figure 8.11.

The generalizations given in the previous paragraph apply to any spin system, not just AB. Spin tickling may thus be used to identify progressive and regressive connected transitions and hence aid in the construction of the energy level diagram. An example of the repeated use of tickling in an ABC system is given in Figure 8.12. The four tickling experiments illustrated are

sufficient to map out an array of connected transitions. The results are conveniently represented in Figure 8.13, where the 2^3 states of the ABC system
form the 8 corners of a cube with the 12 edges of the cube representing the

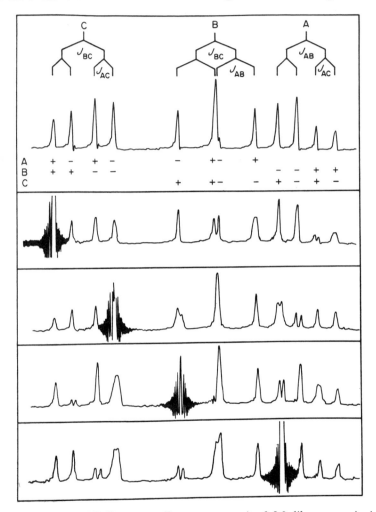

Fig. 8.12   Proton NMR spectra (frequency sweep) of 2,3-dibromopropionic acid.
Top: Single resonance spectrum. Others: ν_2 centered on line giving beat pattern (Freeman
and Anderson[12]).

allowed transitions (excluding combinations; see Section 7.14). From the
arrangement of energy levels the relative signs of the coupling constants can
be determined, and from the observed line frequencies energy values can be
assigned to each state. An iterative computer program then permits the

establishment of the values of chemical shifts and coupling constants (see Section 7.13).

Spin tickling has been applied to more complex systems, as well. The analysis of an AA'BB' spectrum, which is a formidable task by using an iterative computer program and only the ordinary spectrum, can be accomplished readily by systematic repeated tickling experiments.[13] The signs of all J's are determined unambiguously by this procedure, whereas a computer-aided analysis often does not permit the establishment of some signs.

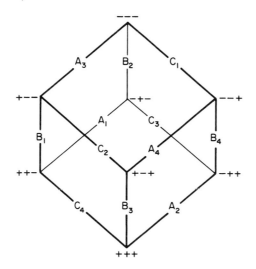

Fig. 8.13 Representation of the 8 spin states of an ABC system and 12 allowed transitions. Spin states are labeled for $J_{AB} > 0$ and both J_{AC} and $J_{BC} < 0$. Combination transitions are not shown (Freeman and Anderson[12]).

Other double resonance techniques may also be used to establish an energy level diagram. The nuclear Overhauser effect can be used in much the same manner as tickling to determine progressive and regressive pairs of transitions. Another double resonance technique, *transitory selective irradiation* (TSI), which consists of applying H_2 for a time short compared with T_1, can be used in establishing an energy level diagram, as well as in other applications.[3]

8.9 Other Applications

Our treatment of double resonance has included only the most widely used techniques as applied to some frequently occurring problems. Many very elegant double resonance techniques have been developed for studies of relaxation effects, chemical exchange, and relative signs of J's in systems not amenable to the simple procedures we have described. An excellent review of double resonance has been published.[3]

References

1. E. B. Baker, *J. Chem. Phys.* **37**, 911 (1962).

2. W. A. Anderson, *Phys. Rev.* **102**, 151 (1956).

3. For a review of NMDR, see R. A. Hoffman and S. Forsen, *Progr. NMR Spectroscopy* **1**, 15–204 (1966).

4. W. A. Anderson and R. Freeman, *J. Chem. Phys.* **37**, 85 (1962).

5. R. Freeman and D. H. Whiffen, *Proc. Phys. Soc.* (*London*) **79**, 794 (1962).

6. A. W. Overhauser, *Phys. Rev.* **92**, 411 (1953).

7. J. N. Shoolery, *Disc. Faraday Soc.* **34**, 104 (1962).

8. F. A. L. Anet and A. J. R. Bourn, *J. Am. Chem. Soc.* **87**, 5250 (1965); K. Nakanishi, *Pure Appl. Chem.* **14**, 89 (1967); J. G. Colson, P. T. Lansbury, and F. D. Saeva, *J. Am. Chem. Soc.* **89**, 4987 (1967).

9. R. Kaiser, *J. Chem. Phys.* **39**, 2435 (1963).

10. R. R. Ernst, *J. Chem. Phys.* **45**, 3845 (1966).

11. R. Johannesen, *J. Chem. Phys.* **47**, 955 (1967).

12. R. Freeman and W. A. Anderson, *J. Chem. Phys.* **37**, 2053 (1962).

13. E. Lustig, E. P. Ragelis, N. Duy, and J. A. Ferretti, *J. Am. Chem. Soc.* **89**, 3953 (1967).

Problems

1. Use Figures 8.1 and 8.2 to prepare plots similar to those in Figure 8.3 for a *field* sweep homonuclear double resonance experiment.

2. The proton NMR spectrum of a complex molecule shows clearly the A doublet of an AB spectrum, but the B portion is obscured by other spectral lines. It is desired to use double resonance to determine the chemical shift ν_B. (a) If $J_{AB} = 10$ Hz, what is the minimum value of H_2 needed to insure complete decoupling of the A doublet? (b) If this amount of power is used and if optimum decoupling is obtained when ν_1 is at 173 Hz (the frequency of the collapsed A doublet) and $\nu_2 = 243$ Hz, what is ν_B? (All frequencies are measured with respect to TMS as zero.)

3. A frequency sweep selective decoupling experiment is to be performed to determine the relative signs of J_{AM} and J_{AX} in a three-proton AMX system. If J_{MX} is the smallest of the three coupling constants in absolute value, sketch the spectrum and indicate where the decoupling field should be applied. Predict the results for J_{AM} and J_{AX} of the same sign and of opposite signs.

4. How would your answer to question 3 have changed, if nucleus M were ^{15}N ($\gamma < 0$), while the other nuclei remained protons?

Chapter 9

Relaxation

In Chapter 2 we found that a perturbed nuclear spin system relaxes to its equilibrium state or steady state by first-order processes characterized by two relaxation times: T_1, the spin-lattice, or longitudinal, relaxation time; and T_2, the spin-spin, or transverse, relaxation time. In this chapter we shall examine briefly the principal processes that govern the magnitude of the relaxation times. We shall also explore some of the chemical applications of relaxation phenomena and indicate the manner in which T_1 and T_2 can be measured.

9.1 Processes for Spin-Lattice Relaxation

We shall restrict ourselves to consideration of relaxation in liquids. The principal processes that lead to spin-lattice relaxation involve a fluctuating magnetic field in the sample due to some sort of molecular motion.[1] This fluctuating field can be thought of as containing components over a range of frequencies, and those components at the Larmor frequency of the nucleus ν_0 can interact with the nuclear spin, which is precessing at ν_0. We shall consider the following types of magnetic fluctuations:

(1) Fields arising from the magnetic moments of nuclei other than the one being relaxed (this is the most general relaxation process, since it must always occur with any sample).

(2) Fields due to an anisotropy in electronic shielding (chemical shift) of the nucleus.

(3) Fields from paramagnetic materials in the sample.

In addition, if the nucleus in question has a quadrupole moment $(I > \frac{1}{2})$, it may be relaxed by an interaction between its quadrupole moment and fluctuating electric, rather than magnetic, fields.

9.2 Nuclear Magnetic Dipole Interactions

Any magnetic nucleus in a molecule supplies an instantaneous magnetic dipole field, which is proportional to the magnetic moment of the nucleus. As the molecule tumbles in solution under the influence of Brownian motion, this field fluctuates in magnitude and direction. The effectiveness of this fluctuating field in relaxing other nuclei depends on (a) the magnitudes of the nuclear moments, (b) the distance between the nuclei, and (c) the frequency distribution of the molecular motion. Factor (a) means that nuclei such as ^1H and ^{19}F are most effective in bringing about relaxation, while factor (b) indicates the dependence on concentration of molecules possessing magnetic nuclei. For example, pure liquid benzene has $T_1 = 19$ sec, while a dilute solution of benzene in CS_2 (which has no magnetic nuclei) shows $T_1 = 60$ sec.[2]

Factor (c) arises from the fact that it is only the components of motion at the Larmor frequency of the relaxing nucleus that are effective in the relaxation process. The theory of Brownian motion has been applied to spin-lattice relaxation by Bloembergen, Purcell, and Pound, whose resulting theory of relaxation (the "BPP theory") serves as the basis for our discussion.[3] They utilized a *correlation time* τ_c, which serves as a measure of the average time that two nuclei remain in a given relative orientation. For molecular rotation the correlation time may be thought of approximately as the length of time that the molecule requires on the average to rotate through an angle of a radian, while for translation the correlation time is roughly the time it takes the molecule to move one molecular diameter. The rotational process is related to an *intra*molecular relaxation, and the translational process is related to *inter*molecular relaxation. In general, both types of relaxation are important, and both depend on the viscosity of the medium and very critically on the size and shape of the molecules involved.

From a quantitative treatment, BPP showed that

$$\frac{1}{T_1} = \frac{(\text{constant})\tau_c}{1 + 4\pi^2 \nu_0^2 \tau_c^2}. \tag{9.1}$$

For rapid molecular motion

$$\frac{1}{\tau_c} \gg 2\pi\nu_0 \tag{9.2}$$

and the equation reduces to

$$\frac{1}{T_1} \propto \tau_c. \tag{9.3}$$

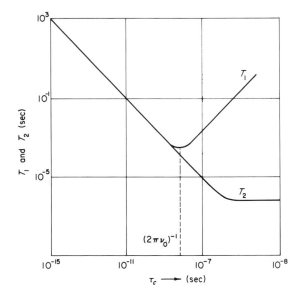

Fig. 9.1   The variation of T_1 and T_2 with correlation time, τ_c (Bloembergen, Purcell, and Pound[3]).

For very slow motion

$$\frac{1}{\tau_c} \ll 2\pi\nu_0 \tag{9.4}$$

and

$$\frac{1}{T_1} \propto \frac{1}{\tau_c}. \tag{9.5}$$

Overall, the variation of T_1 with τ_c can be depicted graphically as shown in Figure 9.1. A correlation time

$$\tau_c = \frac{1}{2\pi\nu_0} \tag{9.6}$$

leads to the most effective spin-lattice relaxation, with T_1 increasing for shorter or longer τ_c.

The dependence of T_2 upon τ_c is also given in Figure 9.1. It coincides with T_1 for short τ_c, but at long τ_c, where the slow molecular motions are inefficient in bringing about spin-lattice relaxation, T_2 departs drastically from T_1. The reason is that a long correlation time permits dipole-dipole interactions to become effective in leading to broad lines, that is, short T_2's. The static local magnetic field at a nucleus i due to another nuclear moment j is

$$H(\text{local}) = \pm \frac{\mu}{r_{ij}^3} (3\cos^2\theta_{ij} - 1). \tag{9.7}$$

In this expression r_{ij} is the magnitude of a vector joining nuclei i and j, while θ_{ij} is the angle between this vector and the applied field H_0.[4] In a solid, where the θ_{ij} are fixed, the local field due to nearby nuclei can be quite large, about 14 gauss for a proton at a distance of 1 Å. Since near neighbors have random orientations of spins with respect to H_0, the spread of fields experienced by nuclei in the sample can be of this order of magnitude. The corresponding line width is about 60 kHz, giving T_2 of the order of 10^{-5} sec.

When the molecules in which the magnetic nuclei reside are in motion, we must consider an average value of θ_{ij}. If the motion is random and rapid (short τ_c) $\cos^2\theta_{ij}$ can be averaged over all space to give $\langle\cos^2\theta_{ij}\rangle_{av} = \frac{1}{3}$. This value inserted in equation 9.7 gives zero local field from this source. (More accurate calculations show that a very small residual effect remains.[4]) Thus for small τ_c, $T_1 \approx T_2$.

For most small molecules $T_1 \approx T_2 \approx 0.1$–10 sec, while small polymers in solution are nearer the minimum in the T_1 curve. Here incomplete averaging of θ_{ij} leads to broader lines. Changes in viscosity, often brought about by temperature variation, may change τ_c substantially. Studies of polymers in solution are usually carried out, when possible, at elevated temperature in order to decrease τ_c and thus sharpen the resonance lines.

When there are several chemically different magnetic nuclei in a molecule, there is no assurance that relaxation times will be identical for all nuclei. Differences in interatomic distances and different internal degrees of freedom can lead to substantial variations in T_1 and T_2. For example, in toluene the aromatic protons have $T_1 = 16$ sec, while for the methyl protons T_1 is only 9 sec.[2]

9.3 The Effect of Anisotropic Shielding

In Chapter 2 we saw that the magnetic field at the nucleus is given by

$$\mathbf{H}(\text{nucleus}) = \mathbf{H}_0 - \boldsymbol{\sigma}\mathbf{H}_0, \tag{9.8}$$

where σ, the shielding factor, is a tensor. We found that an anisotropy in σ may result in pronounced effects on chemical shifts. An anisotropy in σ may also furnish a mechanism for relaxation, since as the molecule tumbles in solution, the field at the nucleus is continually changing in magnitude. The components of random tumbling motion at the Larmor frequency can then lead to spin-lattice relaxation.

This relaxation mechanism is potentially important but has been studied very little. It has been suggested as the explanation for the short relaxation time for ^{13}C in $^{13}CS_2$ relative to that in $^{13}CCl_4$.[5] The latter molecule has tetrahedral symmetry, hence can have no anisotropy in σ.

If σ is axially symmetric, theory predicts that

$$\frac{1}{T_1} = \tfrac{2}{15}\gamma^2 H^2(\sigma^{\|} - \sigma^{\perp})^2 \tau_c \tag{9.9}$$

where $\sigma^{\|}$ and $\sigma^{\perp}$ refer to the components of the shielding tensor parallel and perpendicular to the axis of symmetry. The interesting point in equation 9.9 is that T_1 decreases quadratically with increasing magnetic field. Experimental evidence for such variation has been reported for ^{19}F.[6]

9.4 Electric Quadrupole Relaxation

An electrical analogy to the relaxation mechanism discussed in the preceding section occurs in molecules that have an asymmetric electric field around a nucleus that has an electric quadrupole moment. Molecular tumbling now leads to fluctuating *electric* fields around the nucleus, which can cause transitions (flipping of spins) among the nuclear quadrupole energy levels. The effect is observed in the NMR just as though the relaxation occurred by a magnetic mechanism.

In the region of rapid molecular tumbling characteristic of small molecules $(\tau_c \ll 1/2\pi\nu_0)$, the theory of quadrupole relaxation gives

$$\frac{1}{T_1} = \tfrac{3}{8}e^4\hbar^2 q^2 Q^2 \tau_c \tag{9.10}$$

where Q is the nuclear quadrupole moment, q is a measure of the electric field gradient of the electrons surrounding the nucleus, and e and $\hbar$ are the usual fundamental constants.[1]

Nuclei with large quadrupole moments may relax so rapidly that their resonance lines are extremely broad, since

$$\nu_{1/2} = \frac{1}{\pi T_2} \geqslant \frac{1}{\pi T_1}. \tag{9.11}$$

For example, ^{35}Cl that is covalently bound may have a line width of several KHz. The rapid relaxation of the nucleus also means that it does not remain in a given state long enough to couple with other nuclei in the molecule (see Section 10.3). Of course, a spherically symmetric environment, such as Cl$^-$, eliminates the quadrupole relaxation mechanism and leads to much sharper lines.

Some nuclei, such as ^{14}N and ^{2}H, relax by the quadrupole mechanism at a rate sufficient to lead to only moderate broadening of the resonance lines, for example, ~100 Hz for ^{14}N in many compounds. In this case the effect of spin coupling is not completely eliminated, but the lines of nuclei, such as protons, coupled to the more rapidly relaxing nucleus are considerably broadened. The reason for this broadening will become clear in the next chapter. Again, a symmetric electrical environment precludes quadrupole relaxation. In ^{14}N such symmetry is found in NH_4^+ and symmetric derivatives, and in isonitriles, R—NC. In these cases, coupling of protons to ^{14}N is readily observed (see, e.g., Figure 8.10).

9.5 Relaxation by Paramagnetic Substances

In Section 9.2 we discussed relaxation arising from the fluctuating fields from magnetic nuclei in randomly tumbling molecules. If paramagnetic substances are also present in the solution, the magnetic moments from the unpaired electrons can furnish the basis for fluctuating magnetic fields. The major difference is that the electron magnetic moment is almost 1000 times as large as the largest nuclear moment, so that relaxation by paramagnetic substances can be extremely effective. The BPP theory applied to paramagnetic materials gives

$$\frac{1}{T_1} = \frac{4\pi^2 \gamma^2 \eta N \mu_{\text{eff}}^2}{kT} \tag{9.12}$$

where η is the viscosity of the solution, N is the concentration of paramagnetic material (number per milliliter), and μ_{eff} is the "effective" magnetic moment of the paramagnetic substance.[1] μ_{eff} is essentially the value of μ determined from susceptibility measurements provided the spin-lattice relaxation time of the electron, τ_s, is long compared with the diffusional correlation time τ_c. In this case the orientation of the electron magnetic moment remains fixed during the relaxation process. When $\tau_s < \tau_c$, τ_s should really be used in the treatment, but if τ_c is to be retained, the real μ must be replaced by a smaller effective μ_{eff}. Ions such as Fe^{3+}, Cr^{3+}, Mn^{2+}, and Cu^{2+} have $\mu_{\text{eff}} \approx \mu$, while others, such as Fe^{2+}, Co^{2+}, and Ni^{2+} have $\mu_{\text{eff}} < \mu$.[1]

Molecular oxygen is a fairly effective paramagnetic relaxing agent. Its role in broadening NMR lines was mentioned in Chapter 3.

If the paramagnetic substance forms a complex with the molecule whose NMR is being studied, unpaired electron density may be transferred, and the nucleus relaxed by another mechanism depending on a "contact" interaction. (The effect of contact interaction on chemical shift was mentioned in Section 4.10.) The theory of this effect[7] shows that the magnetic field fluctuates with a correlation time equal to τ_s. For normal values of τ_s, these fluctuations are at too low a frequency to make an appreciable contribution to shortening T_1, but they do lead to a reduced value for T_2.

9.6 Chemical Applications

As we saw in Chapter 2, a knowledge of at least the orders of magnitude of relaxation times is essential to an understanding of the conditions under which NMR spectra can be obtained and of the appearance of the spectra. In addition, information of direct chemical value can often be obtained from measurements of T_1 and T_2 or of their variation under specified conditions. For example, the degree of crystallinity of large polymers or the amount of molecular flexibility in complex systems can often be inferred from NMR relaxation times.

The presence of paramagnetic metal ions and of charge asymmetry in the presence of nuclear quadrupole moments both result in greatly reduced relaxation times. The large effect on T_1 and T_2 permits paramagnetic ions and nonspherical nuclei to be used as sensitive probes of certain types of molecular structure or interaction. As we shall see in Chapter 10, when a nucleus changes rapidly between two or more environments where it has different relaxation times, the *measured* T_1 and T_2 are intermediate between those for the two environments. A paramagnetic metal ion that complexes to a ligand may cause a considerable reduction in T_1 or in T_2 for only specific nuclei in the ligand. For example, Figure 9.2 shows the proton NMR spectra of the glycylglycinate anion in the presence of Cu^{2+} ion. The paramagnetic cupric ion is known to complex with the amino terminal end of the glycylglycinate, so that the CH_2 protons adjacent to the nitrogen are principally relaxed by the copper. The ligand is present in large excess, and the copper ion exchanges rapidly among various ligand molecules. The effect on T_2 is observable because the line width for a 1:1 ratio of ligand to Cu^{2+} would be several kilohertz; hence the average that is observed is still fairly large. Similar studies using paramagnetic metal ions to probe hydration of biopolymers have also been carried out.[9]

The exchange of a nonspherical nucleus between symmetric and asymmetric electrical environments leads to similar results. For example, ^{35}Cl NMR has been used as a probe of protein structure. In this experiment[10] a given chlorine exchanges between a covalently bound environment, where it may have a relaxation time of less than a millisecond, and the symmetric environment of a Cl$^-$ ion, the latter being present in large excess.

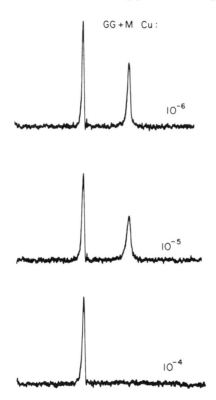

Fig. 9.2 Proton NMR spectrum of glycylglycinate ion, $NH_2CH_2C(O)NHCH_2COO^-$ (0.5 M in D$_2$O) as a function of addition of Cu^{2+} (10^{-6} to 10^{-4} M) (Li, Scruggs, and Becker[8]).

9.7 Measurement of Relaxation Times

Both T_1 and T_2 may be measured directly by high resolution NMR techniques if they are in the appropriate ranges. We saw in Section 2.5 that repetitive scans through a resonance after it has initially been saturated may permit a determination of T_1 from the growth of the signal amplitude. This procedure is limited to values of T_1 greater than a few seconds in order that a sufficient number of scans be obtained to permit accurate measurement. In general, the longer T_1, the better this direct method will be. On the other hand, only short T_2's can be measured directly, either by the relation

$$T_2 = \frac{1}{\pi \nu_{1/2}} \qquad (9.13)$$

or by the time required for decay of ringing. For long T_2 the *true* line width is very small, but the *observed* width is then determined by magnetic field inhomogeneity. Since width due to inhomogeneity is likely to be *at least* 0.1 Hz, only lines that are appreciably broader can be used for this purpose; hence for such direct measurement T_2 must be smaller than about 0.5 sec.

For shorter values of T_1 and longer values of T_2 measurements are usually made by some sort of *pulse* technique. A short rf pulse is applied to the sample and a resultant resonance property studied. We mentioned one type of pulse experiment in connection with Fourier transform spectroscopy in Chapter 3.

The principle of the method can best be understood by considering the behavior of the macroscopic magnetization (as we did in Sections 2.8 and 2.9). The geometric representation is simplified if we adopt a coordinate system that is rotating at the Larmor frequency corresponding to H_0. If we apply an rf field H_1 oscillating at the Larmor frequency, then in the rotating coordinate system H_1 is simply fixed along the x axis. If H_1 is made powerful but is applied only as a short pulse, so that relaxation can be ignored during the period that the pulse is applied (e.g., 100 μsec), the effect of H_1 is to rotate the magnetization M away from the direction of H_0 with an angular velocity of γH_1. If the pulse has a length t_w, then the magnetization is rotated through an angle $\gamma H_1 t_w$. By appropriate choice of the rf power and pulse length, this angle can be made 90° or 180°, and the pulse is called a 90° or 180° pulse.

If a 90° pulse is applied, the magnetization at the end of the pulse lies entirely in the xy plane, where it rotates at the Larmor frequency and continues to give a signal in the receiver coil of the spectrometer. Because of spin-spin relaxation (and magnetic field inhomogeneity), the magnitude of the magnetization in the xy plane decreases with a time constant of T_2^*, the "effective" spin-spin relaxation time, which is often governed by field inhomogeneity. As a result, the signal in the receiver coil decays exponentially; this signal is termed a *free induction decay*.

T_1 is often measured from free induction decays. One common method is the following: A 90° pulse first turns the equilibrium magnetization M_0 from the z axis to the xy plane. The height of the free induction signal immediately after turning off the pulse is proportional to M_0. The signal decays, as pointed out in the preceding paragraph, with time constant T_2^*. However, concurrently with this decay the magnetization along the z axis is being reestablished by spin-lattice relaxation. If a second 90° pulse is now applied at time τ after the first pulse, the height of the free induction signal immediately after the pulse will in general be smaller than M_0 if the equilibrium magnetization along the z axis has not been achieved. By measuring the initial heights at various values of τ between the two pulses, one can determine T_1 with high accuracy over a wide range of values.

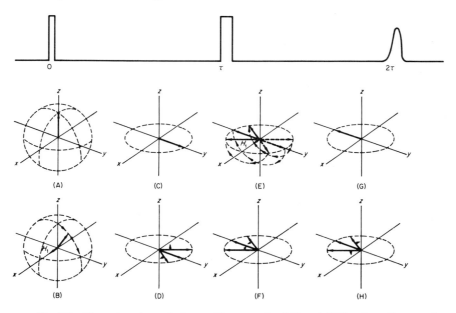

Fig. 9.3 The spin-echo technique with successive 90° and 180° pulses. See text for discussion (Carr and Purcell[12]).

It is clear that free induction decay cannot generally be used to measure T_2, since the lifetime of the decay is often dominated by the effect of magnetic field inhomogeneity. The problem of inhomogeneity is circumvented by an ingenious type of pulse experiment called the *spin-echo* technique.[11, 12] One type of spin-echo experiment that is useful in determining T_2 is illustrated in Figure 9.3. The top portion of the figure gives the actual signals observed, while the lower portion depicts the behavior of **M** in the rotating coordinate system. The experiment proceeds as follows.

(A) Initially the magnetization lies along the z axis parallel to $\mathbf{H_0}$. (B) A pulse is applied which begins to tip **M** toward the y axis in the rotating coordinate system. ($\mathbf{H_1}$ is shown along the rotating x axis.) (C) At time t_w the pulse has achieved a 90° rotation of **M** and is turned off. Since t_w has been selected to be much less than T_2, no loss of phase coherence has yet occurred (see Section 2.8). (D) Because of magnetic field inhomogeneity, nuclei in different parts of the sample have different Larmor frequencies. We can think of a number of macroscopic magnetizations $\mathbf{m}_i$ arising from different portions of the sample. After the pulse, these $\mathbf{m}_i$ begin to "fan out" in the rotating xy plane since they rotate at rates different from that of the coordinate system. The resultant free induction signal decays with time constant T_2^*.

(E) After a time τ a pulse of length $2t_w$ is applied. This is a 180° pulse and rotates each magnetization vector $\mathbf{m}_i$ through 180°. (F) Since each $\mathbf{m}_i$ continues to precess in the same direction as before, the resultant motion causes the vectors to draw together, rather than continue to fan out. (G) At time 2τ the vectors coalesce, leading to a strong resultant magnetization in the negative y direction. This magnetization induces in the receiver coil an observable signal, the "echo." This echo is less intense than the original initial free induction, since spin-spin relaxation has occurred during the interim. Thus, while all $\mathbf{m}_i$ are brought into phase at 2τ, each $\mathbf{m}_i$ is less intense because the nuclei contributing to it have lost phase coherence. (H) Following the echo, the vectors $\mathbf{m}_i$ again fan out, leading to another free induction decay.

In principle, T_2 can be obtained from a 90°–180° spin-echo experiment by measuring the height of the echo as a function of τ. Actually, the experiment as described does not lead directly to measurement of T_2 because of the effect of molecular diffusion. Motion of molecules from one part of the nonhomogeneous field to another leads to an imperfect clustering of the $\mathbf{m}_i$ at 2τ, so that the loss of intensity in the echo is due to diffusion, as well as to spin-spin relaxation. It has been shown that the amplitude of the echo is

$$M(\text{echo}) \propto \exp\left[-\frac{2\tau}{T_2} - \tfrac{2}{3}\gamma^2 G^2 D\tau^3\right] \tag{9.14}$$

where D is the diffusion constant and G is the mean value of the magnetic field gradient across the sample.[12]

The effects of diffusion can be removed by a modification of this experiment in which 180° pulses are applied at τ, 3τ, 5τ, and so on, and echoes are observed at 2τ, 4τ, 6τ, and so on.[12] On the other hand a large, known field gradient can be introduced and the spin-echo technique utilized to obtain values of diffusion coefficients. T_1 can also be measured by the spin-echo technique by appropriate use of spaced 90° pulses.

When two or more chemically shifted or spin-coupled nuclei are involved, the free induction decays and spin echoes are more complex, and the theoretical treatment correspondingly more difficult. However, information not only on relaxation times, but also on chemical shifts and coupling constants can be extracted from experiments on such systems.

References

1. J. A. Pople, W. G. Schneider, and H. J. Bernstein, "High Resolution NMR," Chapter 9. McGraw-Hill, New York, 1959.

2. G. W. Nederbragt and C. A. Reilly, *J. Chem. Phys.* **24**, 1110 (1956).

3. N. Bloembergen, E. M. Purcell, and R. V. Pound, *Phys. Rev.* **73**, 679 (1948).

4. E. R. Andrew, "Nuclear Magnetic Resonance." Cambridge Univ. Press, London and New York, 1956.

5. H. M. McConnell and C. H. Holm, *J. Chem. Phys.* **25**, 1289 (1956).

6. H. S. Gutowsky and D. E. Woessner, *Phys. Rev.* **104**, 843 (1956).

7. N. Bloembergen, *J. Chem. Phys.* **27**, 572 (1957).

8. N. C. Li, R. L. Scruggs, and E. D. Becker, *J. Am. Chem. Soc.* **84**, 4650 (1962).

9. J. Eisinger, R. G. Shulman, and B. M. Szymanski, *J. Chem. Phys.* **36**, 1721 (1962).

10. T. R. Stengle and J. D. Baldeschwieler, *Proc. Nat. Acad. Sci. USA* **55**, 1020 (1966); *J. Am. Chem. Soc.* **89**, 3045 (1967).

11. E. L. Hahn, *Phys. Rev.* **80**, 580 (1950).

12. H. Y. Carr and E. M. Purcell, *Phys. Rev.* **94**, 630 (1954).

Problems

1. Show that H(local) in equation 9.7 averages to zero as θ_{ij} assumes all possible values.

2. Determine the structures of the compounds giving Spectra 31–33, Appendix B.

Chapter 10

Effects of Exchange Processes

Many NMR spectra are extremely sensitive to the rates of processes that cause particular nuclei to exchange among various sites. In this chapter we shall investigate the conditions under which exchange affects spectra and see how NMR spectra can be used to measure certain reaction rates.

10.1 Spectra of Exchanging Systems

Before taking up the quantitative relations between NMR spectra and rate processes, it may be helpful to develop a semiquantitative treatment based on nuclear precession. While not mathematically entirely sound, this treatment provides some insight into the processes that occur.

Suppose a given nucleus can exchange between two sites, A and B, and that in these sites it has resonance (Larmor) frequencies ν_A and ν_B, respectively.*

* The two sites might be, for example, an alcohol, ROH, and a phenol, ϕOH, in a mixture of these two substances, where the OH proton exchanges between them; or the sites might be the axial and equatorial positions for a proton in a molecule such as cyclohexane, which interconverts between two conformations. In the former case there is a breaking of bonds and a "chemical reaction" type of exchange:

$$ROH_a + \phi OH_b \rightleftharpoons ROH_b + \phi OH_a$$

In the latter case the exchange is "positional"; e.g.,

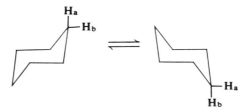

The same treatment applies to both situations, so far as chemical shifts are concerned. (However, see Section 10.3 for a distinction with regard to spin coupling.)

214

We shall arbitrarily take $\nu_A > \nu_B$. To simplify the discussion, we shall assume that the nucleus has an equal probability of being in the two sites; hence the lifetime of the nucleus in state A, τ_A, must equal that in state B:

$$\tau_A = \tau_B = 2\tau. \tag{10.1}$$

(The factor of 2 is used for consistency with the expressions given in the following section.)

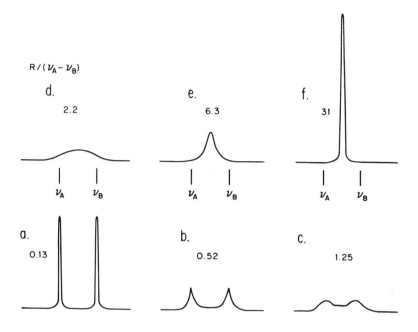

Fig. 10.1 Calculated line shapes for various values of the exchange lifetime relative to the difference in frequency of the two equally populated sites. Exchange rate $R \equiv 1/2\tau$, where $2\tau = \tau_A = \tau_B$. From tables[1] based on an equation similar to equation 10.6.

Consider a coordinate system that rotates about H_0, in the same direction in which the nuclei precess, at a frequency

$$\nu_0 = \tfrac{1}{2}(\nu_A + \nu_B). \tag{10.2}$$

In the rotating coordinate system a nucleus at site A precesses at $(\nu_A - \nu_0)$, while a nucleus at site B precesses at $(\nu_0 - \nu_B)$; that is, it appears in this rotating frame to be precessing in a direction opposite that of the nucleus in site A. We can now distinguish the following four cases regarding exchange rates.

1. *Very slow exchange.* The lifetime at each site, 2τ, is long, so that a given nucleus enters site A and precesses many times at frequency $(\nu_A - \nu_0)$

before leaving site A and entering site B. The result is that interaction with the rf field occurs, and in the fixed laboratory frame of reference a resonance line appears at ν_A. An identical situation occurs for the nucleus at site B. Thus the spectrum consists of two sharp lines at ν_A and ν_B, just as it would in the absence of exchange. (See Figure 10.1a.)

2. *Moderately slow exchange.* The lifetime 2τ is now somewhat smaller than the value in the preceding paragraph. By the familiar Heisenberg uncertainty principle,

$$\Delta E \cdot \Delta t \sim h \tag{10.3}$$

where ΔE is the uncertainty in energy corresponding to an uncertainty in time of measurement Δt. In our case $\Delta t \approx \tau$ so that the uncertainty in energy is reflected in an increased line width*

$$\nu_{1/2} \approx \frac{\Delta E}{h} \approx \frac{h}{\Delta t \cdot h} \approx \frac{1}{\tau}. \tag{10.4}$$

Thus the resonance lines at ν_A and ν_B are broadened, as indicated in Figure 10.1b, c.

3. *Very fast exchange.* A nucleus enters site A, where in the rotating frame it begins to precess at $(\nu_A - \nu_0)$. But before it can complete even a small portion of a single precession, its lifetime in site A expires, and it enters site B. It now begins to precess in the opposite direction in the rotating frame, but again undergoes essentially no precession before it must again leave site B and reenter A. The result is that in the rotating frame the nucleus remains stationary, and thus in the laboratory frame it appears to be precessing at the frequency with which the coordinate system rotates, ν_0. Hence, as shown in Figure 10.1f, a sharp resonance line appears at ν_0, the average of the two Larmor frequencies, even though no nucleus actually precesses at that frequency.

4. *Intermediate exchange rate.* Between cases 3 and 4 there is a range of lifetimes that lead to an intermediate type spectrum, a broad line spanning the frequency range $(\nu_A - \nu_B)$, as indicated in Figure 10.1d.

An example of exchange effects on the spectrum of a molecule that undergoes hindered internal rotation is given in Figure 10.2. The two NH_2 protons are in different environments, thus have different chemical shifts. Broadening and coalescence of the NH_2 lines are observed as the rate of internal rotation increases with increasing temperature.

---

* The argument is similar to that given in Section 2.6 for the relation between T_1 and line width.

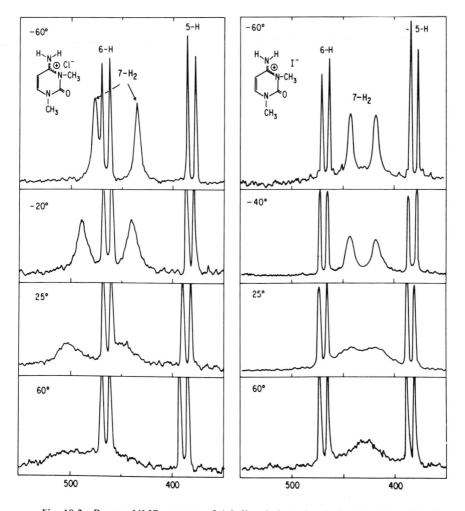

Fig. 10.2 Proton NMR spectra of 1,3-dimethylcytosine hydrochloride and hydro-iodide in SO_2. Note the differences in the spectra of the two molecules at 25° and at 60°, attributable to the fact that the rate of internal rotation of the NH_2 group is probably essentially the same but $(\nu_A - \nu_B)$ is smaller in the hydroiodide than in the hydrochloride (Becker, Miles, and Bradley[2]).

10.2 Theory of Chemical Exchange

The most widely used theoretical treatment of exchange phenomena in NMR[3-5] is based on extensions of the Bloch equations (see Section 2.8) to include exchange terms. We shall not reproduce the derivations of the necessary equations, which are well summarized elsewhere,[6-8] but shall indicate some of the more useful results of this treatment.

For the present we shall continue the assumptions we made in the preceding section: that there are only two equally populated sites (i.e., that equation 10.1 holds). In addition, we assume that in the absence of exchange the lines would have negligible width; that is, that

$$\frac{1}{T_{2(A)}} \approx \frac{1}{T_{2(B)}} \approx 0. \tag{10.5}$$

Under these conditions the shape of the resonance line(s) is

$$g(\nu) = K \frac{\tau(\nu_A - \nu_B)^2}{[\frac{1}{2}(\nu_A + \nu_B) - \nu]^2 + 4\pi^2 \tau^2 (\nu_A - \nu)^2 (\nu_B - \nu)^2} \tag{10.6}$$

where K is a normalizing constant.[6] Figure 10.1 gives plots of equation 10.6 for several values of τ. It is apparent that the shape of the curve depends only on the ratio $R/(\nu_A - \nu_B)$, where $R = 1/2\tau$ is the exchange rate. Thus our terminology of Section 10.1, "slow" and "fast," refers to the number of exchanges per second relative to $(\nu_A - \nu_B)$, measured in hertz (cycles per second). The effect of the differences in $(\nu_A - \nu_B)$ is illustrated in Figure 10.2, where the rate of internal rotation is larger relative to $(\nu_A - \nu_B)$ in the iodide than in the chloride.

It can be seen from Figure 10.1 that for slow exchange the two peaks observed are separated by less than $(\nu_A - \nu_B)$. By finding the maxima of equation 10.6 it can be shown (see problem 3 at the end of this chapter) that

$$\frac{\text{separation of peaks}}{(\nu_A - \nu_B)} = \left[1 - \frac{1}{2\pi^2 \tau^2 (\nu_A - \nu_B)^2}\right]^{1/2}. \tag{10.7}$$

Hence τ may be easily determined.

Equation 10.7 shows that the peaks draw together as τ decreases and coalesce (separation of peaks $= 0$) for

$$\tau = \frac{1}{\sqrt{2}\pi(\nu_A - \nu_B)}. \tag{10.8}$$

Comparisons between exchange rates in different systems are often stated in terms of the conditions (temperature, pH, etc.) for coalescence of the peaks.

Other procedures for finding τ from equation 10.6 are based on the ratio of the height of the peaks to that of the minimum between the peaks[9] or on a computer-aided fitting of the entire curve.[10] All of these procedures have been fairly successfully applied to a variety of systems, but there are several pitfalls inherent in the method. For example, if measurements are made over a range of temperatures to bring about appreciable variation in a particular reaction rate, it is usually necessary to assume that $(\nu_A - \nu_B)$, which is measured under conditions of slow exchange at low temperature, remains constant over the temperature range employed. Such an assumption is often unwarranted. Likewise, the effect of finite T_2 has been ignored in equation 10.6 but can be included in computer-aided calculations.

We began this section with the assumptions that there are only two equally populated sites and that the resonance lines in the absence of exchange have essentially zero width. These assumptions are unnecessary, but their elimination leads to considerably more complex mathematical expressions. In the two cases of slow exchange and of very rapid exchange, however, simple equations result.

For slow exchange, where the lines are broadened but do not overlap appreciably, the observed width of line j (assumed to be Lorentzian in shape) is

$$(\nu_{1/2})_j = (\nu^0_{1/2})_j + \frac{1}{\pi \tau_j} \tag{10.9}$$

where $1/\tau_j$ is the probability per unit time of a nucleus at site j moving to a site where it has a different Larmor frequency, and $(\nu^0_{1/2})_j$ is the width of line j in the absence of exchange. From the relation between $\nu_{1/2}$ and T_2 (equation 2.43), equation 10.9 may be recast as

$$\frac{1}{(T_2)_j} \text{(observed)} = \frac{1}{(T_2)_j} \text{(no exchange)} + \frac{1}{\tau_j}. \tag{10.10}$$

For very fast exchange, the general result is that the frequency of the single line observed is the average of the Larmor frequencies for the different sites, weighted according to the probability that a nucleus is at each site:

$$\nu \text{ (observed)} = p_A \nu_A + p_B \nu_B + p_C \nu_C + \cdots \tag{10.11}$$

where the p_i sum to unity. Since τ does not enter equation 10.11, we cannot actually determine the exchange lifetimes, but merely establish that the exchange rate is greater than about 50 $(\nu_A - \nu_B)$.

10.3 Collapse of Spin Multiplets

In Sections 10.1 and 10.2 we spoke of exchange of a nucleus between sites where it has different Larmor frequencies. The difference in frequencies might arise from differences in chemical shift or from the presence of spin coupling. For example, in CH_3OH the methyl and hydroxyl protons are spin coupled with $J \approx 5$ Hz. If we assume that δ/J is large enough so that first-order analysis is applicable, then the CH_3 resonance consists of a doublet, as shown in Figure 10.3. One line of the doublet arises from those molecules (approximately 50%) that have the hydroxyl proton spin oriented *with* H_0, while the other line arises from the molecules with the OH proton spin oriented *against* H_0. If the OH proton exchanges between molecules, the methyl resonance may be affected. Suppose a given molecule of methanol contains an OH proton whose spin is oriented with the field. If this proton is lost and replaced by another proton, either from another CH_3OH molecule or from somewhere else (e.g., an H^+ or H_2O impurity), the CH_3 Larmor frequency will be unchanged if the replacing proton is also spin oriented with the field, but will change by J Hz if the new proton is spin oriented against the field. In the usual *random* process, then, half of all exchanges will result in a change in the CH_3 Larmor frequency, while the other half will not. With this statistical factor taken into account, equations 10.6–10.10 apply, provided $\delta \gg J$. Where the components of a spin doublet are involved, $(\nu_A - \nu_B)$ in equations 10.6–10.8 is, of course, replaced by J.

Figure 10.3 shows the collapse of the spin multiplets of both the CH_3 and OH resonances in CH_3OH with increase in temperature. For the OH there are four states rather than two, so that the equations we have employed must be modified.

Proton exchanges in OH or NH groups are often catalyzed by H^+ or OH^- and so are highly pH dependent. Sometimes exchange at an intermediate rate broadens the resonance line so much that it may pass unobserved.

Another type of "exchange" does not involve an actual physical removal of the nucleus. If one of a pair of coupled nuclei *relaxes* moderately rapidly due to quadrupole effects (e.g., ^{14}N), the multiplet of the other nucleus is broadened, often by a large amount. We saw an example in the NH_2 proton resonance of formamide (Figure 8.5).

The collapse of a spin multiplet to a single line with rapid proton exchange results from the random spin orientations of the exchanging protons. If a *given* proton exchanges rapidly between two or more sites but is never actually replaced by a proton with different spin orientation, the situation is different. For example, the pair of tautomers (I) and (II) result from rapid exchange of the proton H* between the oxygen and nitrogen atoms. If only (II) existed, the resonance of H* would be split into a doublet of ~90 Hz by coupling to ^{15}N. Actually the spectrum of this substance in $CDCl_3$ shows H* to give rise to a 35-Hz doublet at 25° and a 52-Hz doublet at −50°, resulting from the

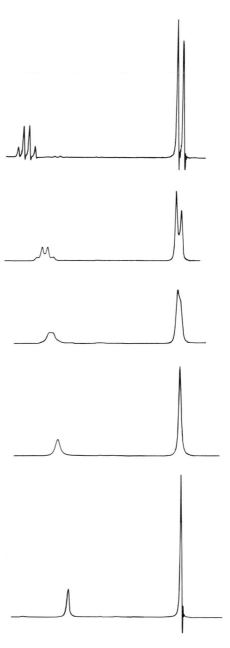

Fig. 10.3 Collapse of spin coupling in methanol with increase in temperature. Both the CH_3 and OH proton resonances are shown. Temperatures (from top): $-54°$, $-20°$, $-10°$, $0°$; $15°$.

rapid tautomerism. In this case

$$J(\text{observed}) = p_{\text{I}}J_{\text{I}} + p_{\text{II}}J_{\text{II}}$$

where p_{I} and p_{II} are the fractions of the two tautomers present.

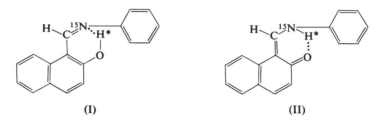

(I)   (II)

  A very common example of this averaging of J's by rapid exchange occurs in molecules where there is rapid rotation about single bonds, such as CH_3—CH_2— (see Table 5.2).

10.4 More Complete Theories of Exchange

  The theory discussed in Section 10.2 has been widely used and is adequate for many exchanging systems. However, when nonfirst-order spin coupling is involved in any of the exchange sites, this theory cannot provide a framework for quantitative treatment of the results. In such cases more general developments, based upon the density matrix formalism of quantum mechanics, are required. Such theory is beyond the scope of this book but is discussed elsewhere.[7] An example of one type of system that has been treated by such procedures is given in Figure 10.4, where calculated spectra are given for two protons that form a coupled AB system. Proton B exchanges with another proton, X, where X is present at much higher concentration than A and B. The qualitative result is the same as would be expected from the simpler theory of Sections 10.2 and 10.3: first, a broadening of the spin "doublets" and ultimately a collapse of the A "doublet." The B lines broaden and eventually, with rapid exchange, are absorbed into the X signal. Thus, while the density matrix treatment must be employed for the calculation of exchange rates, the simpler theories can be useful even in more complex systems in providing a qualitative interpretation.

10.5 Double Resonance and Pulse Techniques

  Thus far we have been concerned with the effect of exchange on the ordinary NMR spectrum. Both double resonance techniques (see Chapter 8) and spin-echo methods (see Chapter 9) provide powerful additional tools for investigating rate processes.

Double resonance is advantageous principally in permitting measurements of rates of slower exchange reactions than can be handled by ordinary single resonance methods. From equation 10.10 it is seen that slow exchange rates are

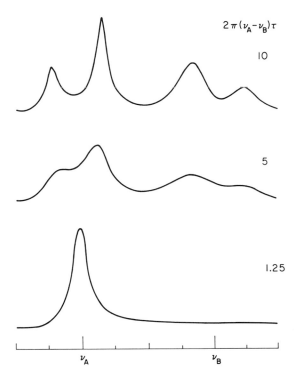

$$2\pi(\nu_A - \nu_B)\tau$$

10

5

1.25

ν_A ν_B

Fig. 10.4 Calculated spectrum of an AB system in which B exchanges with another nucleus, X, present at much higher concentration than A or B. $J_{AB}/(\nu_A - \nu_B) = 0.4$; $J_{AX} = J_{BX} = 0$. Adapted from Kaplan.[11]

normally determined by the change effected in T_2. To bring about an observable change in line width, τ must be less than T_2. As usual, however, it is not the real T_2 of the system that should be used in equation 10.10, but the apparent T_2^*, which is often determined by magnetic field inhomogeneity. The double resonance method, however, permits a determination of τ when $\tau < T_1$. Since T_1 is often much greater than T_2^*, *larger* τ's can thus be determined.

The double resonance procedure for an exchange between sites A and B involves measurement of the change in the signal of the A line immediately after the B resonance is saturated by imposition of a second rf field. The A resonance decays as its Boltzmann distribution is disrupted by exchange of nuclei between sites A and B. From the exponential decay rate of the A resonance, τ can be calculated.[12]

The spin-echo method is quite useful in extending the range of exchange rates to faster reactions (i.e., *smaller* τ's); it also obviates the necessity for certain assumptions made in the treatment of ordinary NMR spectra. We saw in Section 9.7 that in the Carr-Purcell experiment, 180° pulses at times t_p, $3t_p$, $5t_p$, and so on, are followed by echoes at $2t_p$, $4t_p$, $6t_p$, and so on. If t_p is made short, so that $2t_p \ll 2\tau$, the exchange lifetime, then the spin-echo experiment measures the actual T_2, without any contribution from exchange. On the other hand, if $2t_p \gtrsim 2\tau$, exchange affects the results, and from a computer-aided treatment of the data, exchange rates can be found over a wide range.[13] Relatively little application has been made of this technique, but its use seems destined to increase. The spin-echo technique permits the determination of $(\nu_A - \nu_B)$ and T_2 in each experiment; hence the assumption of Section 10.2 that these quantities are constant over a series of measurements at different temperatures or under different conditions is avoided. The spin-echo method suffers the disadvantage of being unable to discriminate between resonances of the exchanging nuclei and other nuclei of the same type in the molecule or solvent. Selective isotopic substitution furnishes the only general way out of this difficulty. For proton exchange studies it may be possible to deuterate all hydrogens in the molecule except those exchanging, or alternatively to deuterate only the exchanging hydrogens and then study the deuterium spin echoes.

10.6 Asymmetry and Internal Rotation

We have seen in Figure 10.2 that highly hindered internal rotation can lead to slow exchange and the observations of separate lines for the exchanging nuclei. In the case shown in Figure 10.2, increase in temperature causes an increase in exchange rate and a change in the character of the spectrum in the direction expected. One might anticipate that if internal rotation is sufficiently rapid, the fast exchange limit embodied in equation 10.11 would apply, and that a single line would result from the exchanging nuclei. This expectation may not be realized, however, when certain types of asymmetry are present in the molecule under consideration.

The most commonly encountered internal rotation is about C—C single bonds. Consider, for example, the case CH_2X—CPQR, where X, P, Q, and R are different substituents. We can picture three stable conformations about the C—C bond (III)–(V). Normally, rotation about a C—C single bond is sufficiently rapid so that the spectra of the individual conformers are not observed. As expected from equation 10.11, the observed spectrum represents the average of the chemical shifts and coupling constants in the three conformations. However, because of the presence of the asymmetric center, the average chemical shift of H_A is *not* necessarily the same as that of H_B.

We can easily see how such nonequivalence can arise. Suppose the three conformations pictured are equally populated, as they would be if completely free rotation occurs about the C—C bond. The chemical shift of H_A in conformation (III) is probably influenced by the groups P and R adjacent to it. It might at first appear that there is an equal contribution to the chemical shift of H_B in conformation (V), where groups P and R are adjacent to H_B.

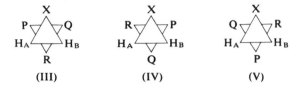

(III)   (IV)   (V)

However, closer examination of the entire molecule shows that differences exist between the conformations: groups P, X, and Q are neighbors in (III), while R, X, and Q are adjacent in (V). Thus while the "immediate" environments of H_A in (III) and H_B in (V) are the same, steric or electronic effects from the remainder of the molecule can in principle lead to different chemical shifts for H_A in (III) and H_B in (V). A similar analysis applies to all other potentially equivalent pairs. Hence we conclude that the average chemical shift of H_A is not necessarily equal to that of H_B. Whether such a difference is observed depends, of course, on the net result of the magnetic effects involved and on the experimental resolution. The point is that we should always expect such differences and regard equivalence in the observed chemical shifts of H_A and H_B as fortuitous.

The asymmetry responsible for the nonequivalence of the chemical shifts of H_A and H_B need not be due to an immediately adjacent asymmetric carbon atom. For example, the CH_2 protons in

$$C_6H_5-\underset{\underset{O}{\|}}{S}-O-CH_2-CH_3$$

have been shown to be nonequivalent.[14] Likewise, it is not necessary that groups A and B be protons. Figure 10.5 gives an example of nonequivalence of methyl groups.

It should be emphasized that the presence of some sort of asymmetry is a necessary condition for chemical nonequivalence of two protons (or two methyl groups, etc.). This does not mean, however, that the molecule must be completely devoid of a plane of symmetry. For example, in the situation we have been considering, suppose that R is the group CH_2X, giving the molecule

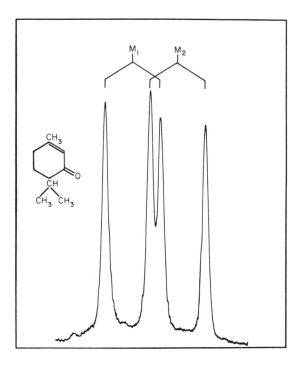

Fig. 10.5 Proton NMR spectrum (60 MHz) of the isopropyl group of piperitone in $CDCl_3$. Each of the nonequivalent methyl groups, M_1 and M_2, is coupled to the isopropyl proton.

(VI). While this molecule has a plane of symmetry, H_A and H_B are, as we have

seen, nonequivalent. Alternatively, suppose that X is CPQR, giving the molecule (VII). This can exist as a *d, l* pair or as a *meso* compound. In the *d* and *l* forms H_A and H_B are equivalent but in the *meso* compound they are nonequivalent.[15]

If the molecule in question has no asymmetry, as for example in a 1,2-

disubstituted ethane, the two protons attached to a given carbon atom are chemically equivalent. Of the three conformations (VIII)–(X), (VIII) and (IX) are mirror images, the average of which must have $\nu_A = \nu_B$ and $\nu_X = \nu_Y$, while (X) contains a plane of symmetry, so that the same equalities hold here. On the other hand, H_A and H_B are *not magnetically* equivalent, since the vicinal coupling constants are not necessarily averaged to the same value. For example, in conformation (VIII), where H_A and H_X are coupled by a *trans* coupling constant, substituents P and R are adjacent, while in (X), where H_A and H_Y are *trans* coupled, P and R are far apart. Thus $J_{AX}(trans) \neq J_{AY}(trans)$, and similar inequalities hold for the other conformations. Hence, this is an AA′XX′

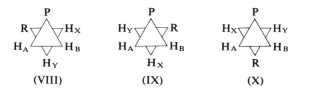

system, not an A_2X_2 system. In some individual cases the differences in the average J's may, of course, be so small that deviations from an A_2X_2 pattern are not observed.

Finally, we should point out that our entire discussion of nonequivalence has been predicated on the assumption of equal populations for all conformers. In most cases where asymmetry is present, there will be differences in energy, hence in populations, of the conformers. Such differences can significantly enhance the magnitude of the nonequivalence.

References

1. "Table of Exchange Broadened NMR Multiplets," Tech. Note No. 2, Contract No. AF 61(052)-03, Weizmann Institute of Science, Rehovoth, Israel.

2. E. D. Becker, H. T. Miles, and R. B. Bradley, *J. Am. Chem. Soc.* **87**, 5575 (1965).

3. H. S. Gutowsky, D. W. McCall, and C. P. Slichter, *J. Chem. Phys.* **21**, 279 (1953).

4. L. H. Piette and W. A. Anderson, *J. Chem. Phys.* **30**, 899 (1959).

5. H. M. McConnell, *J. Chem. Phys.* **28**, 430 (1958).

6. J. A. Pople, W. G. Schneider, and H. J. Bernstein, "High Resolution NMR," Chapter 10. McGraw-Hill, New York, 1959.

7. C. S. Johnson, Jr., *Advan. Magn. Resonance* **1**, 33 (1965).

8. L. W. Reeves, *Advan. Phys. Organic Chem.* **3**, 187 (1965).

9. E. Grunwald, A. Loewenstein, and S. Meiboom, *J. Chem. Phys.* **27**, 630 (1957).

10. J. Jonas, A. Allerhand, and H. S. Gutowsky, *J. Chem. Phys.* **42**, 3396 (1965).

11. J. I. Kaplan, *J. Chem. Phys.* **28**, 278 (1958).

12. R. A. Hoffman and S. Forsen, *Progr. NMR Spectroscopy* **1**, 15 (1966).

13. A. Allerhand and H. S. Gutowsky, *J. Chem. Phys.* **41**, 2115 (1964); H. S. Gutowsky, R. L. Vold, and E. J. Wells, *J. Chem. Phys.* **43**, 4107 (1965).

14. J. S. Waugh and F. A. Cotton, *J. Phys. Chem.* **65**, 562 (1961).

15. An excellent discussion of chemical nonequivalence in rotational isomers, with a number of examples, is given by F. A. Bovey, "NMR Spectroscopy," Chapter 6. Academic Press, New York, 1968.

Problems

1. From Figure 10.2 estimate τ for rotation of the NH_2 group in 1,3-dimethyl-cytosine hydrochloride at 25° and 60°.

2. What are the principal sources of error in making a calculation such as the one in problem 1?

3. Derive equation 10.7 from 10.6 by setting the first derivative of equation 10.6 equal to zero. Note that one of the three possible solutions for v is not a maximum but the minimum at $v = \frac{1}{2}(v_A + v_B)$.

4. Determine the structures of the compounds giving Spectra 34–36, Appendix B.

5. Give the type of spectrum (e.g., AB_2X_2) expected for each of the following ethane derivatives, where Q, R, and S are substituents that do not spin couple with the protons. Assume that rotation about the C—C bond is rapid and that there is a large chemical shift difference between protons on different carbon atoms. (a) CH_3—CH_2R; (b) CH_2Q—CH_2R; (c) CH_3—CQRS; (d) CH_2Q—CHRS; (e) CHQ_2—CHRS.

6. Repeat problem 5 for slow rotation about the C—C bond.

Chapter 11

Solvent Effects and Hydrogen Bonding

Thus far our discussions of the factors governing NMR parameters, such as chemical shifts and coupling constants, have emphasized *intra*molecular contributions. Since almost all NMR measurements are made in the liquid phase, it is clear that *inter*molecular interactions might also be important. In this chapter we shall explore some of the theoretically definable effects arising from the solvent medium. We shall see that such effects are particularly important in *proton* NMR, where intramolecular shieldings are small. We shall devote special attention to the strong specific molecular interaction of hydrogen bonding.

11.1 Medium Effects on Chemical Shifts

In treating the intramolecular contributions to the chemical shift in Chapter 4 we found it helpful to classify the various effects involved. Similarly, following Buckingham et al.,[1] we can express the total effect of the solvent medium on nuclear shielding as the sum of five terms:

$$\sigma(\text{solvent}) = \sigma_B + \sigma_W + \sigma_A + \sigma_E + \sigma_H. \tag{11.1}$$

σ_B is the contribution of the bulk magnetic susceptibility of the medium. As we saw in Chapters 3 and 4, this effect can be allowed for theoretically when dealing with an external reference and is zero for an internal reference. Since in general we use internal references, we shall ignore this effect. It should be noted, however, that by choosing an internal reference we make the implicit assumption that the reference compound itself is not subject to solvent interactions. For a *complete* analysis of solvent effects, an *external* reference must be used and σ_B calculated as discussed in Section 4.4. In general, solvent effects are small for a reference such as TMS, but can be pronounced in some cases, especially where aromatic molecules are present in high concentration.[2]

σ_W arises from the effect of the weak Van der Waals forces between solute and solvent molecules. Such effects can distort and change the symmetry of the electronic environment of a given nucleus. Theory predicts that σ_W should be negative, and experimental tests of equation 11.1 under conditions where σ_W should be one of the dominant terms indicate that a change in proton shielding of the order of 0.1–0.2 ppm might be expected from the effect of Van der Waals forces.[1] Generally, large polarizable halogen atoms in the solvent lead to increased negative values of σ_W.

σ_A refers to the magnetic anisotropy in the solvent molecules and arises from the nonzero orientational averaging of solvent with respect to solute. The magnetic anisotropy itself was discussed in Sections 4.8 and 4.9, where we saw that aromatic rings and groups such as $C=C$, $C=O$, $C\equiv C$, and $C\equiv N$ cause especially large effects. While it is difficult to isolate this effect from others, studies show that aromatic solvents usually lead to positive σ_A's of about 0.5 ppm, while solvents containing triple bonds have negative σ_A's of about 0.2–0.4 ppm.

The large positive σ_A normally found for aromatic solvents has been widely exploited. In complex molecules it is often found that solvent effects are selective. For example, in Figure 1.6 we saw that the chemical shifts of different methyl groups in a steroid may respond quite differently to change of solvent. Systematic studies of the variation in chemical shifts of protons in well-known locations in large molecules have shown considerable regularity in solvent effects.[3] For example, we can denote a solvent shift

$$\Delta_{C_6H_6}^{CDCl_3} = \delta_{CDCl_3} - \delta_{C_6H_6} \tag{11.2}$$

where the δ's are defined according to equation 4.7 with respect to TMS. Thus a positive value of Δ indicates an upfield shift in the proton resonance on going from $CDCl_3$ to benzene as solvent. It has been found that in molecules containing a $C=O$ group, Δ is negative for protons located on the oxygen side of a plane through the carbon atom of the carbonyl group perpendicular to the $C=O$ axis, and positive on the other side of this plane[3] (see Figure 11.1). This result can be interpreted in terms of a "complex" between the solute and aromatic solvent such that the π electrons of the aromatic ring are near the slightly positively charged carbon atom of the $C=O$ group, while at the same time remaining as far as possible from the negative oxygen, as indicated in Figure 11.1 Similar generalizations may be made for polar aromatic solvents interacting with polar solutes. In general, the solute-solvent complex is best thought of as a transitory species that biases the otherwise random distribution of solvent molecules around the solute, rather than a distinct separate species. These predicted solvent effects are quite useful in structure elucidation, but like many empirical generalizations, must be used with considerable caution. Steric effects, for example, can sometimes modify substantially the expected orientation of the interacting solute-solvent pair.

σ_E arises from the effect of an electric field on the nuclear shielding. Buckingham *et al.*[1] have shown that when a polar molecule or a molecule containing polar groups is dissolved in a dielectric medium, it induces a "reaction field," the effect of which is usually to reduce the shielding around a proton in the solute. Thus σ_E is ordinarily negative, but could be positive for certain molecular geometries. Equations for determining the magnitude of σ_E in terms of molecular properties such as dipole moment and polarizability

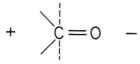

Fig. 11.1 Effect of solvent change on chemical shifts of protons in a molecule containing a C=O group.[3] Dashed line indicates a plane perpendicular to the plane of the C=O group; + or − refers to the sign of $\Delta_{C_6H_6}^{CDCl_3}$.

have been derived but will not be reproduced here. Experimental studies of the electric field effect indicate that σ_E might be as large as 1 ppm for polar molecules in solvents of high dielectric constant.[1]

σ_H refers to *specific* solute-solvent interactions, the most important of which is hydrogen bonding. We shall discuss hydrogen bonding in Section 11.4. When such interactions are present, σ_H usually is the dominant term in equation 11.1. There is often a tendency in such cases to ignore the other effects but, as we have seen, they can be quite significant even if not dominant.

11.2 Solvent Effects on Coupling Constants

While solvent effects on chemical shifts can be quite large, the effect of solvents on coupling constants is usually small. Careful measurements of coupling constants show, however, that the effects in some cases are not negligible. For example, geminal H—H coupling constants in a number of compounds, such as styrene oxide,[4] formaldehyde,[5] and α-chloroacrylonitrile,[6] vary with solvent by 1–2 Hz. In addition, some one-bond ^{13}C—H and ^{15}N—H coupling constants vary with solvent; in these cases the variation seems to be related to hydrogen bonding and will be discussed in Section 11.4.

Observed vicinal coupling constants in some ethane derivatives are also found to vary with solvent. In such cases, however, the observed J is the weighted average of the J's for the various conformers, so that the observed changes in J reflect mainly the effect of the solvent in altering the proportions of the conformers.[7]

11.3 Solvent Effects on Relaxation and Exchange Rates

We saw in Chapter 9 that T_1 and T_2 depend on the rate of molecular tumbling, which, in turn, is a function of the viscosity of the solution. For small molecules and small polymers, T_1 and T_2 are to the left of the minimum in Figure 9.1, so that an increase in viscosity reduces the relaxation times and thus broadens the resonance lines. Such effects are found in materials of high viscosity, such as glycerol or ethylene glycol, the line widths of which are markedly temperature dependent. Of the commonly used solvents for proton NMR listed in Table 3.1, dimethyl sulfoxide is the most viscous; at room temperature lines of compounds dissolved in this solvent are generally noticeably broader than in other solvents.

If the solute contains exchangeable protons, its spectrum may be quite dependent on the nature of the solvent insofar as exchange lifetimes are concerned (see Chapter 10). If, in addition, the solvent contains exchangeable protons, there may be a rapid exchange between solute and solvent so that the solvent resonance line due to its exchangeable protons in effect includes also the exchangeable protons of the solute.

11.4 Hydrogen Bonding

Hydrogen bonding is recognized as a relatively strong, specific interaction between molecules or between suitable portions of the same molecule. Proton chemical shifts are extremely sensitive to hydrogen bonding. In almost all cases, formation of a hydrogen bond causes the resonance of the bonded proton to move downfield (i.e., to larger δ values) by as much as 10 ppm. In general there is a rough correlation between the NMR shift and the strength of the bond as measured by the enthalpy of its formation.[8] Table 11.1 shows

Table 11.1

EFFECT OF HYDROGEN BONDING ON PROTON CHEMICAL SHIFTS[a]

Compound	δ(bonded)[b]	δ(bonded) $-$ δ(free)
$C_2H_5OH\cdots O{-}C_2H_5$ (H below O)	5.3	4.6
$C_6H_5OH\cdots O{=}P(OC_2H_5)_3$	8.7	4.3
$Cl_3CH\cdots O{=}C(CH_3)_2$	8.0	0.7
$Cl_3CH\cdots$ (benzene ring)	6.4	-0.9
$C_6H_5C{\diagup O{-}H\cdots O\diagdown \atop \diagdown O\cdots H{-}O\diagup}CC_6H_5$	14.0	7.8
$C_6H_5NH_2\cdots N$ (pyridine ring)	5.3	2.0
$C_6H_5NH_2\cdots O{=}S(CH_3)_2$	5.0	1.7
$C_6H_5SH\cdots O{=}C{-}N(CH_3)_2$ (H below C)	3.8	0.5
$CH_3C{=}CH\ CCH_3$ $\quad\ \ \ \vert\quad\quad \Vert$ $\quad\ \ O{-}H\cdots O$	15.5	—

[a] Data compiled from work in the author's laboratory and from various literature sources. These data are illustrative but should not be regarded as accurate because of variations caused by differences in solvent, concentration, and temperature.

[b] In parts per million with respect to TMS (internal).

typical changes in proton resonance frequency on hydrogen bonding. Intramolecularly bonded enols and phenols display resonances at especially low field.

Proton NMR has proved to be one of the most sensitive methods of studying hydrogen bonding, both qualitatively and quantitatively. Since hydrogen bonds are usually made and broken very rapidly relative to the chemical shift difference between bonded and nonbonded forms (expressed in hertz), separate lines are not observed for different species; the frequency ν of the single observed line is given by equation 10.11. In suitable systems the variation of ν with concentration and temperature can be analyzed to give equilibrium constants and other thermodynamic properties for hydrogen bond formation.[9]

The reason for the pronounced downfield shift of a bonded proton has not been completely explained. However, it seems clear that it is not merely a result of decreased electron density around the proton, for overall the proton is probably in a region of higher electron density in the hydrogen bond X—H⋯Y than in X—H alone. Nevertheless, the electron distribution in the X—H covalent bond is evidently altered by the electric field from Y in such a way that the proton is deshielded. In addition, the proton may experience a neighbor anisotropy effect (see Section 4.8) from Y. For most acceptors this effect results in a small upfield shift, and for aromatic molecules where the proton is bonded approximately to the center of the π-electron cloud, the ring current effect (Section 4.9) leads to a large upfield shift, which predominates over any deshielding due to other factors. A hydrogen bond to π electrons of an aromatic ring is the only type of hydrogen bond that results in an observed upfield, rather than downfield, shift.

The effects of hydrogen bonding on the chemical shifts of X and Y have not been studied carefully. It appears that changes in their chemical shifts may amount to a few parts per million, but in contrast to proton chemical shifts, such effects are small relative to the ranges covered for typical acceptor atoms, such as N and O.

A few studies of the effect of hydrogen bonding on coupling constants have been directed to X—H one-bond couplings. For both ^{15}N—H in aniline and ^{13}C—H in CHCl$_3$, ^1J increases by about 5% on formation of a hydrogen bond.[10, 11]

References

1. A. D. Buckingham, T. Schaefer, and W. G. Schneider, *J. Chem. Phys.* **32**, 1227 (1960).

2. See, for example, E. D. Becker, *J. Phys. Chem.* **63**, 1379 (1959).

3. See, for example, J. H. Bowie, D. W. Cameron, P. E. Schutz, D. H. Williams, and N. S. Bhacca, *Tetrahedron* **22**, 1771 (1966).

4. S. L. Smith and R. H. Cox, *J. Mol. Spectroscopy* **16**, 216 (1965).

5. B. L. Shapiro, S. J. Ebersole, and R. M. Kopchik, *J. Mol. Spectroscopy* **11**, 326 (1963).

6. V. S. Watts, G. S. Reddy, and J. H. Goldstein, *J. Mol. Spectroscopy* **11**, 325 (1963).

7. See, for example, J. W. Emsley, J. Feeney, and L. H. Sutcliffe, "High Resolution NMR Spectroscopy," pp. 568–573. Macmillan (Pergamon), New York, 1965; also, R. J. Abraham, L. Cavalli, and K. G. R. Pachler, *Mol. Phys.* **11**, 471 (1966).

8. D. P. Eyman and R. S. Drago, *J. Am. Chem. Soc.* **88**, 1617 (1966).

9. See, for example, G. C. Pimentel, and A. L. McClellan, "The Hydrogen Bond," Freeman, San Francisco, 1960; see also reference 7, pp. 539–51.

10. D. F. Evans, *J. Chem. Soc.* p. 5575 (1963).

11. E. D. Becker, unpublished work.

Problem

Determine the structure of the molecule giving Spectrum 37, Appendix B.

Chapter 12

Use of NMR in Quantitative Analysis

We saw in Chapter 6 that quantitative measurements of the relative areas of the lines in an NMR spectrum can be of great aid in problems of structure elucidation. In many instances such intensity measurements can also be valuable for the quantitative analysis of mixtures of compounds of known constitution. In this chapter we shall indicate some of the advantages and disadvantages of NMR as a quantitative analytical method and describe a few of the systems that have been analyzed in this way. Quantitative analysis by NMR is as yet neither a widely investigated nor a widely utilized field.

12.1 Advantages of NMR in Quantitative Analysis

Probably the principal advantage of NMR as a quantitative analytical method relative to most other spectroscopic techniques is the absence in NMR of quantities analogous to the absorption coefficients or extinction coefficients found in other types of spectra. As we saw in Section 2.4, the intensity of an NMR signal for a given nuclear isotope is proportional to the number of nuclei contributing to the signal but is independent of the chemical nature of a given isotopic nucleus. Thus in principle a proton NMR analysis for, say, benzene can be based on a standard signal from naphthalene, acetone, or any other convenient proton-containing molecule. This is a very distinct advantage, for it often means in practice that the compound being analyzed in a mixture need not be available in pure form for use as a standard.

Another advantage of NMR stems from the fact that resonance lines are

236

usually narrow relative to chemical shift differences. As the values of obtainable magnetic fields are increased, the likelihood of appreciable overlap of the proton NMR spectra of different components of a mixture is reduced. For nuclei other than hydrogen, the range of chemical shifts is much larger (see Section 4.5), so that overlap is even less likely. Of course, molecules that contain *only* nuclei that are very similar chemically (e.g., benzene and naphthalene) will generally have spectra that overlap significantly.

12.2 Drawbacks and Problems in the Use of NMR in Quantitative Analysis

There are a number of disadvantages to the use of NMR as a quantitative analytical method, but as we shall see, most of these can be overcome by taking suitable precautions.

Most quantitative spectroscopic methods depend on measurements of the easily determined peak *heights* of spectral lines or bands. While peak heights can be used in NMR in some special cases (see Section 12.3), this procedure is generally avoided since peak heights are highly dependent on instrumental conditions and nuclear relaxation times. As we have seen, it is the *area* under a line that serves as a measure of the number of nuclei responsible for it. The electronic integrators supplied with most commercial NMR instruments are accurate to about 1% or 2% of full scale measurement. This figure can be misleading, however, in two ways. First, poor signal/noise ratio leads to greatly reduced accuracy, since amplifier drift and fluctuations in the size of the integral increase. Second, if one component is present at much lower concentration than another, the percentage error in measurement of the quantity of this minor component could be quite high. On the other hand, the accuracy of the NMR method, like all analytical methods subject to random errors, can be improved by averaging the results of several independent determinations.

The presence of more than one isotope of a given element can cause difficulties in analyses. This problem arises most frequently in organic molecules, where the 1.1% natural abundance of ^{13}C leads to ^{13}C satellites around the main peaks in proton NMR spectra (see Section 7.24). A ^{13}C satellite of a strong line could cause considerable error if it happens to overlap a weak line or group of lines. Provided the analyst is aware of this possibility, the presence of ^{13}C satellites poses no fundamental barrier to accurate analyses since the natural abundance of ^{13}C is known and the area under the satellite peaks can be precisely related to that under the main peaks.* In fact, in analyzing for

---

* If there are n equivalent carbon atoms in the molecule, a simple statistical treatment shows that to a very high degree of approximation $(1.1 \times n)\%$ of the molecules contain one ^{13}C atom and contribute to the ^{13}C satellites.

components present in vastly different concentrations, it is sometimes possible to compare the area under the main lines of one compound with that under the ^{13}C satellite lines of the other.

Related to the problem of ^{13}C satellites is the occurrence of spinning sidebands (see Section 3.2). The area of the spinning sidebands should be added to that of the main peak to obtain the true area representative of the quantity of material responsible for the resonance. Usually by careful adjustment of magnetic field homogeneity, use of very high-precision sample tubes, and optimization of spinning rate, it is possible to reduce spinning sidebands to the point where the neglect of their area is unimportant.

The problem of selective saturation of different NMR lines was discussed in Section 3.7. We saw that this potential source of error can be eliminated by careful choice of the magnitude of H_1 and of sweep speed. Sweep speeds of 10 Hz/sec with H_1 of 0.1–0.2 milligauss have been found to be optimum for quantitative analysis.[1]

We noted in Section 3.5 that NMR is inherently a rather insensitive method. Relatively large samples are required, which could preclude its use as an analytical method in some cases. The insensitivity is especially marked with nuclei other than hydrogen and fluorine, which might otherwise offer many advantages. Because of its insensitivity, NMR is only very rarely used for analyzing trace components, but the rapid relaxation of paramagnetic ions does permit this type of analysis in special circumstances, as we shall discover in Section 12.3.

Particular care must be taken in proton NMR analyses if exchangeable protons are present in one or more of the components. Usually it is poor practice to base the analytical method on an exchangeable proton, since small amounts of water or other substances containing active protons might be present as an impurity. By exchanging rapidly with the proton in question, such impurities can alter the area of its resonance line (see Chapter 10). Even if the exchangeable proton is not used in the analysis, its presence could cause some difficulty if it exchanges at an intermediate rate and gives a very broad line that overlaps or underlies regions that are to be used in the analysis. If such interference occurs, conditions of solvent, temperature, or added acid can usually be adjusted to change the frequency and width of the interfering line.

12.3 Some Analytical Uses of NMR

Probably the simplest use of NMR as a quantitative analytical method is the analysis of isotopic composition. For example, the residual hydrogen in D_2O has been determined by NMR.[2] If instrumental parameters, especially field homogeneity, are maintained constant, peak heights can be used. The procedure involves adding known amounts of H_2O to the sample of D_2O and thus constructing a calibration curve of signal amplitude versus amount of H_2O (or HDO) originally in the D_2O sample. Clearly, this technique can be adapted to other substances provided allowance is made for the effects of spin-spin coupling where the protons are not exchangeable. For example, if proton NMR is used to determine benzene-d_5 in a sample of benzene-d_6, the line of C_6D_5H will be split or broadened relative to that of C_6H_6 because of H—D coupling. The difficulty can be overcome by use of areas, rather than peak heights.

Another early use of NMR in quantitative analysis involved the determination of moisture in solid carbohydrate or proteinaceous material.[3] For this purpose broad line NMR equipment suffices, and the distinction between water and the solid substrate is made on the basis of the vastly different line widths. A similar technique is used commercially to analyze for oil in corn kernels.[4]

Proton NMR has been shown to be useful and fairly accurate in the analysis of mixtures of dinitrotoluenes.[5] It was found that the methyl peaks afforded the best quantitative measure of the amounts of the various isomers and that peak heights, rather than areas, provided the most accurate determinations. In this system NMR apparently overestimates the amounts of minor components (<10 mole percent) by about 0.5% absolute, while it underestimates by about 2% a component present at >50 mole percent.

Proton NMR has been used to determine the amount of "active hydrogen" in a sample by addition of D_2O and measurement of the intensity of the water line.[6] Careful experimental technique is required in determining the amount of HDO in the D_2O added and in some cases correcting for slow exchange of protons.

Number average molecular weights of glycol polyesters and polyalkylene glycols have been found by proton NMR analysis of the relative intensities of the CH_2 groups in the chain and of terminal CH_2 groups.[7] Pyridine was used as the solvent to enhance chemical shift differences, and a trace of HCl was added to promote OH exchange and thus narrow the terminal CH_2 line.

NMR has been employed in the analysis of mixtures of drugs,[8, 9] in one case with the assistance of a computer program to solve the simultaneous equations involved in the analysis.[9]

When rapid proton exchange occurs, the *frequency* of the observed line, rather than line areas, may sometimes be used as a means of quantitative analysis. An example of this technique in the measurement of equilibrium constants was mentioned in Section 11.4. Mixtures of materials with rapidly exchanging protons can be analyzed similarly.[10] Line widths can also be used in special analytical methods. We saw in Section 9.5 that a paramagnetic ion, such as Cu^{2+}, causes broadening of some of the lines of a ligand to which the metal ion is attached. With rapid metal ion exchange, the large paramagnetic broadening effect acts as a "chemical amplifier" to permit the determination of very small amounts of paramagnetic ion by measurement of line widths, rather than line areas.[10] This is one of the few quantitative analytical applications of NMR that permits determination of a substance in "trace" amounts.

Quantitative analysis of multicomponent mixtures by NMR seems destined to increase. The development of more refined instruments and especially of techniques for coupling NMR spectrometers to digital computers should have a major impact on developments in this area.

References

1. J. L. Jungnickel and J. W. Forbes, *Anal. Chem.* **35**, 938 (1963).

2. Varian Associates, *NMR at Work* No. 57 (1958).

3. See J. A. Pople, W. G. Schneider, and H. J. Bernstein, "High Resolution NMR," p. 460. McGraw-Hill, New York, 1959.

4. T. F. Conway and F. R. Earle, *J. Am. Oil Chem. Soc.* **40**, 265 (1963).

5. A. Mathias and D. Taylor, *Anal. Chim. Acta* **35**, 376 (1966).

6. P. J. Paulsen and W. D. Cooke, *Anal. Chem.* **36**, 1721 (1964).

7. T. F. Page, Jr., and W. E. Bresler, *Anal. Chem.* **36**, 1981 (1964).

8. D. P. Hollis, *Anal. Chem.* **35**, 1682 (1963).

9. G. D. Haines, Dissertation, Georgetown Univ., 1966.

10. R. J. Day and C. N. Reilley, *Anal. Chem.* **38**, 1323 (1966).

Appendix A

Nuclear Spins, Magnetic Moments, and Resonance Frequencies[a]

Isotope			Spin I	NMR frequency (MHz for a 10-kG field)	Natural abundance (%)	Relative sensitivity at constant field	Magnetic moment μ (multiples of the nuclear magneton $eh/4\pi Mc$)	Electric quadrupole moment Q (multiples of barns (10^{-24} cm²))
Z	Element	A						
0	n	1*	$\frac{1}{2}$	29.167	—	0.322	-1.91315	—
1	¹H	1	$\frac{1}{2}$	42.5759	99.985	1.00	2.79268	—
1	²H	2	1	6.53566	1.5×10^{-2}	9.65×10^{-3}	0.857387	2.73×10^{-3}
1	³H	3*	$\frac{1}{2}$	45.4129	—	1.21	2.97877	—
2	³He	3	$\frac{1}{2}$	32.433	1.3×10^{-4}	0.442	-2.1274	—
3	⁶Li	6	1	6.2653	7.42	8.50×10^{-3}	0.82192	6.9×10^{-4}
3	⁷Li	7	$\frac{3}{2}$	16.546	92.58	0.293	3.2560	-3×10^{-2}
3	⁸Li	8*	2	6.300	—	2.59×10^{-2}	1.653	—
4	⁹Be	9	$\frac{3}{2}$	5.9834	100	1.39×10^{-2}	-1.1774	5.2×10^{-2}
5	¹⁰B	10	3	4.5754	19.58	1.99×10^{-2}	1.8007	7.4×10^{-2}
5	¹¹B	11	$\frac{3}{2}$	13.660	80.42	0.165	2.6880	3.55×10^{-2}
6	¹³C	13	$\frac{1}{2}$	10.7054	1.108	1.59×10^{-2}	0.702199	—
7	¹³N	13	$\frac{1}{2}$*	4.91	—	1.53×10^{-3}	(-)0.322	—
7	¹⁴N	14	1	3.0756	99.63	1.01×10^{-3}	0.40347	7.1×10^{-2}
7	¹⁵N	15	$\frac{1}{2}$	4.3142	0.37	1.04×10^{-3}	-0.28298	—
8	¹⁵O	15*	$\frac{1}{2}$	11.0	—	1.70×10^{-2}	0.719	—
8	¹⁷O	17	$\frac{5}{2}$	5.772	3.7×10^{-2}	2.91×10^{-2}	-1.8930	-2.6×10^{-2}

	Isotope			NMR frequency (MHz for a 10-kG field)	Natural abundance (%)	Relative sensitivity at constant field	Magnetic moment μ (multiples of the nuclear magneton $eh/4\pi Mc$)	Electric quadrupole moment Q (multiples of barns (10^{-24} cm^2))
Z	Element	A	Spin I					
9	·F	17*	$\frac{5}{2}$	14.40	—	0.451	4.720	
9	·F	19	$\frac{1}{2}$	40.0541	100	0.833	2.62727	—
9	·F	20*	2	7.977	—	5.26×10^{-2}	2.093	
10	Ne	19*	$(\frac{1}{2})$	28.75	—	0.308	-1.886	
10	Ne	21	$\frac{3}{2}$	3.3611	0.257	2.50×10^{-3}	-0.66140	
11	Na	21*	$\frac{3}{2}$	12.126	—	0.116	2.3861	
11	Na	22*	3	4.436	—	1.81×10^{-2}	1.746	
11	·Na	23	$\frac{3}{2}$	11.262	100	9.25×10^{-2}	2.2161	0.14–0.15
11	Na	24*	4	3.221	—	1.15×10^{-2}	1.690	
12	·Mg	25	$\frac{5}{2}$	2.6054	10.13	2.67×10^{-3}	-0.85449	
13	·Al	27	$\frac{5}{2}$	11.094	100	0.206	3.6385	0.149
14	·Si	29	$\frac{1}{2}$	8.4578	4.70	7.84×10^{-3}	-0.55477	
15	·P	31	$\frac{1}{2}$	17.235	100	6.63×10^{-2}	1.1305	—
15	·P	32*	1	1.923	—	2.46×10^{-4}	-0.2523	—
16	·S	33	$\frac{3}{2}$	3.2654	0.76	2.26×10^{-3}	0.64257	
16	S	35*	$\frac{3}{2}$	5.08	—	8.50×10^{-3}	1.00	-6.4×10^{-2}
17	·Cl	35	$\frac{3}{2}$	4.1717	75.53	4.70×10^{-3}	0.82091	4.5×10^{-2}
17	·Cl	36*	2	4.8931	—	1.21×10^{-2}	1.2838	-7.89×10^{-2}
17	·Cl	37	$\frac{3}{2}$	3.472	24.47	2.71×10^{-3}	0.6833	-1.72×10^{-2}
18	Ar	37*	$\frac{3}{2}$	5.08	—	8.50×10^{-3}	1.0	-6.21×10^{-2}
19	·K	38*	3	3.491	—	8.82×10^{-3}	1.374	
19	·K	39	$\frac{3}{2}$	1.9868	93.10	5.08×10^{-4}	0.39097	
19	·K	40*	4	2.470	1.18×10^{-2}	5.21×10^{-3}	-1.296	0.11
19	·K	41	$\frac{3}{2}$	1.0905	6.88	8.40×10^{-5}	0.21459	
19	·K	42*	2	4.345	—	8.50×10^{-3}	-1.140	
19	·K	43*	$\frac{3}{2}$	0.828	—	3.68×10^{-5}	0.163	
20	·Ca	41*	$\frac{7}{2}$	3.4681	—	1.14×10^{-2}	-1.5924	

Z	Element	Isotope	I	ν (MHz)	Abundance (%)	Rel. sensitivity	μ	Q
20	·Ca	43		2.8646	0.145	6.40×10^{-3}	−1.3153	−0.26
21	Sc	43*	7/2	10.04	—	0.275	4.61	0.14
21	Sc	44*	2	9.76	—	9.63×10^{-2}	2.56	0.37
21	Sc	44*m	6	5.03	—	9.24×10^{-2}	3.96	−0.22
21	·Sc	45	7/2	10.343	100	0.301	4.7492	0.12
21	Sc	46*	4	5.77	—	6.65×10^{-2}	3.03	−0.22
21	Sc	47*	7/2	11.6	—	0.426	5.33	1.5×10^{-2}
22	Ti	45*	7/2	0.207	—	2.40×10^{-6}	0.095	
22	·Ti	47	5/2	2.4000	7.28	2.09×10^{-3}	−0.78710	
22	Ti	49	7/2	2.4005	5.51	3.76×10^{-3}	−1.1022	
23	V	49*	7/2	9.71	—	0.249	4.46	
23	·V	50	6	4.2450	0.24	5.55×10^{-2}	3.3413	
23	·V	51	7/2	11.19	99.76	0.382	5.139	-4×10^{-2}
24	·Cr	53	3/2	2.4065	9.55	9.03×10^{-4}	−0.47354	
25	Mn	52*	6	3.907	—	4.33×10^{-2}	3.075	
25	Mn	52*m	2	0.030	—	2.9×10^{-9}	0.008	
25	Mn	53*	7/2	11.0	—	0.362	5.05	
25	Mn	54*	(2)	8.4	—	6.11×10^{-2}	(2.2)	
25	Mn	54*m	(3)	6.6	—	5.98×10^{-2}	(2.6)	
25	·Mn	55	5/2	10.501	100	0.175	3.444	0.55
25	Mn	56*	3	8.233	—	0.116	3.240	
26	·Fe	57	1/2	1.3758	2.19	3.37×10^{-5}	0.09024	—
27	Co	55*	7/2	10.0	—	0.274	4.6	
27	Co	56*	4	7.34	—	0.136	3.85	
27	Co	57*	7/2	10.1	—	0.283	4.65	
27	Co	58*	2	15.4	—	0.381	4.05	
27	·Co	59	7/2	10.054	100	0.277	4.6163	0.40
27	Co	60*	5	5.793	—	0.101	3.800	
28	·Ni	61	3/2	3.8047	1.19	3.57×10^{-3}	−0.74868	
29	Cu	61*	3/2	10.8	—	8.22×10^{-2}	2.13	
29	·Cu	63	3/2	11.285	69.09	9.31×10^{-2}	2.2206	−0.16
29	Cu	64*	1	3.1	—	9.79×10^{-4}	0.40	

| Isotope | | | Spin I | NMR frequency (MHz for a 10-kG field) | Natural abundance (%) | Relative sensitivity at constant field | Magnetic moment μ (multiples of the nuclear magneton $eh/4\pi Mc$) | Electric quadrupole moment Q (multiples of barns $(10^{-24}\ cm^2)$) |
Z	Element	A						
29	·Cu	65	$\frac{3}{2}$	12.089	30.91	0.114	2.3789	−0.15
29	Cu	66*	1	1.65	—	1.54×10^{-4}	−0.216	—
30	Zn	65*	$\frac{5}{2}$	2.345	—	1.95×10^{-3}	0.7692	-2.4×10^{-2}
30	·Zn	67	$\frac{5}{2}$	2.663	4.11	2.85×10^{-3}	0.8733	0.15
31	Ga	68*	1	0.0892	—	2.45×10^{-8}	0.0117	3.1×10^{-2}
31	Ga	69	$\frac{3}{2}$	10.22	60.4	6.91×10^{-2}	2.011	0.178
31	Ga	71	$\frac{3}{2}$	12.984	39.6	0.142	2.5549	0.112
31	Ga	72*	3	0.33591	—	7.80×10^{-6}	−0.13220	0.72
32	Ge	71*	$\frac{1}{2}$	8.4	—	7.64×10^{-3}	0.55	—
32	·Ge	73	$\frac{9}{2}$	1.4852	7.76	1.40×10^{-3}	−0.87679	−0.2
33	·As	75	$\frac{3}{2}$	7.2919	100	2.51×10^{-2}	1.4349	0.3
34	Se	76*	2	3.45	—	4.27×10^{-3}	−0.906	—
34	·Se	77	$\frac{1}{2}$	8.118	7.58	6.93×10^{-3}	0.5325	—
34	Se	79	$\frac{7}{2}$	2.22	—	2.98×10^{-3}	−1.02	0.9
35	Br	76*	1	4.18	—	2.52×10^{-3}	(−)0.548	0.27
35	·Br	79	$\frac{3}{2}$	10.667	50.54	7.86×10^{-2}	2.0990	0.33
35	Br	80*	1	3.92	—	2.08×10^{-3}	0.514	0.20
35	Br	80*m	5	2.008	—	4.20×10^{-3}	1.317	0.76
35	·Br	81	$\frac{3}{2}$	11.498	49.46	9.85×10^{-2}	2.2626	0.28
35	Br	82*	5	2.479	—	7.90×10^{-3}	(+)1.626	(+)0.76
36	·Kr	83	$\frac{9}{2}$	1.638	11.55	1.88×10^{-3}	−0.9671	0.15
36	Kr	85*	$\frac{9}{2}$	1.6956	—	2.08×10^{-3}	−1.001	0.25
37	Rb	81*	$\frac{3}{2}$	10.4	—	7.32×10^{-2}	2.05	—
37	Rb	82*m	5	2.29	—	6.20×10^{-3}	1.50	—
37	·Rb	83*	$\frac{5}{2}$	4.33	—	1.23×10^{-2}	1.42	—
37	Rb	84*	2	5.03	—	1.32×10^{-2}	−1.32	—

Z	Element	A	Spin		Abundance %		μ	Q
37	·Rb	85	5/2	4.1108	72.15	1.05×10^{-2}	1.3482	0.27
37	Rb	86*	2	6.44	—	2.77×10^{-2}	-1.69	
37	·Rb	87	3/2	13.931	27.85	0.175	2.7414	0.13
38	·Sr	87	9/2	1.8452	7.02	2.69×10^{-3}	-1.0893	0.2
39	·Y	89	1/2	2.0859	100	1.18×10^{-4}	-0.13682	—
39	Y	90*	2	6.17	—	2.44×10^{-2}	-1.62	-0.16
39	Y	91*	1/2	2.49	—	1.99×10^{-4}	0.163	—
40	·Zr	91	5/2	3.97249	11.23	9.48×10^{-3}	-1.30284	
41	·Nb	93	9/2	10.407	100	0.482	6.1435	-0.2
42	·Mo	95	5/2	2.774	15.72	3.23×10^{-3}	-0.9097	0.12
42	·Mo	97	5/2	2.832	9.46	3.43×10^{-3}	-0.9289	1.1
43	·Tc	99*	9/2	9.5830	—	0.376	5.6572	0.3
44	Ru	99	3/2	1.44	12.72	1.95×10^{-4}	-0.284	
44	Ru	101	5/2	2.1	17.07	1.41×10^{-3}	-0.69	—
45	·Rh	103	1/2	1.3401	100	3.11×10^{-5}	-0.08790	
46	·Pd	105	5/2	1.95	22.23	1.12×10^{-3}	-0.639	
47	Ag	104*	5	6.1	—	0.118	4.0	
47	Ag	104*m	2	14.0	—	0.291	3.7	
47	Ag	105*	1/2	1.54	—	4.73×10^{-5}	0.101	—
47	·Ag	107	1/2	1.7229	51.82	6.62×10^{-5}	-0.11301	
47	Ag	108*	1	32.0	—	1.13	4.2	
47	·Ag	109	1/2	1.9807	48.18	1.01×10^{-4}	-0.12992	
47	Ag	110*m	6	4.557	—	6.87×10^{-2}	3.587	
47	Ag	111*	1/2	2.21	—	1.40×10^{-4}	-0.145	
47	Ag	112*	2	0.2077	—	9.00×10^{-7}	0.0545	
47	Ag	113*	1/2	2.41	—	1.81×10^{-4}	0.158	
48	Cd	107*	5/2	1.879	—	1.00×10^{-3}	-0.6162	0.8
48	Cd	109*	5/2	2.529	—	2.44×10^{-3}	-0.8293	0.8
48	·Cd	111	1/2	9.028	12.75	9.54×10^{-3}	-0.5922	—
48	·Cd	113	1/2	9.445	12.26	1.09×10^{-2}	-0.6195	
48	Cd	113*m	11/2	1.51	—	2.13×10^{-3}	-1.09	-0.79
48	Cd	115*	1/2	9.862	—	1.24×10^{-2}	-0.6469	—

	Isotope			NMR frequency (MHz for a 10-kG field)	Natural abundance (%)	Relative sensitivity at constant field	Magnetic moment μ (multiples of the nuclear magneton $eh/4\pi Mc$)	Electric quadrupole moment Q (multiples of barns $(10^{-24}\ cm^2)$)
Z	Element	A	Spin I					
48	Cd	115*m	$\frac{11}{2}$	1.447	—	1.87×10^{-3}	-1.044	-0.61
49	·In	113	$\frac{9}{2}$	9.3099	4.28	0.345	5.4960	1.14
49	In	113*m	$\frac{1}{2}$	3.209	—	4.28×10^{-4}	-0.2105	—
49	In	114*m	5	7.2	—	0.191	4.7	1.16
49	·In	115*	$\frac{9}{2}$	9.3301	95.72	0.347	5.5079	1.16
49	In	115*m	$\frac{1}{2}$	3.715	—	6.64×10^{-4}	-0.2437	—
49	In	116*	5	6.42	—	0.137	4.21	
49	In	116*m	5	6.7	—	0.156	4.4	
50	·Sn	115	$\frac{1}{2}$	13.922	0.35	3.50×10^{-2}	-0.91320	—
50	·Sn	117	$\frac{1}{2}$	15.168	7.61	4.52×10^{-2}	-0.99490	—
50	·Sn	119	$\frac{1}{2}$	15.869	8.58	5.18×10^{-2}	-1.0409	—
51	·Sb	121	$\frac{5}{2}$	10.189	57.25	0.160	3.3415	-0.5
51	Sb	122*	2	7.24	—	3.94×10^{-2}	-1.90	
51	·Sb	123	$\frac{7}{2}$	5.5176	42.75	4.57×10^{-2}	2.5334	-0.7
52	Te	119*	$\frac{1}{2}$	4.12	—	9.04×10^{-4}	0.27	—
52	·Te	123	$\frac{1}{2}$	11.16	0.87	1.8×10^{-2}	-0.7319	—
52	·Te	125	$\frac{1}{2}$	13.45	6.99	3.15×10^{-2}	-0.8824	—
53	I	125*	$\frac{5}{2}$	9.0	—	0.116	3	-0.66
53	·I	127	$\frac{5}{2}$	8.5183	100	9.34×10^{-2}	2.7937	-0.69
53	·I	129*	$\frac{7}{2}$	5.6694	—	4.96×10^{-2}	2.6031	-0.48
53	I	131*	$\frac{7}{2}$	5.963	—	5.77×10^{-2}	2.738	-0.41
54	·Xe	129	$\frac{1}{2}$	11.777	26.44	2.12×10^{-2}	-0.77247	
54	·Xe	131	$\frac{3}{2}$	3.4911	21.18	2.76×10^{-3}	0.68697	-0.12
55	Cs	127*	$\frac{1}{2}$	21.8	—	0.134	1.43	—
55	Cs	129*	$\frac{1}{2}$	22.4	—	0.146	1.47	—
55	Cs	130*	1	10.7	—	4.20×10^{-2}	1.4	
55	Cs	131*	$\frac{5}{2}$	10.72	—	0.186	3.517	

			Spin		%			
55	Cs	132*	2	8.46	—	6.28×10^{-2}	2.22	-3×10^{-3}
55	·Cs	133	$\frac{7}{2}$	5.58469	100	4.74×10^{-2}	2.56422	0.43
55	·Cs	134*	4	5.666	—	6.28×10^{-2}	2.973	
55	Cs	134*m	8	1.0447	—	1.42×10^{-3}	1.0964	
55	Cs	135*	$\frac{7}{2}$	5.9096	—	5.62×10^{-2}	2.7134	
55	Cs	137*	$\frac{7}{2}$	6.1459	—	6.32×10^{-2}	2.8219	
56	·Ba	135	$\frac{3}{2}$	4.2296	6.59	4.90×10^{-3}	0.83229	0.25
56	·Ba	137	$\frac{3}{2}$	4.7315	11.32	6.86×10^{-3}	0.93107	0.2
57	·La	138	5*	5.6171	0.089	9.19×10^{-2}	3.6844	2.7
57	·La	139	$\frac{7}{2}$	6.0144	99.911	5.92×10^{-2}	2.7615	0.21
58	Ce	137*	$\frac{3}{2}$	4.6	—	6.20×10^{-3}	0.9	
58	Ce	137*m	$\frac{11}{2}$	0.96	—	5.40×10^{-4}	0.69	
58	Ce	139*	$\frac{3}{2}$	5.1	—	8.50×10^{-3}	1.0	
58	Ce	141*	$\frac{7}{2}$	2.1	—	2.57×10^{-3}	0.97	
58	Ce	143*	$\frac{7}{2}$	2.2	—	2.81×10^{-3}	1.0	
59	·Pr	141	$\frac{5}{2}$	12.5	100	0.293	4.09	-5.9×10^{-2}
59	Pr	142*	2	1.1	—	1.55×10^{-4}	0.30	4×10^{-2}
60	Nd	143	$\frac{7}{2}$	2.315	12.17	3.38×10^{-3}	-1.063	-0.48
60	Nd	145	$\frac{7}{2}$	1.42	8.30	7.86×10^{-4}	-0.654	-0.25
60	Nd	147*	$\frac{5}{2}$	1.77	—	8.32×10^{-4}	0.579	
61	Pm	143*	$(\frac{5}{2})$	11.6	—	0.235	(3.8)	
61	Pm	143*	$(\frac{7}{2})$	8.5	—	0.167	(3.9)	
61	Pm	144*	(5)	2.6	—	9.02×10^{-3}	(1.7)	
61	Pm	144*	(6)	2.3	—	8.68×10^{-3}	(1.8)	
61	Pm	147*	$\frac{7}{2}$	5.62	—	4.83×10^{-2}	2.58	0.7
61	Pm	148*	1	16	—	0.142	2.1	0.2
61	Pm	148*m	6	2.3	—	8.68×10^{-3}	1.8	
61	Pm	149*	$\frac{7}{2}$	7.2	—	0.101	3.3	
61	Pm	151*	$\frac{5}{2}$	5.5	—	2.50×10^{-2}	1.8	
62	Sm	147	$\frac{7}{2}$	1.76	14.97	1.48×10^{-3}	-0.807	1.9
62	Sm	149	$\frac{7}{2}$	1.40	13.83	7.47×10^{-4}	-0.643	-0.208
63	·Eu	151	$\frac{5}{2}$	10.559	47.82	0.178	3.4630	6.0×10^{-2}
63	Eu	152*	3	4.858	—	2.38×10^{-2}	1.912	1.16

Isotope			Spin I	NMR frequency (MHz for a 10-kG field)	Natural abundance (%)	Relative sensitivity at constant field	Magnetic moment μ (multiples of the nuclear magneton $eh/4\pi Mc$)	Electric quadrupole moment Q (multiples of barns (10^{-24} cm^2))
Z	A	Element						
63	153	·Eu	$\frac{5}{2}$	4.6627	52.18	1.53×10^{-2}	1.5292	2.9
63	154*	Eu	3	5.084	—	2.72×10^{-2}	2.001	
64	155	·Gd	$\frac{3}{2}$	1.6	14.73	2.79×10^{-4}	−0.32	1.6
64	157	·Gd	$\frac{3}{2}$	2.0	15.68	5.44×10^{-4}	−0.40	2
65	156*	Tb	3	3.8	—	1.15×10^{-2}	1.5	1.4
65	159	Tb	$\frac{3}{2}$	9.66	100	5.83×10^{-2}	1.90	1.3
65	160*	Tb	3	4.1	—	1.39×10^{-2}	1.6	1.9
66	155*	Dy	$(\frac{3}{2})$	1.1	—	7.87×10^{-5}	0.21	
66	157*	Dy	$(\frac{3}{2})$	1.6	—	2.79×10^{-4}	0.32	
66	161	Dy	$\frac{5}{2}$	1.4	18.88	4.17×10^{-4}	−0.46	1.4
66	163	Dy	$\frac{5}{2}$	2.0	24.97	1.12×10^{-3}	0.64	1.6
67	165	Ho	$\frac{7}{2}$	8.73	100	0.181	4.01	2.82
68	165*	Er	$\frac{5}{2}$	2.0	—	1.18×10^{-3}	0.65	2.2
68	167	Er	$\frac{7}{2}$	1.23	22.94	5.07×10^{-4}	−0.565	2.83
68	169*	Er	$\frac{1}{2}$	7.8	—	6.09×10^{-3}	0.51	—
68	171*	Er	$\frac{5}{2}$	2.1	—	1.47×10^{-3}	0.70	
69	166*	Tm	2	0.19	—	7.17×10^{-7}	0.05	4.6
69	169	·Tm	$\frac{1}{2}$	3.52	100	5.66×10^{-4}	−0.231	—
69	170*	Tm	1	2.0	—	2.69×10^{-4}	0.26	0.61
69	171*	Tm	$\frac{1}{2}$	3.46	—	5.37×10^{-4}	0.227	—
70	171	·Yb	$\frac{1}{2}$	7.4990	14.31	5.46×10^{-3}	0.49188	—
70	173	Yb	$\frac{5}{2}$	2.0659	16.13	1.33×10^{-3}	−0.67755	2.8
70	175*	Yb	$(\frac{7}{2})$	0.33	—	9.40×10^{-6}	−0.15	
71	175	·Lu	$\frac{7}{2}$	4.86	97.41	3.12×10^{-2}	2.23	5.68
71	176*	Lu	7	3.4	2.59	3.72×10^{-2}	3.1	8.0
71	177*	Lu	$\frac{7}{2}$	4.84	—	3.08×10^{-2}	2.22	5.51
72	177	Hf	$\frac{7}{2}$	1.3	18.50	6.38×10^{-4}	0.61	3

Z	Isotope	A	Spin I	Resonance freq.	Abundance (%)	Rel. sensitivity	Magnetic moment	Quadrupole moment
72	Hf	179	9/2	0.80	13.75	2.16×10^{-4}	-0.47	3
73	·Ta	181	7/2	5.096	99.988	3.60×10^{-2}	2.340	3
74	·W	183	1/2	1.7716	14.40	7.20×10^{-5}	0.116205	—
75	·Re	185	5/2	9.5855	37.07	0.133	3.1437	2.8
75	·Re	186*	1	13.17	—	7.90×10^{-2}	1.728	
75	·Re	187*	5/2	9.6837	62.93	0.137	3.1759	2.6
75	·Re	188*	1	13.55	—	8.59×10^{-2}	1.777	
76	·Os	187	1/2	0.98059	1.64	1.22×10^{-5}	0.06432	—
76	·Os	189	3/2	3.3034	16.1	2.34×10^{-3}	0.65004	0.8
77	·Ir	191	3/2	0.7318	37.3	2.53×10^{-5}	0.1440	1.5
77	·Ir	193	3/2	0.7968	62.7	3.27×10^{-5}	0.1568	1.5
78	·Pt	195	1/2	9.153	33.8	9.94×10^{-3}	0.6004	—
79	·Au	190*	1	0.496	—	4.20×10^{-6}	0.065	
79	·Au	194*	1	0.56	—	5.95×10^{-6}	0.073	
79	·Au	195*	3/2	0.742	—	2.65×10^{-5}	0.146	
79	·Au	196*	2	2.3	—	1.24×10^{-3}	0.6	
79	·Au	197	3/2	0.729188	100	2.51×10^{-5}	0.143489	0.59
79	·Au	198*	2	2.227	—	1.14×10^{-3}	0.5842	
79	·Au	199*	3/2	1.358	—	1.62×10^{-4}	0.2673	
80	Hg	193*	3/2	3.1	—	1.93×10^{-3}	-0.61	1.37
80	Hg	193*m	13/2	1.23	—	1.57×10^{-3}	-1.05	1.41
80	Hg	195*	1/2	8.1	—	6.84×10^{-3}	0.53	
80	Hg	195*m	13/2	1.22	—	1.53×10^{-3}	-1.04	
80	·Hg	197*	1/2	7.9	—	6.46×10^{-3}	0.52	
80	·Hg	199	1/2	7.59012	16.84	5.67×10^{-3}	0.497859	
80	Hg	201	3/2	2.8099	13.22	1.44×10^{-3}	-0.55293	0.50
80	Hg	203*	5/2	2.5	—	2.45×10^{-3}	0.83	0.5
81	Tl	197*	1/2	23.6	—	0.171	1.55	—
81	Tl	199*	1/2	23.9	—	0.178	1.57	—
81	Tl	200*	2	0.57	—	1.94×10^{-5}	(0.15)	—
81	Tl	201*	1/2	24.1	—	0.181	1.58	—
81	Tl	202*	2	0.57	—	1.94×10^{-5}	(0.15)	
81	·Tl	203	1/2	24.332	29.50	0.187	1.5960	—

	Isotope		Spin I	NMR frequency (MHz for a 10-kG field)	Natural abundance (%)	Relative sensitivity at constant field	Magnetic moment μ (multiples of the nuclear magneton $eh/4\pi Mc$)	Electric quadrupole moment Q (multiples of barns (10^{-24} cm²))
Z	Element	A						
81	Tl	204*	2	0.34	—	4.05×10^{-6}	0.089	
81	·Tl	205	$\frac{1}{2}$	24.570	70.50	0.192	1.6116	—
82	·Pb	207	$\frac{1}{2}$	8.90771	22.6	9.16×10^{-3}	0.584284	—
83	Bi	203*	$\frac{9}{2}$	7.78	—	0.201	4.59	−0.64
83	Bi	204*	6	5.40	—	0.114	4.25	−0.41
83	Bi	205*	$\frac{9}{2}$	9.3	—	0.346	(5.5)	
83	Bi	206*	6	5.79	—	0.141	4.56	−0.19
83	·Bi	209*	$\frac{9}{2}$	6.84178	100	0.137	4.03896	−0.4
83	Bi	210*	1	0.337	—	1.32×10^{-6}	0.0442	0.13
84	Po	205*	$\frac{5}{2}$	0.79	—	7.55×10^{-5}	0.26	0.17
84	Po	207*	$\frac{5}{2}$	0.82	—	8.43×10^{-5}	0.27	0.28
89	Ac	227*	$\frac{3}{2}$	5.6	—	1.13×10^{-2}	1.1	−1.7
90	Th	229*	$\frac{5}{2}$	1.2	—	2.74×10^{-4}	0.4	4.6
91	Pa	231*	$\frac{3}{2}$	9.96	—	6.40×10^{-2}	1.96	
91	Pa	233*	$\frac{3}{2}$	17	—	0.334	3.4	−3.0
92	U	233*	$\frac{5}{2}$	1.6	—	6.75×10^{-4}	0.54	3.5
92	U	235*	$\frac{7}{2}$	0.76	0.72	1.21×10^{-4}	0.35	4.1
93	Np	237*	$\frac{5}{2}$	18	—	0.926	(6)	
94	Pu	239*	$\frac{1}{2}$	3.05	—	3.67×10^{-4}	0.200	—
94	Pu	241*	$\frac{5}{2}$	2.09	—	1.38×10^{-3}	−0.686	
95	Am	241*	$\frac{5}{2}$	4.82	—	1.69×10^{-2}	1.58	4.9
95	Am	242*	1	2.90	—	8.46×10^{-4}	0.381	−2.8
95	Am	243*	$\frac{5}{2}$	4.79	—	1.66×10^{-2}	1.57	4.9

| Free electron with $g = 2.00232$ | $\frac{1}{2}$ | 2.80246×10^4 | — | 2.84×10^8 | -1836.09 | — |

[a] Compiled by K. Lee and W. A. Anderson, October, 1967. Z, atomic number; A, atomic weight (mass number); I, nuclear spin in units of $h/2\pi$; μ, magnetic moments in units of the nuclear magneton $eh/4\pi Mc$; Q, quadrupole moment in units of barns (10^{-24} cm^2); *, magnetic moment observed by NMR; *, radioactive isotope; ( ), assumed or estimated values; m, metastable excited state.

Assuming a nuclear magneton value of 5.0505×10^{-24} erg/gauss, the NMR frequency was calculated for a total field of 10^4 gauss. The sensitivities, relative to the proton, are calculated from:

$$\text{Sensitivity at constant field} = 7.652 \times 10^{-3} \; \mu^3 \; (I + 1)/I^2.$$

This expression assumes an equal number of nuclei, a constant temperature, and that $T_1 = T_2$ (the longitudinal relaxation time equals the transverse relaxation time). This sensitivity represents the ideal induced voltage in the receiver coil at saturation and with a constant noise source. The calculated values are therefore determined under complete optimum conditions and should be regarded as such.

Further details and literature references are given in the original tabulation, printed and distributed by Varian Associates, Palo Alto, California.

Proton NMR Spectra of "Unknowns"

All spectra in this section were obtained at 60 MHz except where specified. Tetramethylsilane was used as an internal reference for all spectra except Spectrum 35. Except where noted samples were solutions in chloroform-*d*. Chemicals were reagent grade but were not repurified. Some weak lines due to impurities appear in the spectra but are not identified in order to simulate the situation encountered in practice.

Spectra have been selected to illustrate points covered in the text. Appropriate spectra are assigned in the problems at the end of Chapters 4–7 and 9–11. Answers to the *odd-numbered* spectra are given in Appendix D.

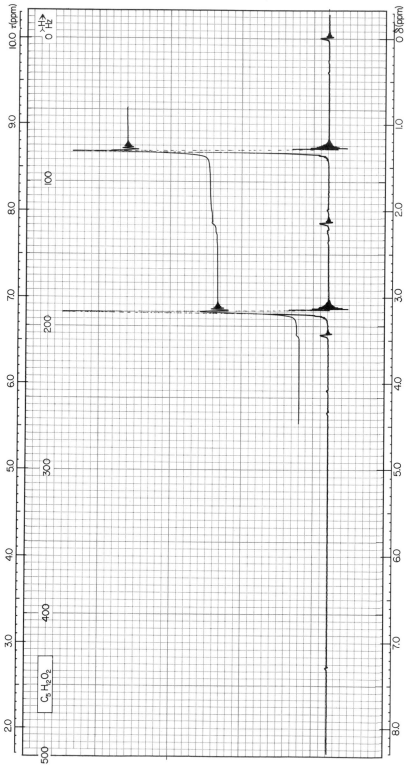

$C_5 H_{12} O_2$

Spectrum 1

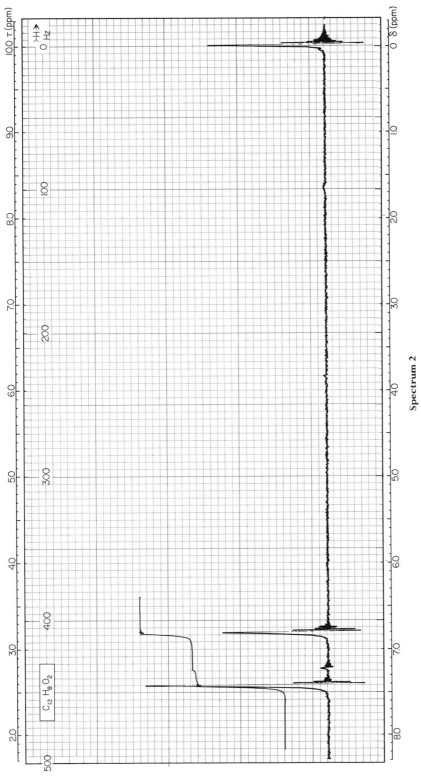

Spectrum 2

255

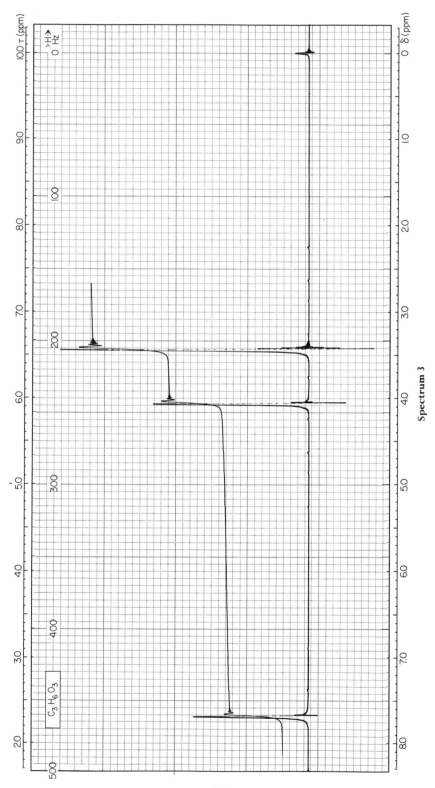

Spectrum 3

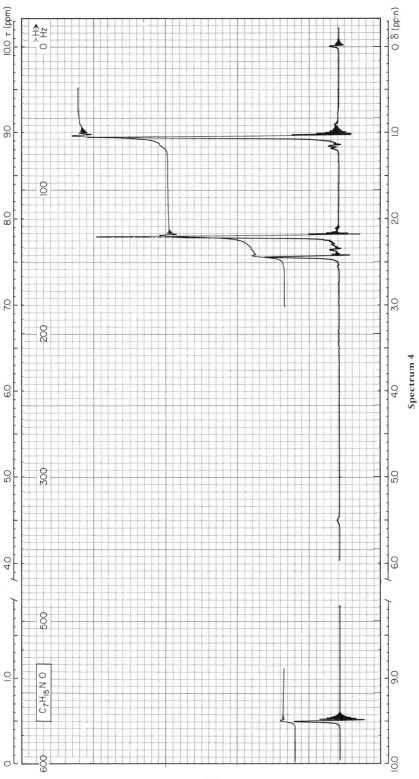

Spectrum 4

$C_7H_{15}NO$

257

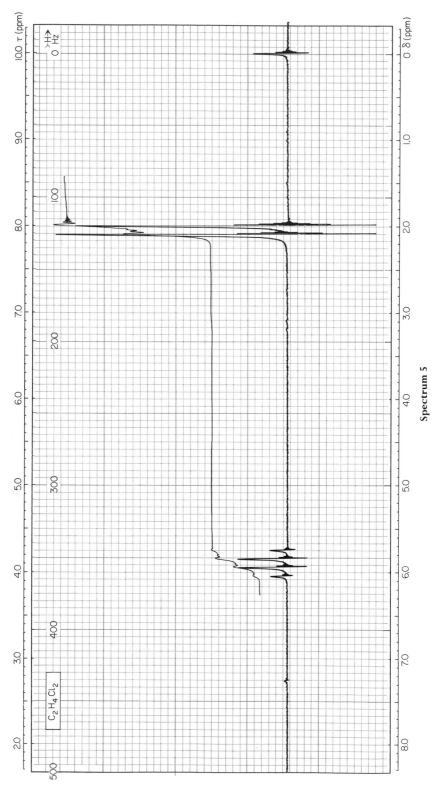

Spectrum 5

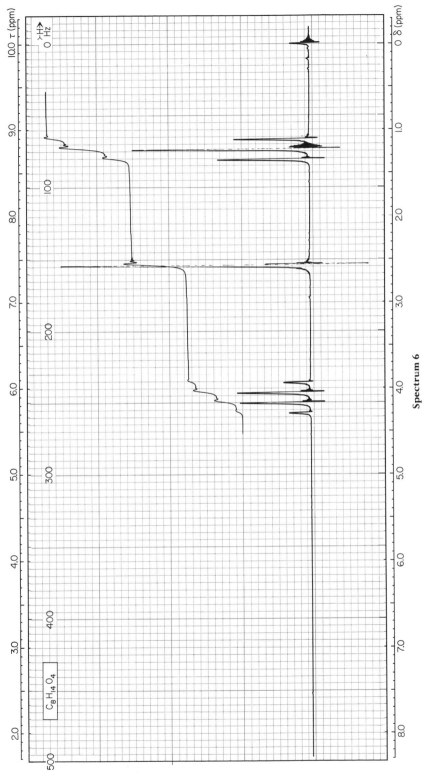

Spectrum 6

$C_8H_{14}O_4$

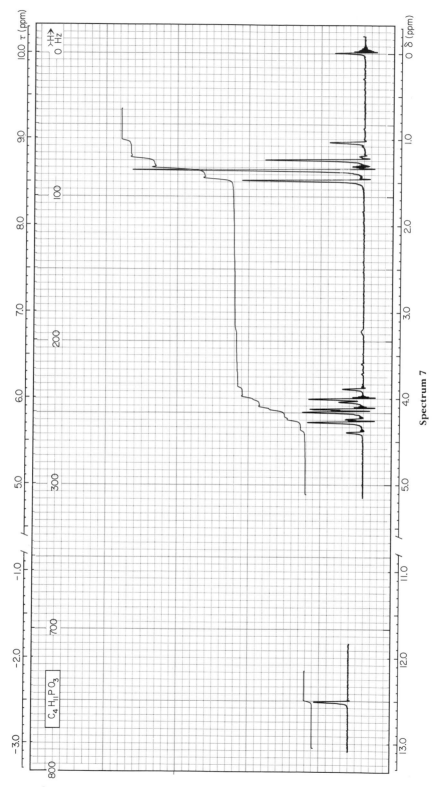

Spectrum 7

260

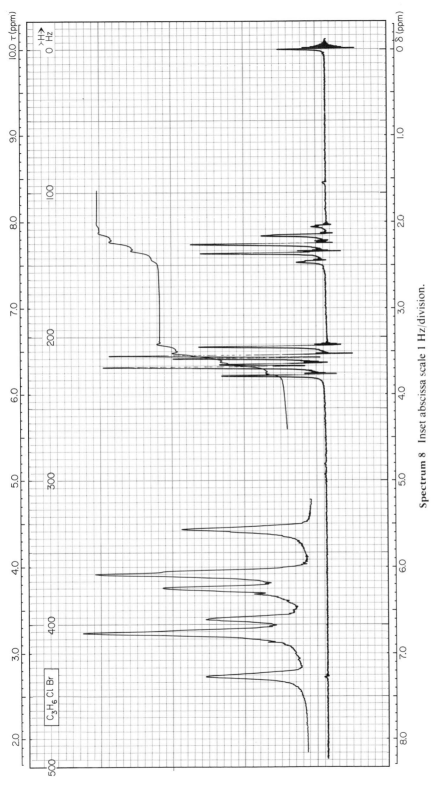

Spectrum 8 Inset abscissa scale 1 Hz/division.

C_3H_6ClBr

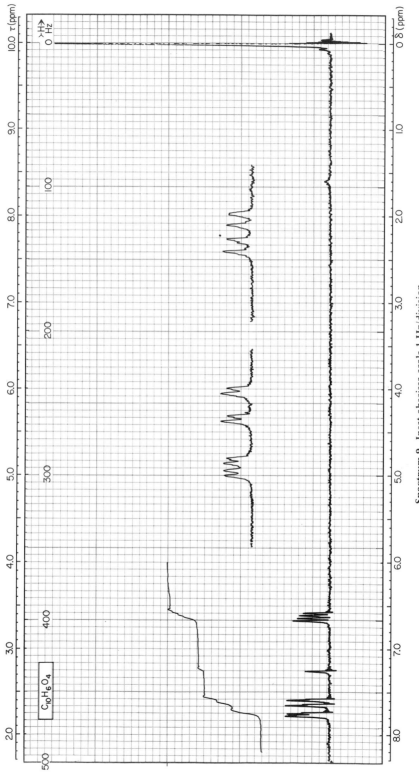

Spectrum 9 Inset abscissa scale 1 Hz/division.

$C_{10}H_6O_4$

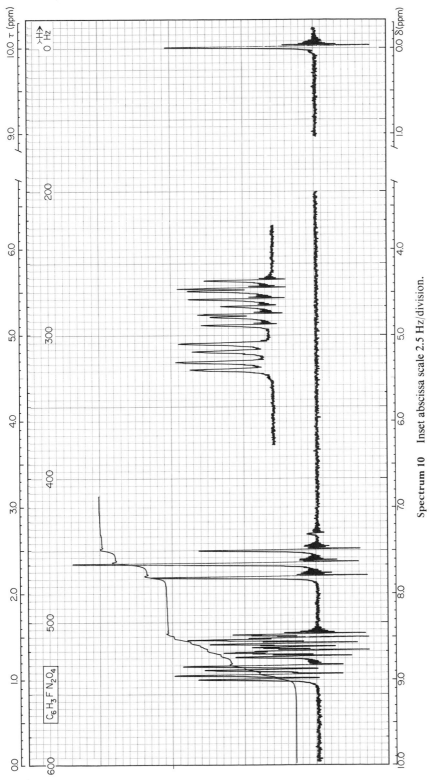

Spectrum 10 Inset abscissa scale 2.5 Hz/division.

263

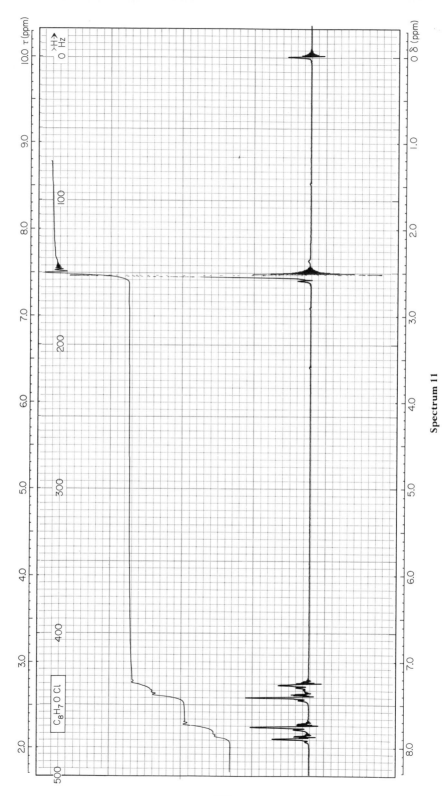

Spectrum 11

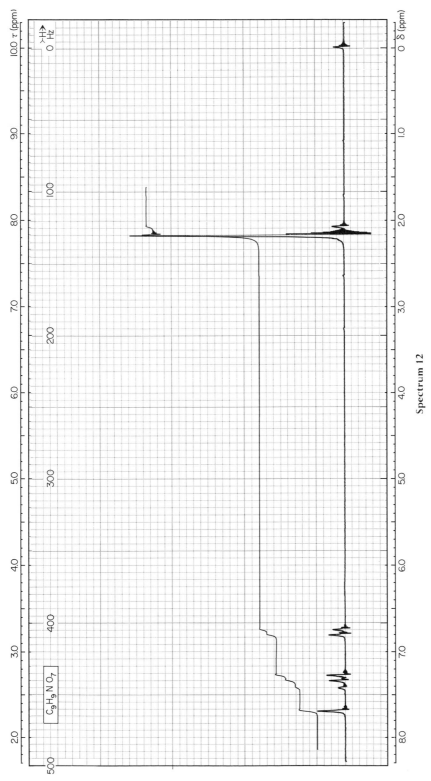

Spectrum 12

265

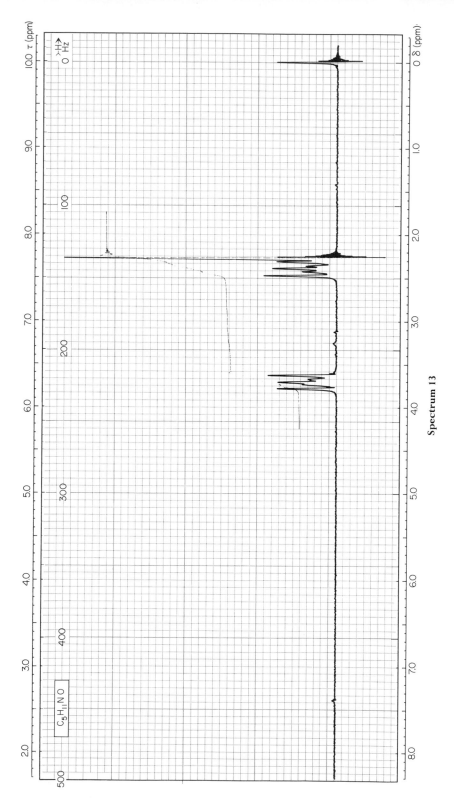

C₅H₁₁NO

Spectrum 13

266

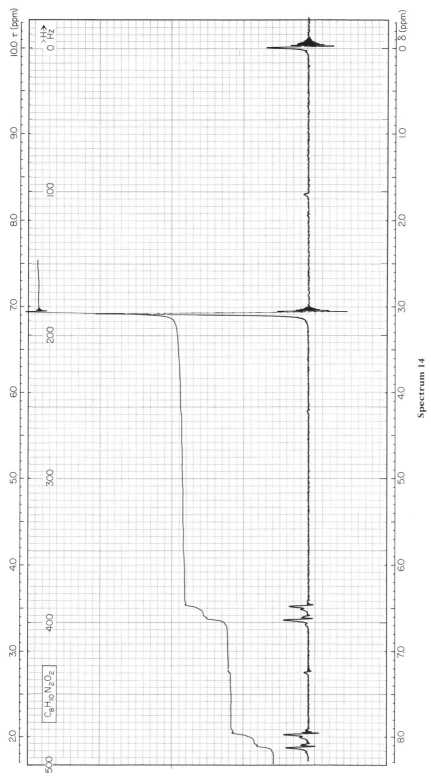

Spectrum 14

$C_8H_{10}N_2O_2$

267

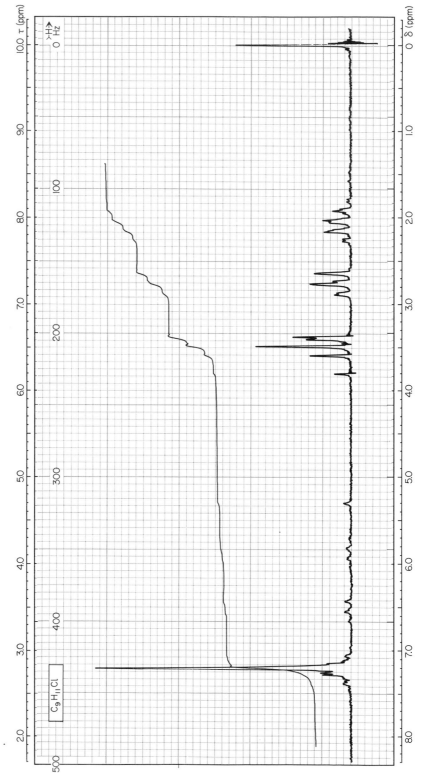

C₉H₁₁Cl

Spectrum 15

268

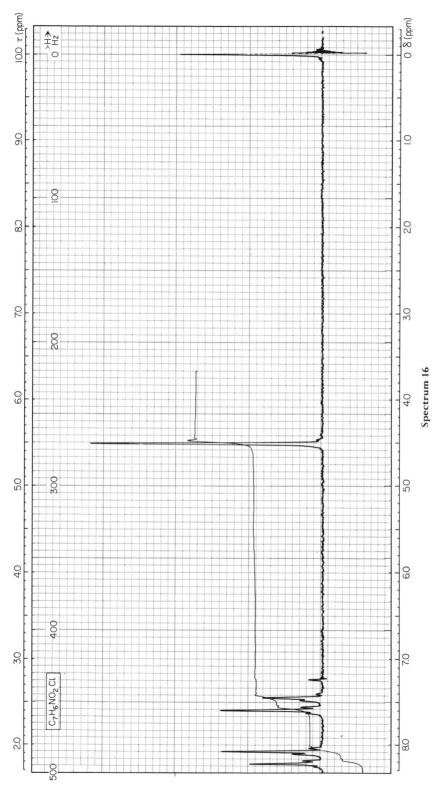

Spectrum 16

C₇H₆NO₂Cl

269

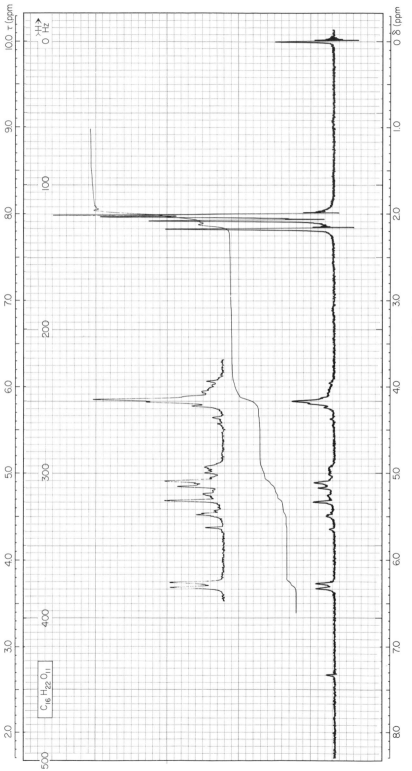

Spectrum 17 A sugar derivative.

$C_{16}H_{22}O_{11}$

270

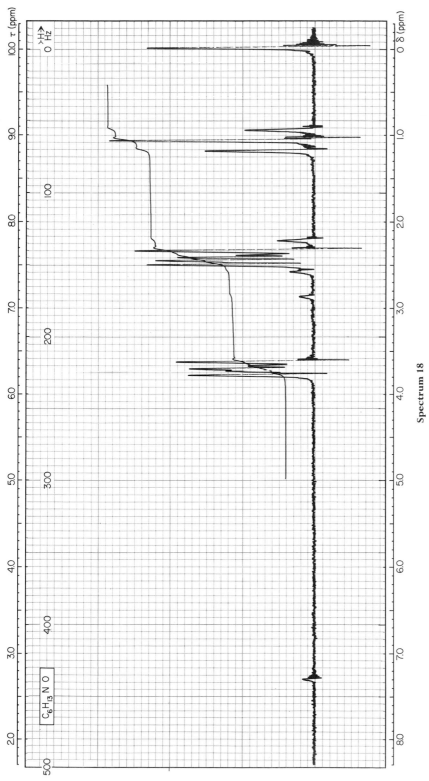

Spectrum 18

$C_6H_{13}NO$

271

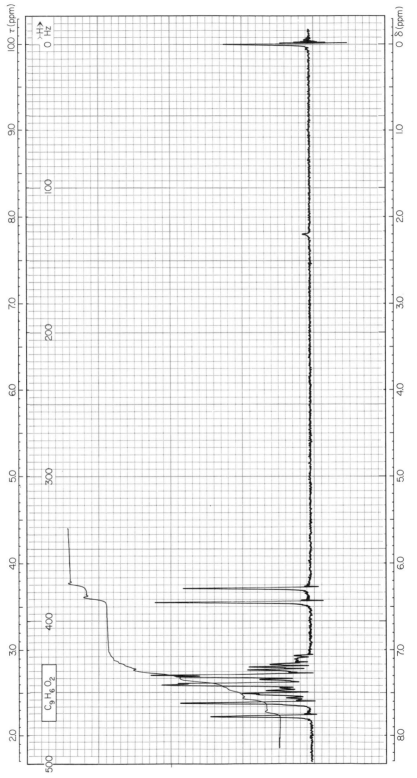

Spectrum 19

$C_9H_6O_2$

272

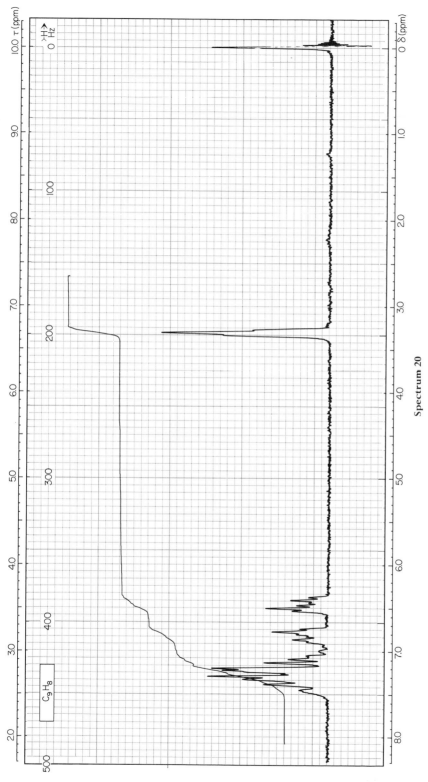

Spectrum 20

C₉H₈

273

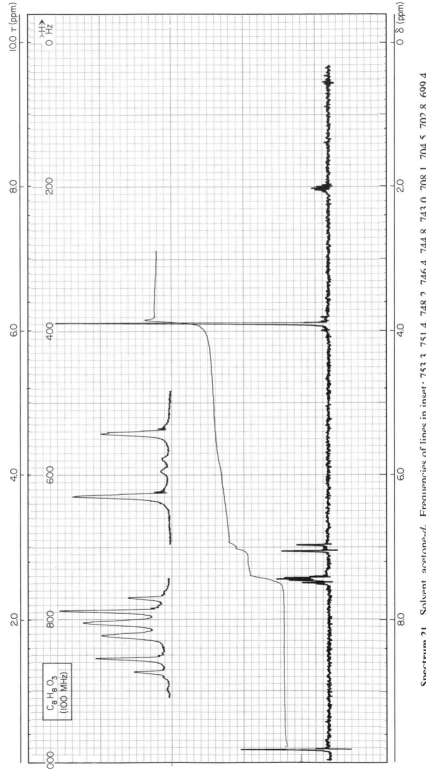

Spectrum 21 Solvent, acetone-d_6. Frequencies of lines in inset: 753.3, 751.4, 748.2, 746.4, 744.8, 743.0, 708.1, 704.5, 702.8, 699.4.

$C_8H_8O_3$
(100 MHz)

274

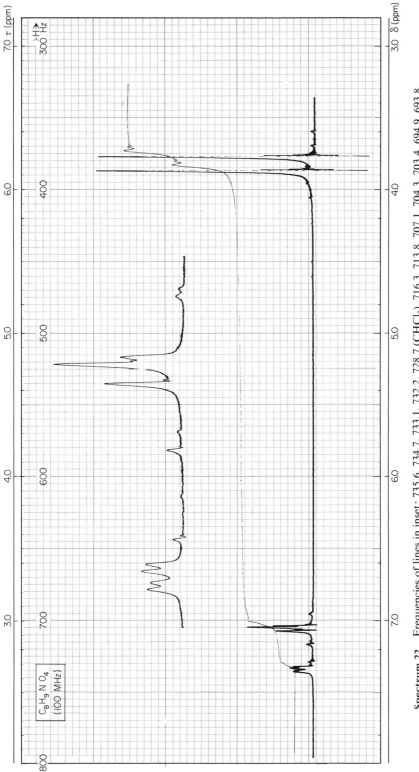

Spectrum 22 Frequencies of lines in inset: 735.6, 734.7, 733.1, 732.2, 728.7 (CHCl₃), 716.3, 713.8, 707.1, 704.3, 703.4, 694.9, 693.8.

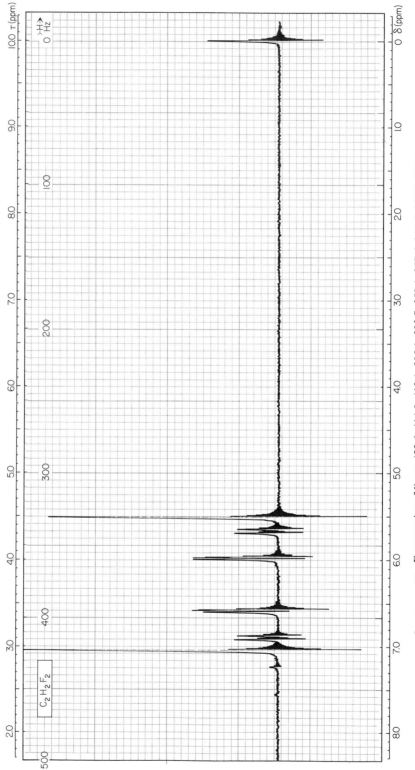

Spectrum 23 Frequencies of lines: 422.6, 414.8, 412.1, 395.1, 393.7, 359.1, 357.6, 340.9, 337.9, 330.1.

276

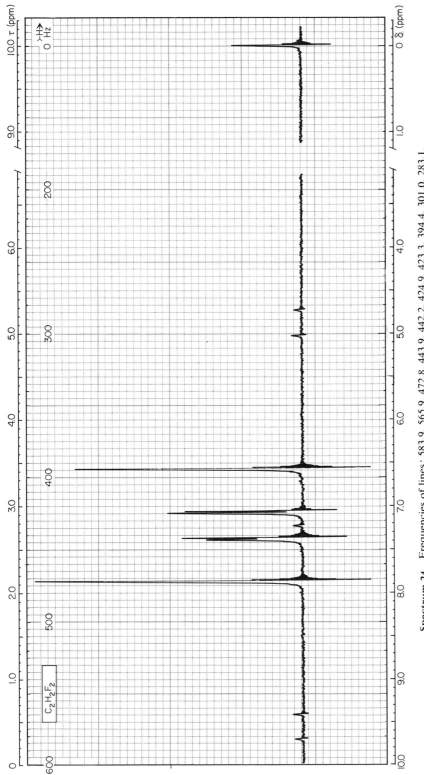

Spectrum 24 Frequencies of lines: 583.9, 565.9, 472.8, 443.9, 442.2, 424.9, 423.3, 394.4, 301.0, 283.1.

$C_2H_2F_2$

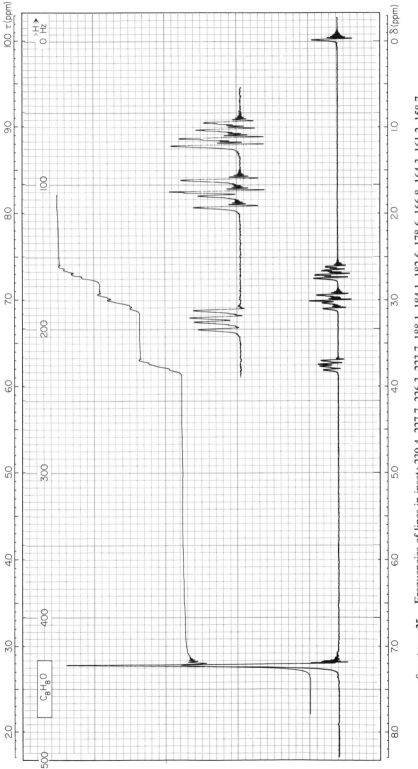

C_8H_8O

Spectrum 25 Frequencies of lines in inset: 230.4, 227.7, 226.3, 223.7, 188.1, 184.1, 182.6, 178.6, 166.8, 164.3, 161.2, 158.7.

278

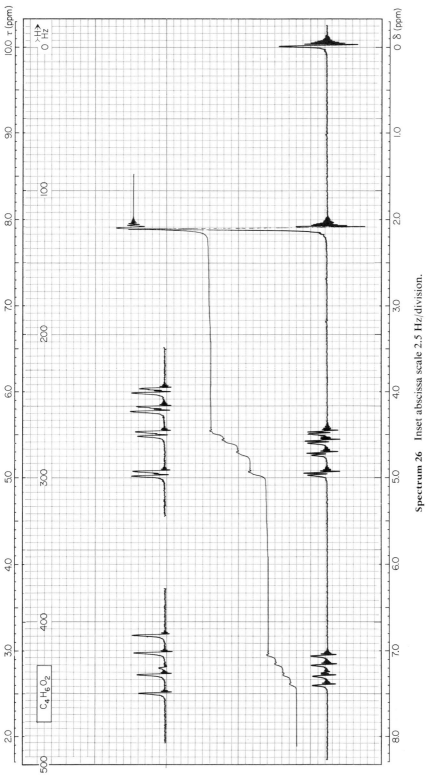

Spectrum 26 Inset abscissa scale 2.5 Hz/division.

279

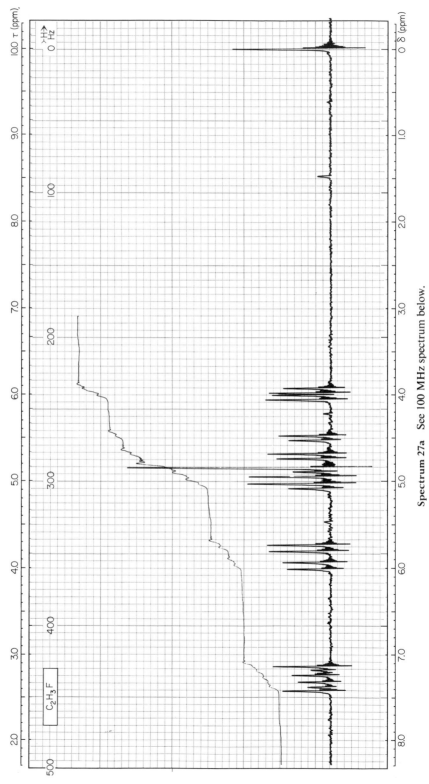

Spectrum 27a   See 100 MHz spectrum below.

C₂H₃F

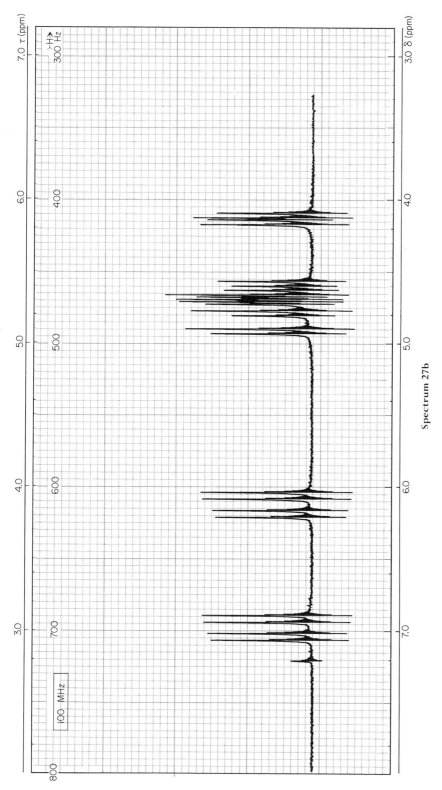

Spectrum 27b

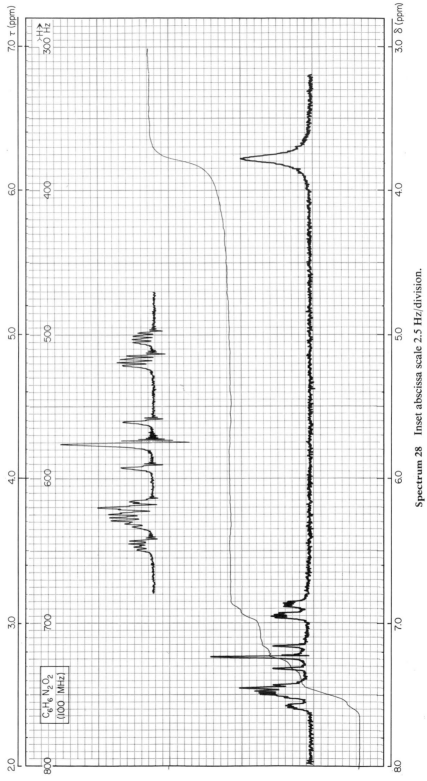

Spectrum 28   Inset abscissa scale 2.5 Hz/division.

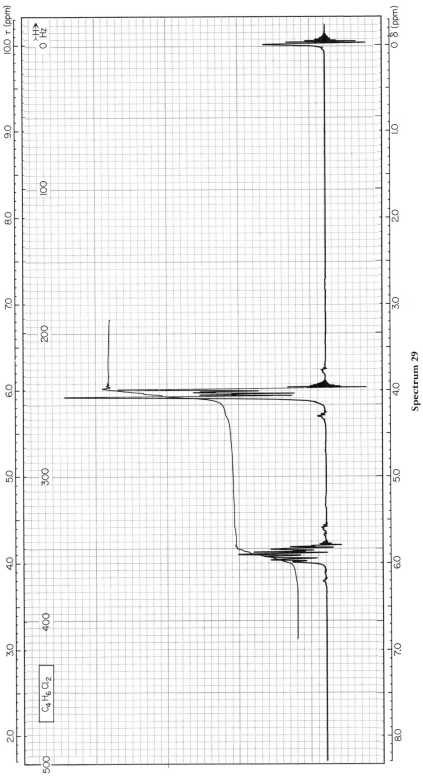

Spectrum 29

$C_4H_6Cl_2$

283

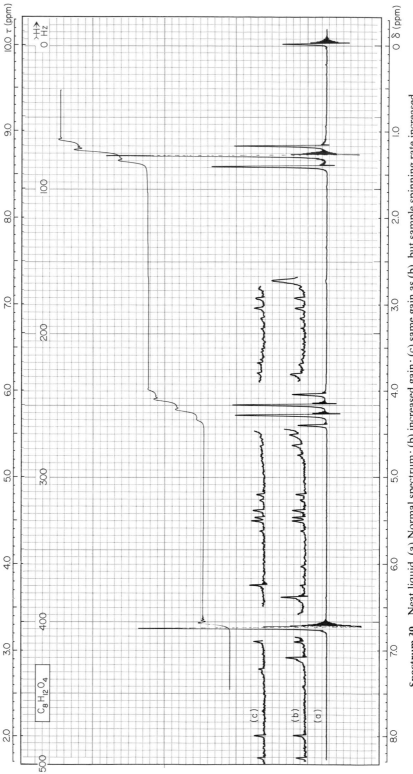

Spectrum 30 Neat liquid. (a) Normal spectrum; (b) increased gain; (c) same gain as (b), but sample spinning rate increased.

284

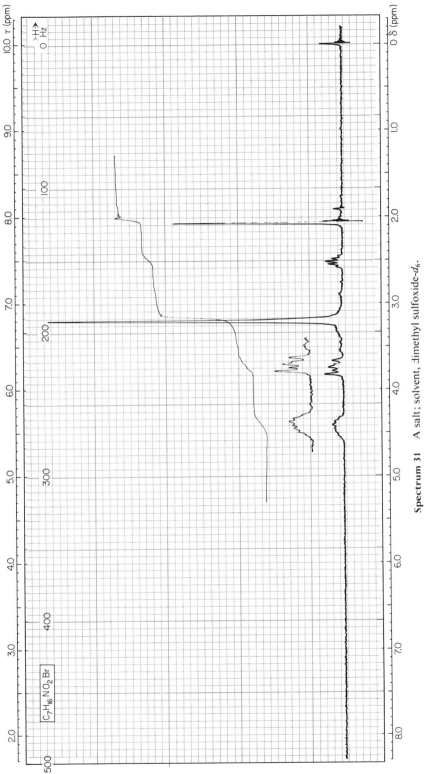

C$_7$H$_{16}$NO$_2$Br

>H→
─O Hz

τ (ppm)

Spectrum 31   A salt; solvent, dimethyl sulfoxide-d_6.

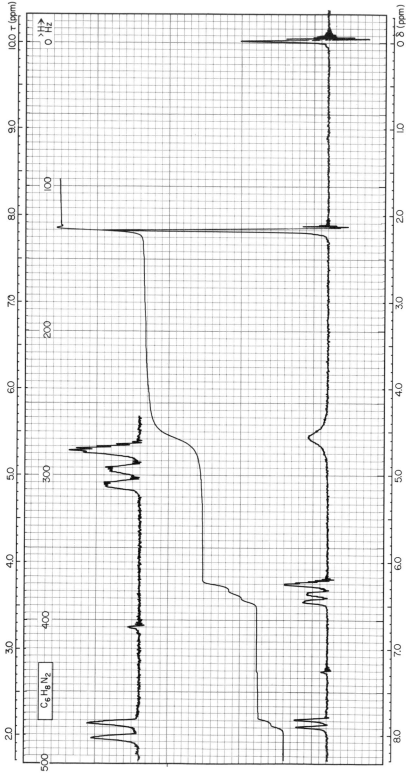

Spectrum 32 Inset abscissa scale 2.5 Hz/division.

C₆H₈N₂

286

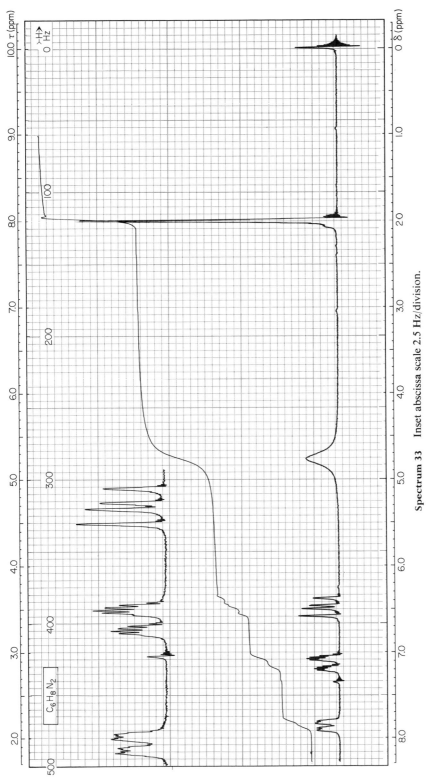

Spectrum 33   Inset abscissa scale 2.5 Hz/division.

287

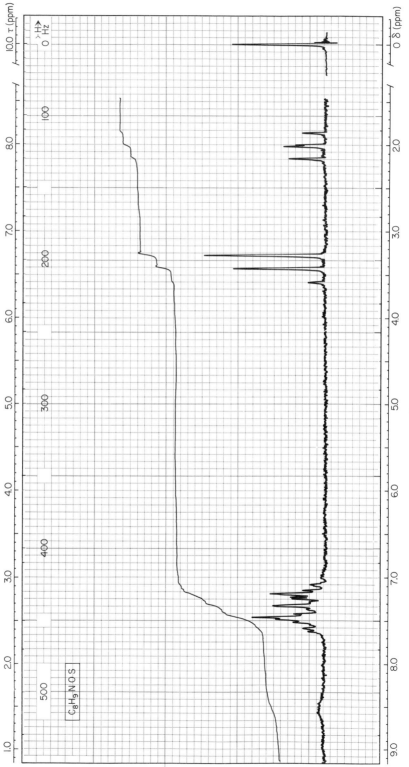

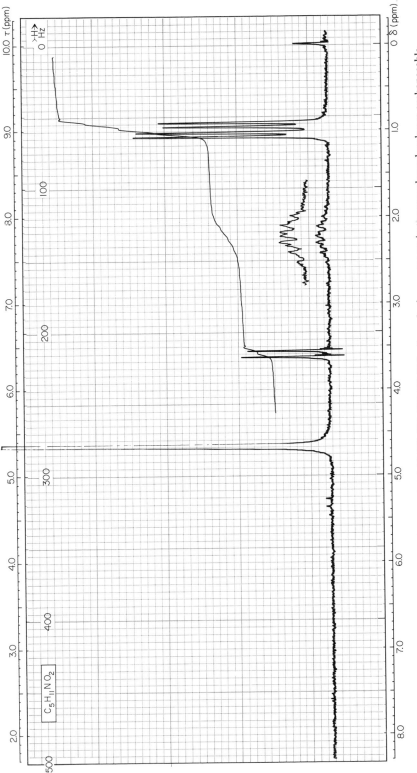

Spectrum 35   Solvent D$_2$O; internal reference, (CH$_3$)$_3$SiCH$_2$CH$_2$CH$_2$COONa. Some hydrogen atoms in the sample molecule are exchangeable.

C$_5$H$_{11}$NO$_2$

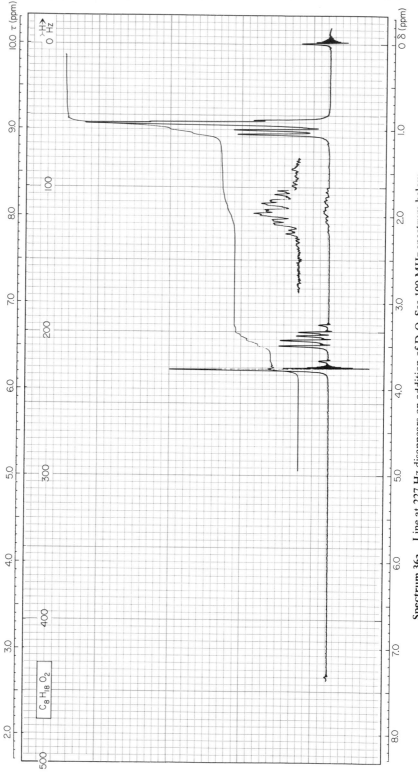

Spectrum 36a   Line at 227 Hz disappears on addition of D$_2$O. See 100 MHz spectrum below.

C$_8$H$_{18}$O$_2$

290

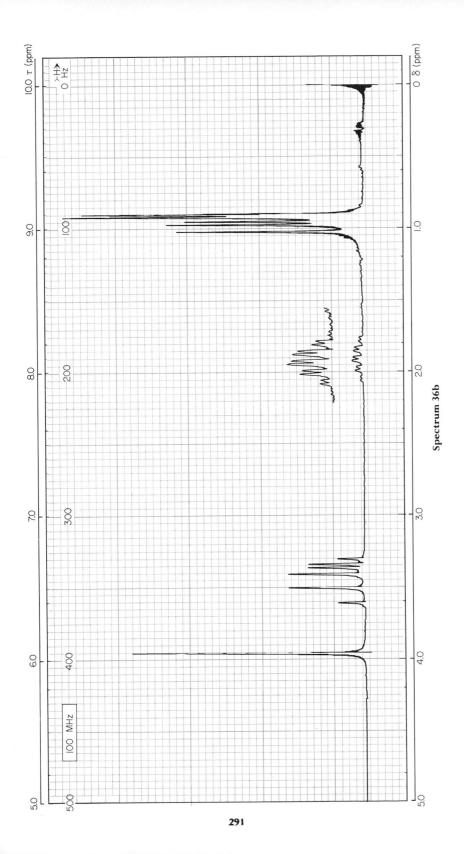

Spectrum 36b

100 MHz

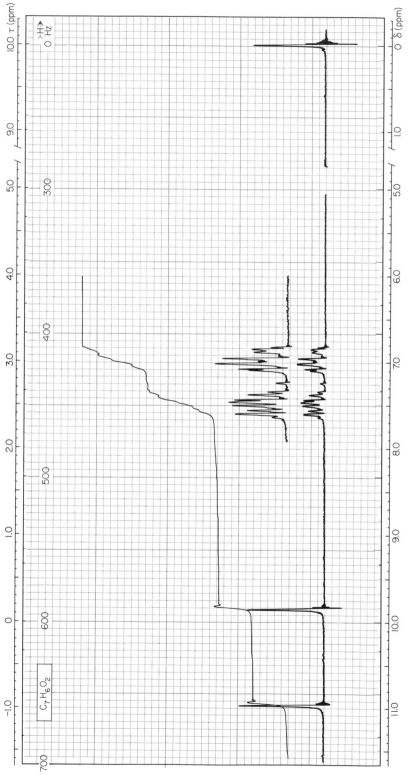

Spectrum 37

Appendix C

General NMR References

A. Comprehensive Treatments

1. J. A. Pople, W. G. Schneider, and H. J. Bernstein, "High Resolution NMR." McGraw-Hill, New York, 1959.
2. J. W. Emsley, J. Feeney, and L. H. Sutcliffe, "High Resolution NMR," Vols. 1 and 2. Macmillan (Pergamon), New York, 1966.
3. P. L. Corio, "Structure of High Resolution NMR Spectra." Academic Press, New York, 1967.
4. F. A. Bovey, "NMR Spectroscopy." Academic Press, New York, 1968.

B. Introductory Books

1. R. H. Bible, "Introduction to NMR Spectroscopy." Plenum Press, New York, 1965.
2. R. H. Bible, "Guide to the NMR Empirical Method." Plenum Press, New York, 1967.
3. J. D. Roberts, "Nuclear Magnetic Resonance." McGraw-Hill, New York, 1959.
4. J. D. Roberts, "Introduction to Spin-Spin Splitting in High Resolution NMR." Benjamin, New York, 1961.
5. A. Carrington and A. D. McLachlen, "Introduction to Magnetic Resonance." Harper & Row, New York, 1966.
6. D. Chapman and P. D. Magnus, "Introduction to Practical High Resolution NMR Spectroscopy." Academic Press, New York, 1966.

C. Organic Applications

1. N. S. Bhacca and D. H. Williams, "Applications of NMR Spectroscopy in Organic Chemistry." Holden-Day, San Francisco, 1964.
2. L. M. Jackman, "Applications of NMR Spectroscopy in Organic Chemistry." Macmillan (Pergamon), New York, 1959.

3. D. W. Mathieson (editor), "Interpretation of Organic Spectra." Academic Press, New York, 1965.
4. D. W. Mathieson (editor), "NMR for Organic Chemists." Academic Press, New York, 1967.
5. J. R. Dyer, "Application of Absorption Spectroscopy of Organic Compounds." Prentice-Hall, Englewood Cliffs, 1965.
6. H. Suhr, "Anwendung der Kermagnetischen Resonanz in der Organischen Chemie." Springer, New York, 1965.

D. Compilations of Data (in addition to those in above books)

1. "Varian High Resolution NMR Spectra Catalog," Vols. 1 and 2. Varian Associates, Palo Alto, California, 1963.
2. M. G. Howell, A. S. Kende, and J. S. Webb, "Formula Index to NMR Literature Data," Vols. 1 and 2. Plenum Press, New York, 1966.
3. H. M. Hershenson, "NMR and ESR Spectra Index." Academic Press, New York, 1965.
4. "Sadtler Standard NMR Spectra." Sadtler Research Laboratories, Philadelphia, Pennsylvania, 1967.
5. F. A. Bovey, "NMR Data Tables for Organic Compounds." Wiley (Interscience), New York, 1967.
6. W. Brügel, "NMR Spectra and Chemical Structure." Academic Press, New York, 1967.

E. Serial Publications

1. J. S. Waugh (editor), *Advances in Magnetic Resonance* **1**, 1965; **2**, 1966; **3**, 1968. Academic Press, New York.
2. J. W. Emsley, J. Feeney, and L. H. Sutcliffe (editors), *Progress in NMR Spectroscopy* **1**, 1966; **2**, 1967; **3**, 1967. Macmillan (Pergamon), New York.
3. *Analytical Chemistry Annual Reviews*: e.g., E. Lustig and W. B. Moniz, "NMR Spectrometry," **38**, 331R (1966).

Answers to Selected Problems

Chapter 2

4. Since signal strength is proportional to n, the difference in population of the two energy levels, equation 2.39 gives the desired relation. It is convenient to cast it into the form

$$\ln(n - n_{eq}) = -\frac{1}{T_1} t + \ln(n - n_{eq})_{t=0}$$

or

$$\log_{10}(n - n_{eq}) = -\frac{1}{2.303 \, T_1} t + \log_{10}(n - n_{eq})_{t=0}.$$

Thus a plot against time of the difference between the signal height at time t and the asymptotic value it assumes after a sufficiently long time should give a straight line, from the slope of which we obtain T_1.

7. For a Gaussian line the shape function is

$$g(v) = A \exp[-\alpha(v - v_0)^2].$$

From equation 2.42,

$$A = 2T_2.$$

At the half-maximum point, where $v = v_0 + \frac{1}{2}v_{1/2}$, we obtain

$$\exp\left(-\frac{\alpha v_{1/2}^2}{4}\right) = \frac{1}{2}$$

or

$$\alpha = \frac{4\ln 2}{v_{1/2}^2}.$$

From equation 2.19,

$$\int_0^\infty g(v)\,dv = 1.$$

A table of definite integrals shows that

$$\int_{-\infty}^\infty \exp[-ax^2]\,dx = \left(\frac{\pi}{a}\right)^{1/2}.$$

Making the substitution $x = v - v_0$,

$$\int_{-v_0}^\infty 2T_2 \exp\left(-\frac{4\ln 2}{v_{1/2}^2}x^2\right)dx = 1,$$

$$2\left(\frac{\pi}{4\ln 2}\right)^{1/2} v_{1/2}\,T_2 = 1,$$

$$v_{1/2} = \left(\frac{\ln 2}{\pi}\right)^{1/2}\frac{1}{T_2} = \frac{1}{2.14T_2}.$$

(Note that the limit of integration, $-v_0$, is replaced by $-\infty$. Why is this change valid?)

Chapter 3

2. The expression for the amplitude modulated rf wave is

$$AB\cos(2\pi v_0 t)\cos(2\pi v_m t).$$

From the well-known trigonometric identities for the sum and difference of two angles we have

$$\cos(a + b) = \cos a \cos b - \sin a \sin b,$$

$$\cos(a - b) = \cos a \cos b + \sin a \sin b.$$

The sum of these identities is

$$\cos(a + b) + \cos(a - b) = 2\cos a \cos b.$$

Thus the expression for the modulated wave can be written

$$\frac{AB}{2}\{\cos[2\pi(v_0 + v_m)t] + \cos[2\pi(v_0 - v_m)t]\}.$$

In this form we see that there are components oscillating at $(\nu_0 + \nu_m)$ and $(\nu_0 - \nu_m)$.

Chapter 4

4. We are given that dioxane in CCl_4 has a chemical shift $\tau = 6.43$ ppm, or that $\delta = 3.57$ ppm downfield from TMS as an internal reference. From Figure 4.1 we see that liquid dioxane is 3.37 ppm lower in field than TMS dissolved in CCl_4. Thus dioxane dissolved in CCl_4 must be 0.20 ppm lower in field than liquid dioxane.

6. Using the same reasoning as in Problem 4, we find that the chemical shift of benzene in CCl_4 is 0.75 ppm lower in field than that of liquid benzene. We can use equation 4.13 to correct for the effect of magnetic susceptibility:

$$\delta(\text{true}) = 0.75 - \tfrac{2}{3}\pi \times 10^6[-0.611 - (-0.691)] \times 10^{-6}$$

$$= 0.58 \text{ ppm}.$$

Thus of the measured difference in chemical shift between benzene in CCl_4 and in the neat liquid, 23% is due to susceptibility effects. The remainder represents a real change in shielding due to the solvent environment (see Chapter 11).

Chapter 5

2. The splitting is measured in CH_3D, and equation 5.2 is applied.

5. The ^1H spectrum consists of a doublet with equal intensities and a separation of 12 Hz. The ^{31}P spectrum contains 10 lines, each separated from the next by 12 Hz. The relative intensities, by extension of Table 5.1, are $1:9:36:84:126:126:84:36:9:1$. Experimentally the spectrum often appears as an octet since the outermost lines are so weak.

9. A nucleus with $I = 1$ may be oriented three ways relative to H_0, with a projection, m_i, on H_0 of $+1$, 0, or -1. We must consider what arrangements of n spins are possible to give the same total projection, M. For $n = 2$, the total projection M can equal 2 only if both spins have projections of $+1$; i.e., $m_1 = m_2 = 1$. But $M = 1$ can be obtained with $m_1 = 1$ and $m_2 = 0$, or with $m_1 = 0$ and $m_2 = 1$. Thus the state with $M = 1$ is twice as likely to occur as that with $M = 2$. $M = 0$ can occur three ways: $m_1 = 1$ and $m_2 = -1$; $m_1 = -1$ and $m_2 = 1$; or $m_1 = 0$ and $m_2 = 0$. Other cases

can be treated in the same way. A table analogous to Table 5.1 for the $I = 1$ case is

n	Relative intensity
0	1
1	1 1 1
2	1 2 3 2 1
3	1 3 6 7 6 3 1

(The table may be extended by noting that each entry is the sum of the one immediately above and its two neighbors.)

Chapter 7

1. CH_2=CHF, ABCX or ABMX; PF_3, A_3X; cubane, A_8; $CH_3CHOHCH_3$, A_6MX or A_6XY if OH is not exchanging, or A_6X with exchange; chlorobenzene, AA'BB'C; $CH_3CH_2CH_3$, A_6B_2.

4. (a) and (d) are AB spectra. (b) has incorrect line spacings, and (c) has the wrong intensity ratio.

16. See answer to Spectrum 21, Appendix B.

17. See answer to Spectrum 23, Appendix B.

19. See answer to Spectrum 25, Appendix B.

20. See answer to Spectrum 27, Appendix B.

Chapter 8

2. (a) $\gamma H_2/2\pi \geqslant 20$ Hz. (b) From equation 8.5,

$$(173 - 243) = (173 - \nu_B) - \frac{(20)^2}{2(173 - \nu_B)}.$$

To a high degree of approximation, ν_B in the last term can be replaced by ν_2. Then solution of the equation gives $\nu_B = 245.9$ Hz.

4. The labeling of the states would change, but the experimental result would appear to be the same. [For a discussion of this point, see R. Johannesen, *J. Chem. Phys.* **48**, 1414 (1968).]

Chapter 10

5. (a) A_3X_2; (b) $AA'XX'$; (c) A_3; (d) ABX; (e) AX.

6. (a) $ABB'XX'$; (b) $AA'XX'$ and ABXY, with intensity ratio of 1:2 if all three conformations are equally populated; (c) ABC; (d) three different ABX spectra; (e) three different AX spectra.

Appendix B

1. $(CH_3)_2C(OCH_3)_2$.

3. CH_3OCH_2COOH. Note that the integral of the carboxyl proton peak is too large. This discrepancy is due to the fact that this hygroscopic sample has absorbed water. The line at 462 Hz is actually due to the rapidly exchanging water and carboxyl protons. See Chapter 10 for a discussion of exchange phenomena.

5. CH_3CHCl_2. The symmetric isomer, CH_2ClCH_2Cl, would have only a single line in its spectrum.

7. $(C_2H_5O)_2PH$. $^1J_{PH} = 688$ Hz, while $^3J_{PH} = 9$ Hz.
$\overset{\|}{O}$

9.

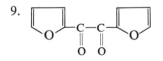

11.　　　　$O=C-CH_3$　　　　Note the pattern typical of a *para*-substi-

tuted aromatic.

Cl

13.　　　　　　　　　　　Note the complex but symmetric pattern of lines due to the ring protons, which results from the magnetic nonequivalence of the two protons attached to the same carbon atom.

CH_3

15. 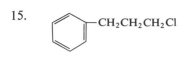 This spectrum is typical of many mono-substituted benzenes in which the substituent is neither strongly electron-withdrawing nor strongly electron-donating. As a result the five aromatic protons have almost identical chemical shifts.

17.

CH$_2$OAc
AcO—O OAc
OAc

OAc

(Ac: CH$_3$C=O)

19.

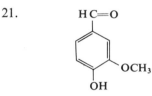

An α,β-unsaturated ketone usually displays the resonance of the β proton at lower field than most olefinic protons. As seen in this spectrum it can be downfield as far as or farther than the aromatic proton lines.

21.

HC=O

OCH$_3$

OH

The lines due to the aldehyde, aromatic and methoxyl protons are readily identified. The broad resonance around δ = 4.5 ppm, unobservable in the spectrum itself but quite apparent in the integral, is due to the OH proton. (The effect of exchange on line widths is taken up in detail in Chapter 10.)

So far as the positions of the substituents on the aromatic ring are concerned, it is nearly impossible to distinguish between the OH and OCH$_3$ since both have almost the same effect on the chemical shifts of nearby aromatic protons. Treating these two substituents as equivalent, we can still distinguish six position isomers:

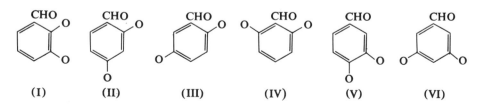

(I)   (II)   (III)   (IV)   (V)   (VI)

Isomers (IV) and (VI) can be excluded since they would give essentially A$_2$X spectra, which would differ from the experimental spectrum. The observed spectrum should be analyzed as ABX (see next paragraph), but for our present purposes we can use first-order analysis. The single proton responsible for the resonance near 450 Hz is evidently *ortho* to exactly one other proton and *meta* to no protons. Since it is shielded, it is probably *ortho* to the OH or OCH_3 rather than to the CHO group. These considerations rule out (I) and (II). Isomer (III) would be expected to have the chemical shifts of protons 3 and 4 nearly equal and at high field, whereas it is actually the two low-field chemical shifts that are almost equal. Thus (V) is preferred. The correct formula, given above, is vanillin; iso-vanillin, which differs only in interchange of OH and OCH_3, gives a very similar NMR spectrum.

ABX analysis: The AB portion shows only six lines, but the two central lines are obviously broader than the others and must each consist of two almost coincident lines. Thus the two ab subspectra may be identified, and J_{AB} is found to be 1.8 Hz. From the distance between the centers of the subspectra $|J_{AX} + J_{BX}| = 8.4$ Hz, while the X portion shows that this quantity is 8.7 Hz (reasonable agreement for a single spectral trace with some ambiguity in selecting certain line positions). From the AB portion we obtain $2D_+ = 5.1$ and $2D_- = 3.4$, while from the X portion we get 5.2 and 3.5 Hz. Using average values for these quantities and following the procedure of Table 7.6, we obtain the two solutions (1) $v_A - v_B = 3.9$ and $J_{AX} - J_{BX} = 0.9$, or (2) $v_A - v_B = 0.9$ and $J_{AX} - J_{BX} = 3.9$. The former leads to the result $J_{AX} = 5.2$ Hz and $J_{BX} = 3.4$ Hz, which would be highly unusual for an aromatic system of this sort. The latter solution gives the perfectly acceptable values $J_{AX} = 8.2$ Hz and $J_{BX} = 0.4$ Hz, with $v_A = 748.2$ Hz and $v_B = 747.8$ Hz. We did not need to consider the relative intensities of the X lines in this case since we could reject one possible solution on the basis of our prior knowledge of the magnitudes of certain coupling constants.

23. From the empirical formula this compound must be one of the three isomers of difluoroethylene. The analysis of the AA'XX' spectrum follows the procedure outlined in Section 7.22. With the notation of Table 7.7, $N = 92.5$, $K = 21.2$, $M = 17.0$, and $L = 51.7$ Hz, provided we take one of the ab subspectra as lines 2, 5, 6, and 9 (reading lines in order across Spectrum 23) and the other as lines 3, 4, 7, and 8. This gives $J_{AA'} = 19.1$, $J_{XX'} = 2.1$, $J_{AX} = 72.0$, and $J_{AX'} = 20.5$ Hz. The association of these values with the two *geminal*, the *cis*, and the *trans* couplings, and the determination of the correct geometric isomer is best done in conjunction with Spectrum 24 and Figure 5.3.

It might appear that the intensity relations would permit the ab subspectra to be chosen as follows: lines 2, 4, 7, and 9 as one subspectrum and lines 3, 5, 6, and 8 as the other. However, this choice is not valid, for it would lead to different values of L from the two subspectra. Can you show that this is a general result for all AA′XX′ spectra?

25. ![benzene ring with CH—CH2 and O] Within the accuracy of the data given, this spectrum can be analyzed by the first-order procedure. Alternatively the two ab subspectra can be identified, and an ABX analysis carried out. There is ambiguity in the association of the left and right halves of the ab subspectra, but that simply means that the relative signs cannot be determined.

27. The compound is vinyl fluoride, $CH_2\!=\!CHF$. The 60 MHz spectrum departs considerably from first order due to the fortuitous coincidence of several lines. The 100 MHz spectrum, on the other hand, shows the 24 lines predicted by the first-order rules and may be analyzed accordingly to give the values

$$J_{HF}(gem) = 85, J_{HF}(cis) = 20.5, J_{HF}(trans) = 53.5,$$

$$J_{HH}(gem) = 3, J_{HH}(cis) = 5, \text{ and } J_{HH}(trans) = 12.5.$$

The exact treatment of this molecule as an ABCX system shows that the proton resonance spectrum consists of two overlapping abc (approximately abx) subspectra, which may be analyzed to give the proton chemical shifts and all six coupling constants (signs, as well as magnitudes). For details see J. W. Emsley, J. Feeney, and L. H. Sutcliffe, "High Resolution NMR Spectroscopy," p. 423. Macmillan (Pergamon), New York, 1965.

29. $CH_2ClCH\!=\!CHCH_2Cl$ *(trans)*. Note the effect of virtual coupling.

31. $(CH_3)_3N^+CH_2CH_2OCCH_3Br^-$.
    $$\overset{\|}{O}$$

33.   The chemical shifts of the three ring protons suggest that the substituents are located on the 2 and 3 positions, and this conclusion is confirmed by the observed splittings. The long-range coupling of 4-H to the CH_3 establishes the methyl group in the 3 position. Note the broadening of the amino protons and the proton α to the ring nitrogen as a result of ^{14}N relaxation.

35. $(CH_3)_2CHCHCOOH.$
$$\underset{NH_2}{|}$$

The two methyl groups are chemically nonequivalent because of the presence of the asymmetric center.

37.

The OH proton has a large (low field) chemical shift because of the strong intramolecular hydrogen bonding.

Subject Index

A

AA′BB′ spin system
  analysis by spin tickling, 199
  spectra, appearance of in special cases, 169–170
AA′XX′ spin system
  analysis, 168–169
  frequencies and intensities of lines, 167
  spectrum, schematic representation, 168
AB spin system
  energy levels, 131–133
  spectrum, 135–138
    analysis of, 137–138
  spin tickling, 197
  subspectra in ABX spectrum, 153
    in A_3B spectrum, 148
  transitions, 133
A_2B spin system, 144–147
  basis functions, 145
  frequencies and intensities of lines, 147
  spectrum, 145–146
A_3B spin system, 148
ABC spin system
  basis functions, 143
  spectrum, 143–144
  spin tickling, 197–199
Absorption mode signal, 27–28
ABX spin system
  analysis, procedure for (table), 157

approximation for ABC, 144
basis functions, 149
deceptive simplicity in spectra, 161–163
frequencies and intensities of lines, 150
signs of coupling constants, 152, 154, 158–161
spectra
  analysis of, 152–158
  determination of, 150–152
  schematic representation, 153
  virtual coupling in, 163–164
Acrylamide, spectrum of, 5, 8
Adiabatic condition for spectral sweep, 28
Adiabatic rapid passage, 56
AMX spin system, transitions and signs of coupling constants, 193
Analysis, quantitative, *see* Quantitative analysis
Analysis of spectra, *see also* specific spin systems, First order analysis
  AA′XX′, example, 92
  A_2X_2, example, 92
  AB, example, 93
  aids in, 170–173
  [13]C satellites in, 171–172
  of complex spectra, 119–174
  computer programs for, 142
  double quantum transitions in, 172–173
  field dependence, use in, 170–171

304